The American Assembly, *Columbia University*

THE CONGRESS AND AMERICA'S FUTURE

Prentice-Hall, Inc., *Englewood Cliffs, N.J.*

A SPECTRUM BOOK

Preface

The Congress and America's Future was the subject of the Twenty-sixth American Assembly at Arden House, the Harriman (New York) campus of Columbia University, October 29 to November 1, 1964. The findings and policy recommendations of the meeting have been published in a separate pamphlet by The American Assembly.

This volume, prepared under the editorial supervision of David B. Truman, was designed as background reading for the Arden House meeting and other sessions of The American Assembly across the country, as well as for general readership.

The opinions contained herein are those of the individual authors and not of The American Assembly, a non-partisan, educational institution. The same may be said of the Ford Foundation, which generously supported the entire program.

The American Assembly

Clifford C. Nelson
President

Henry M. Wriston
Chairman

Table of Contents

David B. Truman

Introduction: The Problem in Its Setting

Criticism of the Congress is a hardy perennial of American life. The cartoon symbol of the bewhiskered, frock-coated, and bungling old man, familiar to all newspaper readers, effectively illustrates a persistent stereotype. It is by no means new. But in the past half-dozen years the pattern and volume of criticism directed at the Congress have taken on a character unlike anything since the close of the first decade of this century. To the perennial objections of individuals and groups whose desires have not met with legislative approval have been added a growing number of criticisms from responsible senators and representatives, as well as from journalists and scholars. The concerns and the proposals emanating from these sources are not consistent in detail nor are they uniformly well considered. But most of them display a common element of worry that, unless ways are found to alter the functioning of the Congress, the fortunes of the nation may be inadequately guarded or seriously diminished.

Concern about the Congress has its ultimate roots in three rather distinct sets of circumstances. Examination of these essays and reflections on the Congress will be more productive if these are kept in mind.

In the first place, the trials of our national legislature are in part a reflection of the "parliamentary crisis" that has affected the West for at least five decades. The twentieth century, it is often noted, has been hard on legislatures. Compelled in some fashion to deal with the complexities of increasingly urbanized, rapidly industrialized, and irrevocably

DAVID B. TRUMAN *is Dean of Columbia College and President of The American Political Science Association for 1964-65. Also Professor of Government in the Faculty of Political Science, Columbia University, Dean Truman is the author of numerous works on the functions and processes of government, including* The Governmental Process *and* The Congressional Party.

interdependent societies, they have found themselves alternating in varying degrees between two equally dangerous and distasteful situations:
yielding the initiative as well as the implementing responsibilities to bureaucrats whose actions might be imperfectly mediated by political officials, or attempting to retain one or both of these functions at the expense
of delay, indecision, and instability. The conferences of the Inter-Parliamentary Union, which have included delegates from the Congress of the
United States, have been concerned with these problems since the close
of World War I. The charges of "rubber stamp" against the Congresses
of Franklin Roosevelt's first Administration have been matched by criticisms from within and without the National Assembly of the Fifth French
Republic, from critics of West Germany's "chancellor democracy," and
even from within the British Parliament; the delays and debilitating
compromises of other American Congresses have had at least their equiva-
lents in the Third and Fourth French Republics, in Italy, and in most
of the governments of Northwestern Europe. To this awkward alternation
has been added the inevitable increase in executive power that comes,
especially in a stable system, from the continued dominance on questions
of foreign policy.

There are those in American society and in other countries of the
West who would like to wish out of existence the industrial and technological changes that are at the roots of this "parliamentary crisis" and
return to a simpler day. Such sentiments, though entirely understandable,
are more than unrealistic. They are, as the European experience in the
inter-war decades demonstrates, a seedbed for movements that would sub-
vert and destroy the values underlying representative and constitutional
systems. Solutions must be sought to the "parliamentary crisis," if these
sentiments are not to produce such movements, by means that will ac-
knowledge the irreversibility of the twentieth century's precipitating
changes and will simultaneously preserve the essential values of the system—the stabilizing and legitimating processes of autonomous criticism
and consent.

Secondly, concern over the performance of the Congress derives in
part from two constitutional and closely related political features of the
American system: the constitutional separation of the Congress and the
President and the diffusing effects of federalism. The former is not strictly
a separation of powers but, as Richard Neustadt has phrased it, "separated institutions sharing powers." [1] This arangement, a source of tension and rivalry since the earliest days of the Republic, has complicated
congressional adaptation to the twentieth century. The rhetoric of separation, as Neustadt argues in his essay (Chapter Five), helps to perpetuate
in the Congress the illusion that it must and should be the principal
source of policy initiatives, of grand designs for national programs, an
illusion pregnant with frustration. At the same time, separation has

---

[1] Richard E. Neustadt, *Presidential Power* (New York, 1960), pp. 33, 39, 186, *ff.*

played no small part in keeping the Congress more vital, more a political force to be reckoned with, than perhaps any national legislature in the world. This vitality, misdirected though it may sometimes be, is an asset not to be lightly overlooked in the search for function and organization appropriate to contemporary problems.

The handicapping effects of separation are complicated and reinforced by the federal character not only of the constitutional order but equally and consequently of the political order and especially of the major parties. This does not only mean that local or sectional interests are represented on Capitol Hill, but also that the most serious risks confronting the member of Congress are local. Except as these can be combined, as occasionally they are, with central demands in the Congress itself or in the White House, they tend to insulate the representative or senator from any policy constraint, from any political sanction, whose reach is not primarily local. To the strains of separation are thus added the diversity and incongruity of political risk that are induced by a federalized governmental and political structure. The political risks of senators and representatives, as Douglas Price's analysis demonstrates (Chapter Two), may not be quite what they once were or what they appear to be, but the thrust of localism has not been altered.

In many respects, of course, this pull of localism is as it should be. Diverse interests within a continental country are often geographically defined, and they need to have access to the national legislature if that body is to be, in any reasonable sense, a representative one. Criticism arises when it appears that congressional stakes in national action are too weak to provide sufficient support for a national power to govern. Again, the problem is more complex because it is not one of clear and mutually exclusive alternatives but one of balance, of relative weights.

The third and most obvious source of concern about the Congress is those structural and procedural practices—including such matters as the seniority rule, "extended debate" in the Senate, and the powers of the House Committee on Rules—that appear to weaken the power to govern, to subject national objectives to local priorities, and to grant inequitable power advantages to interests and to persons strategically situated to exploit these practices. Most discussions of congressional "reform" focus on these items, or a fraction of them, without substantial reference to the two more fundamental sources of dissatisfaction and as if the criticized practices were awkward bits of machinery wholly without deeper origins or justifying function. Yet, as Richard F. Fenno, Jr. and Ralph K. Huitt both point out in their discussions of the separate and quite distinct influence structures in the House and Senate (respectively Chapters Three and Four) these arrangements are parts of two coherent and well-developed systems. "The Congress" is in a very real sense a fiction, but each of the houses is an integral fact. To modify any of these conspicuous practices would be to alter fundamentally the internal power structure of each chamber. It would also, as Price's essay indicates, require a fundamental alteration in the pattern of most contemporary congressional careers. This might be desirable, yet it might also take more effective power than is required to produce particular substantive results from the existing arrangements.

Despite the implications of some criticisms of the Congress, it is not precisely the institution it was at the turn of the century. But how is it different? Samuel P. Huntington (Chapter One) argues that the Congress has experienced a steady insulation from nationalizing changes and sources of power in the society at the same time that power within the legislature has become increasingly dispersed. These trends are serious, and perhaps represent insuperable obstacles to congressional achievement of the institutional adaptations called for by the problems and patterns of the contemporary scene, by the American version of the "parliamentary crisis."

The crucial test of the Congress and of the federal government as a whole will not be in abstract terms, however, but rather in the quality of its policy output in matters of basic consequence for the nation's welfare. In order to assess a part of that output, in Chapters Six and Seven Harvey C. Mansfield and Holbert N. Carroll examine the role and the effect of the Congress in two broad areas of continuing basic importance, economic policy and national security policy. Both are concerned with the problem of limiting or eliminating the fragmentation of power and perspective that characterizes congressional operation. Their assessment of the House and Senate records in these two crucial areas does not, however, support a wholesale indictment of congressional performance. But it does lead much of the analysis outside the Congress and toward the White House. It underscores the possibility, argued by Neustadt (Chapter Five), that in the days ahead the convergent but non-identical interests of Presidents and members of Congress will require a greatly increased measure of collaboration between these two sets of elective politicians, if their distinctive skills are to control the demands of a consolidating officialdom.

The tempo of debate over these matters and particularly over the Congress and its functioning seems certain to rise in the months ahead. The essays in this book were planned to make a constructive contribution to such discussion, but they are not intended to promote any one of the many alternative proposals for reorganizing the Congress. Nor are they designed to champion a particular line of criticism. Rather they attempt a further analysis of the problems of the Congress by seeing its life and work in context, by identifying its characteristic ways and the reasons for them, and by examining the nature of its product in two areas crucial to the future of the nation. No single group of essays can pretend to have exhausted the subject of congressional reform. If these contribute to a more comprehending discussion of the problem, they will have served their purpose.

Samuel P. Huntington

1

Congressional Responses
to the Twentieth Century

Congress is a frequent source of anguish to both its friends and its foes. The critics point to its legislative failure. The function of a legislature, they argue, is to legislate, and Congress either does not legislate or legislates too little and too late. The intensity of their criticism varies inversely with the degree and despatch with which Congress approves the President's legislative proposals. When in 1963 the 88th Congress seemed to stymie the Kennedy legislative program, criticism rapidly mounted. "What kind of legislative body is it," asked Walter Lippmann, neatly summing up the prevailing exasperation, "that will not or cannot legislate?" When in 1964 the same 88th Congress passed the civil rights, tax, and other bills, criticism of Congress correspondingly subsided. Reacting differently to this familiar pattern, the friends of Congress lamented its acquiescence to presidential dictate. Since 1933, they said, the authority of the executive branch—President, administration, and bureaucracy—has waxed, while that of Congress has waned. They warned of the constitutional perils stemming from the permanent subordination of one branch of government to another. Thus, at the same time that it is an obstructive ogre to its enemies, Congress is also the declining despair of its friends. Can both images be true? In large

---

SAMUEL P. HUNTINGTON *is Professor of Government at Harvard University and consultant in the field of military policy to numerous government and private organizations. He was Associate Director, Institute of War and Peace Studies, Columbia University, from 1959 to 1962. Author of many books and articles, Professor Huntington's most recent publication is* Political Power: USA/USSR *(with Zbigniew Brzezinski).*

part, they are. The loss of power by Congress, indeed, can be measured by the extent to which congressional assertion coincides with congressional obstruction.

This paradox has been at the root of the "problem" of Congress since the early days of the New Deal. Vis-à-vis the Executive, Congress is an autonomous, legislative body. But apparently Congress can defend its autonomy only by refusing to legislate, and it can legislate only by surrendering its autonomy. When Congress balks, criticism rises, and the clamoring voices of reformers fill the air with demands for the "modernization" of the "antiquated procedures" of an "eighteenth century" Congress so it can deal with "twentieth century realities." The demands for reform serve as counters in the legislative game to get the President's measures through Congress. Independence thus provokes criticism; acquiescence brings approbation. If Congress legislates, it subordinates itself to the President; if it refuses to legislate, it alienates itself from public opinion. Congress can assert its power or it can pass laws; but it cannot do both.

LEGISLATIVE POWER AND INSTITUTIONAL CRISIS

The roots of this legislative dilemma lie in the changes in American society during the twentieth century. The twentieth century has seen: rapid urbanization and the beginnings of a post-industrial, technological society; the nationalization of social and economic problems and the concomitant growth of national organizations to deal with these problems; the increasing bureaucratization of social, economic, and governmental organizations; and the sustained high-level international involvement of the United States in world politics. These developments have generated new forces in American politics and initiated major changes in the distribution of power in American society. In particular, the twentieth century has witnessed the tremendous expansion of the responsibilities of the national government and the size of the national bureaucracy. In 1901, the national government had 351,798 employees or less than $1\frac{1}{2}$ per cent of the national labor force. In 1962, it had 5,232,819 employees, constituting 7 per cent of the labor force. The expansion of the national government has been paralleled by the emergence of other large, national, bureaucratic organizations: manufacturing corporations, banks, insurance companies, labor unions, trade associations, farm organizations, newspaper chains, radio-TV networks. Each organization may have relatively specialized and concrete interests, but typically it functions on a national basis. Its headquarters are in New York or Washington; its operations are scattered across a dozen or more states. The emergence of these organizations truly constitutes, in Kenneth Boulding's expressive phrase, an "organizational revolution." The existence of this private "Establishment," more than anything else, distinguishes twentieth-century America from nineteenth-century America. The leaders of these organizations are the notables of American society: they are the prime wielders of social and economic power.

These momentous social changes have confronted Congress with an institutional "adaptation crisis." Such a crisis occurs when changes in the environment of a governmental institution force the institution either to alter its functions, affiliation, and modes of behavior, or to face decline, decay, and isolation. Crises usually occur when an institution loses its previous sources of support or fails to adapt itself to the rise of new social forces. Such a crisis, for instance, affected the Presidency in the second and third decades of the nineteenth century. Under the leadership of Henry Clay the focal center of power in the national government was in the House of Representatives; the congressional caucus dictated presidential nominations; popular interest in and support for the Presidency were minimal. The "Executive," Justice Story remarked in 1818, "has no longer a commanding influence. The House of Representatives has absorbed all the popular feelings and all the effective power of the country." The Presidency was on the verge of becoming a weak, secondary instrumental organ of government. It was rescued from this fate by the Jacksonian movement, which democratized the Presidency, broadened its basis of popular support, and restored it as the center of vitality and leadership in the national government. The House of Commons was faced with a somewhat similar crisis during the agitation preceding the first Reform Bill of 1832. New social groups were developing in England which were demanding admission to the political arena and the opportunity to share in political leadership. Broadening the constituency of the House of Commons and reforming the system of election enabled the House to revitalize itself and to continue as the principal locus of power in the British government.

In both these cases a governmental institution got a new lease on life, new vigor, new power, by embodying within itself dynamic, new social forces. When an institution fails to make such an alignment, it must either restrict its own authority or submit to a limitation upon its authority imposed from outside. Thus in 1910, when the House of Lords refused to approve Lloyd George's budget, it was first compelled by governmental pressure, popular opinion, and the threat of the creation of new peers to acquiesce in the budget and then through a similar process to acquiesce in the curtailment of its own power to obstruct legislation approved by the Commons. In this case the effort to block legislation approved by the dominant forces in the political community resulted in a permanent diminution of the authority of the offending institution. A somewhat similar crisis developed with respect to the Supreme Court in the 1930's. Here again a less popular body attempted to veto the actions of more popular bodies. In three years the Court invalidated twelve acts of Congress. Inevitably this precipitated vigorous criticism and demands for reform, culminating in Roosevelt's court reorganization proposal in February of 1937. The alternatives confronting the Court were relatively clear-cut: it could "reform" or be "reformed." In "the switch in time that saved nine," it chose the former course, signaling its change by approving the National Labor Relations Act in April 1937 and the Social Security Act in May. With this switch, support for the reorganization of the Court drained away. The result was, in the words of Justice Jackson, "a failure of the reform forces and a victory of the reform."

Each of these four institutional crises arose from the failure of a governmental institution to adjust to social change and the rise of new viewpoints, new needs, and new political forces. Congress's legislative dilemma and loss of power stem from the nature of its over-all institutional response to the changes in American society. This response involves three major aspects of Congress as an institution: its affiliations, its structure, and its functions. During the twentieth century Congress has insulated itself from the new political forces which social change has generated and which are, in turn, generating more change. Hence the leadership of Congress has lacked the incentive to take the legislative initiative in handling emerging national problems. Within Congress power has become dispersed among many officials, committees, and subcommittees. Hence the central leadership of Congress has lacked the ability to establish national legislative priorities. As a result, the legislative function of Congress has declined in importance, while the growth of the federal bureaucracy has made the administrative overseeing function of Congress more important. These three tendencies—toward insulation, dispersion, and oversight—have dominated the evolution of Congress during the twentieth century.

Affiliations: Insulation from Power

Perhaps the single most important trend in congressional evolution during the twentieth century has been the growing insulation of Congress from other social groups and political institutions. In 1900 no gap existed between congressmen and the other leaders of American society and politics. Half a century later the changes in American society, on the one hand, and the institutional evolution of Congress, on the other, had produced a marked gap between congressional leaders and the bureaucratically oriented leadership of the executive branch and of the Establishment. The growth of this gap can be seen in seven trends in congressional evolution.

(1) *Increasing tenure of office.* In the nineteenth century few congressmen stayed in Congress very long. During the twentieth century the average tenure of congressmen has inexorably lengthened. In 1900 only 9 per cent of the members of the House of Representatives had served five terms or more and less than 1 per cent had served ten terms or more. In 1957, 45 per cent of the House had served five terms or more

and 14 per cent ten terms or more. In 1897, for each representative who had served ten terms or more in the House, there were 34 representatives who had served two terms or less. In 1961, for each ten-termer there were only 1.6 representatives who had served two terms or less.[1] In the middle of the nineteenth century, only about half the representatives in any one Congress had served in a previous Congress, and only about one-third of the senators had been elected to the Senate more than once. By 1961 close to 90 per cent of the House were veterans, and almost two-thirds of the senators were beyond their first term. The biennial infusion of new blood had reached an all-time low.

Table I

VETERAN CONGRESSMEN IN CONGRESS

Congress	Date	Representatives elected to House more than once	Senators elected to Senate more than once
42nd	1871	53%	32%
50th	1887	63	45
64th	1915	74	47
74th	1935	77	54
87th	1961	87	66

Source: Figures for representatives for 1871-1915 are from Robert Luce, *Legislative Assemblies* (Boston: Houghton Mifflin Company, 1924), p. 365. Other figures were calculated independently.

(2) *The increasingly important role of seniority.* Increasing tenure of congressmen is closely linked to increasingly rigid adherence to the practices of seniority. The longer men stay in Congress, the more likely they are to see virtue in seniority. Conversely, the more important seniority is, the greater is the constituent appeal of men who have been long in office. The current rigid system of seniority in *both* houses of Congress is a product of the twentieth century.

In the nineteenth century seniority was far more significant in the Senate than in the House. Since the middle of that century apparently only in five instances—the last in 1925—has the chairmanship of a Senate committee been denied to the most senior member of the committee. In the House, on the other hand, the Speaker early received the power to appoint committees and to designate their chairmen. During the nineteenth century Speakers made much of this power. Committee appointment and the selection of chairmen were involved political processes, in which the Speaker carefully balanced factors of seniority, geography, expertise, and policy viewpoint in making his choices. Not infre-

---

[1] George B. Galloway, *History of the United States House of Representatives* (House Document 246, Eighty-seventh Congress, 1st Session, 1962), p. 31; T. Richard Witmer, *New York Times*, Dec. 27, 1963, p. 24.

quently prolonged bargaining would result as the Speaker traded committee positions for legislative commitments. Commenting on James G. Blaine's efforts at committee construction in the early 1870's, one member of his family wrote that Blaine "left for New York on Wednesday. He had cotton and wool manufacturers to meet in Boston, and, over and above all, pressure to resist or permit. As fast as he gets his committees arranged, just so fast some after consideration comes up which overtopples the whole list like a row of bricks." [2] Only with the drastic curtailment of the powers of the Speaker in 1910 and 1911 did the seniority system in the House assume the inflexible pattern which it has today. Only twice since the 1910 revolt—once in 1915 and once in 1921—has seniority been neglected in the choice of committee chairmen.

(3) *Extended tenure: a prerequisite for leadership.* Before 1896 Speakers, at the time of their first election, averaged only seven years' tenure in the House. Since 1896 Speakers have averaged twenty-two years of House service at their first election. In 1811 and in 1859 Henry Clay and William Pennington were elected Speaker when they first entered the House. In 1807 Thomas Jefferson arranged for the election of his friend, William C. Nicholas, to the House and then for his immediate selection by the party caucus as floor leader. Such an intrusion of leadership from outside would now be unthinkable. Today the Speaker and other leaders of the House and, to a lesser degree, the leaders of the Senate are legislative veterans of long standing. In 1961 fifty-seven House leaders averaged twenty years of service in the House and thirty-four Senate leaders sixteen years of service in the Senate. The top House leaders (Speaker, floor leaders, chairmen and ranking minority members of Ways and Means, Appropriations, and Rules Committees) averaged thirty-one years in the House and nineteen years in leadership positions. The top Senate leaders (President *pro tem.,* floor leaders, chairmen and ranking minority members of Finance, Foreign Relations, and Appropriations Committees) averaged twenty years in the Senate and nine years in leadership positions. Between 1948 and 1961 the average tenure of top leaders increased by two years in the House and by three years in the Senate. Increasing tenure means increasing age. In the nineteenth century the leaders of Congress were often in their thirties. Clay was thirty-four when he became Speaker in 1811; Hunter, thirty when he became Speaker in 1839; White, thirty-six at his accession to the Speakership in 1841; and Orr, thirty-five when he became Speaker in 1857. In contrast, Rayburn was fifty-eight when he became Speaker, Martin sixty-three, and McCormack seventy-one.

(4) *Leadership within Congress: a one-way street.* Normally in American life becoming a leader in one institution opens up leadership possibilities in other institutions: corporation presidents head civic agencies or become

[2] Gail Hamilton, *Life of James G. Blaine,* p. 263, quoted in DeAlva S. Alexander, *History and Procedure of the House of Representatives* (Boston: Houghton Mifflin Company, 1916), p. 69.

cabinet officers; foundation and university executives move into government; leading lawyers and bankers take over industrial corporations. The greater one's prestige, authority, and accomplishments within one organization, the easier it is to move to other and better posts in other organizations. Such, however, is not the case with Congress. Leadership in the House of Representatives leads nowhere except to leadership in the House of Representatives. To a lesser degree, the same is true of the Senate. The successful House or Senate leader has to identify himself completely with his institution, its mores, traditions, and ways of behavior. "The very ingredients which make you a powerful House leader," one representative has commented, "are the ones which keep you from being a public leader." [3] Representatives typically confront a "fourth-term crisis": if they wish to run for higher office—for governor or senator—they must usually do so by the beginning of their fourth term in the House. If they stay in the House for four or more terms, they in effect choose to make a career in the House and to forswear the other electoral possibilities of American politics. Leadership in the Senate is not as exclusive a commitment as it is in the House. But despite such notable exceptions as Taft and Johnson, the most influential men in the Senate have typically been those who have looked with disdain upon the prospect of being anything but a United States Senator. Even someone with the high talent and broad ambition of Lyndon Johnson could not escape this exclusive embrace during his years as majority leader. In the words of Theodore H. White, the Senate, for Johnson, was "faith, calling, club, habit, relaxation, devotion, hobby, and love." Over the years it became "almost a monomania with him, his private life itself." [4] Such "monomania" is normally the prerequisite for Senate leadership. It is also normally an insurmountable barrier, psychologically and politically, to leadership anywhere outside the Senate.

(5) *The decline of personnel interchange between Congress and the administration.* Movement of leaders in recent years between the great national institutions of "The Establishment" and the top positions in the administration has been frequent, easy, and natural. This pattern of lateral entry distinguishes the American executive branch from the governments of most other modern societies. The circulation of individuals between leadership positions in governmental and private institutions eases the strains between political and private leadership and performs a unifying function comparable to that which common class origins perform in Great Britain or common membership in the Communist Party does in the Soviet Union.

The frequent movement of individuals between administration and

---

[3] Quoted in Charles L. Clapp, *The Congressman: His Work as He Sees It* (Washington: Brookings Institution, 1963), p. 21.

[4] Theodore H. White, *The Making of the President, 1960* (New York: Atheneum Press, 1961), p. 132.

establishment contrasts sharply with the virtual absence of such movement between Congress and the administration or between Congress and
the establishment. The gap between congressional leadership and administration leadership has increased sharply during this century. Seniority makes it virtually impossible for administration leaders to become
leaders of Congress and makes it unlikely that leaders of Congress will
want to become leaders of the administration. The separation of powers
has become the insulation of leaders. Between 1861 and 1896, 37 per
cent of the people appointed to posts in the President's cabinet had
served in the House or Senate. Between 1897 and 1940, 19 per cent of
the Cabinet positions were filled by former congressmen or senators. Between 1941 and 1963, only 15 per cent of the cabinet posts were so filled.
Former congressmen received only 4 per cent of over 1,000 appointments
of political executives made during the Roosevelt, Truman, Eisenhower,
and Kennedy Administrations.[5] In 1963, apart from the President and
Vice-President, only one of the top seventy-five leaders of the Kennedy
Administration (Secretary of the Interior Udall) had served in Congress.

Movement from the administration to leadership positions in Congress
is almost equally rare. In 1963 only one of eighty-one congressional leaders (Senator Anderson) had previously served in the President's Cabinet.
Those members of the administration who do move on to Congress are
typically those who have come to the administration from state and local
politics rather than from the great national institutions. Few congressmen and even fewer congressional leaders move from Congress to positions of leadership in national private organizations, and relatively few
leaders of these organizations move on to Congress. Successful men who
have come to the top in business, law, or education naturally hesitate
to shift to another world in which they would have to start all over again
at the bottom. In some cases, undoubtedly, Establishment leaders also
consider legislative office simply beneath them.

(6) *The social origins and careers of congressmen.* Congressmen are
much more likely to come from rural and small-town backgrounds than
are administration and establishment leaders. A majority of the senators holding office between 1947 and 1957 were born in rural areas. 64
per cent of the 1959 senators were raised in rural areas or in small towns,
and only 19 per cent in metropolitan centers. In contrast, 52 per cent
of the presidents of the largest industrial corporations grew up in metropolitan centers, as did a large proportion of the political executives appointed during the Roosevelt, Truman, Eisenhower, and Kennedy Administrations. The contrast in origins is reflected in fathers' occupations.
In the 1950s, the proportion of farmer fathers among senators (32 per

[5] See Pendleton Herring, *Presidential Leadership* (New York: Farrar and Rinehart,
1940), pp. 164-65 for figures for 1861-1940; figures for 1940-1963 have been calculated
on same basis as Herring's figures; see also Dean E. Mann, "The Selection of Federal
Political Executives," *American Political Science Review*, 58 (March, 1964), 97.

cent) was more than twice as high as it was among administration leaders (13 per cent) and business leaders (9 to 15 per cent).[6]

Of perhaps greater significance is the difference in geographical mobility between congressmen and private and public executives. Forty-one per cent of the 1959 senators, but only 12 per cent of the 1959 corporation presidents, were currently residing in their original hometowns. Seventy per cent of the presidents had moved 100 miles or more from their hometowns but only 29 per cent of the senators had done so.[7] In 1963, over one-third (37 per cent) of the top leaders of Congress but only 11 per cent of administration leaders were still living in their places of birth. Seventy-seven per cent of the congressional leaders were living in their states of birth, while 70 per cent of the administration leaders

Table II

GEOGRAPHICAL MOBILITY OF NATIONAL LEADERS

	Congressional Leaders (1963) N-81	Administration Leaders (1963) N-74	Political Executives (1959) N-1, 865	Business Leaders (1952) N-8300
None	37%	11%	} 14%	} 40%
Intrastate	40	19		
Interstate, intraregion	5	9	10	15
Interregion	19	61	73	45
International	0	0	3	0

Sources: "Political Executives," Warner *et al., op. cit.,* p. 332; business leaders, Warner and Abegglen, *op. cit.,* p. 82; congressional and administration leaders, independent calculation. Geographical mobility is measured by comparing birthplace with current residence. For administration leaders, current residence was considered to be last residence before assuming administration position. The nine regions employed in this analysis are defined in Warner *et al., op. cit.,* pp. 42-43.

had moved out of their states of birth. Sixty-one per cent of administration leaders and 73 per cent of political executives had moved from one region of the country to another, but only 19 per cent of congressional leaders had similar mobility.

[6] See Andrew Hacker, "The Elected and the Anointed," *American Political Science Review,* 55 (September 1961), 540-41; Mann, *ibid.,* 58 (March 1964) 92-93; Donald R. Matthews, *U.S. Senators and Their World* (Chapel Hill: University of North Carolina Press, 1960), pp. 14-17; W. Lloyd Warner, *et al., The American Federal Executive* (New Haven: Yale University Press, 1963), pp. 11, 56-58, 333; W. Lloyd Warner and James C. Abegglen, *Occupational Mobility in American Business and Industry* (Minneapolis: University of Minnesota Press, 1955), p. 38; Suzanne Keller, "The Social Origins and Career Patterns of Three Generations of American Business Leaders" (Ph.D. dissertation, Columbia University, 1953), cited in Wendell Bell, Richard J. Hill, and Charles R. Wright, *Public Leadership* (San Francisco: Chandler Press, 1961), p. 106.

[7] Hacker, *op. cit.,* 544.

During the course of this century the career patterns of congressmen and of executive leaders have diverged. At an earlier period both leaderships had extensive experience in local and state politics. In 1903 about one-half of executive leaders and three-quarters of congressional leaders had held office in state or local government. In 1963 the congressional pattern had not changed significantly, with 64 per cent of the congressional leaders having held state or local office. The proportion of executive leaders with this experience, however, had dropped drastically.

Table III

EXPERIENCE OF NATIONAL POLITICAL LEADERS
IN STATE AND LOCAL GOVERNMENT

Offices Held	*Congressional Leaders*		*Administration Leaders*	
	1903	*1963*	*1903*	*1963*
Any state or local office	75%	64%	49%	17%
Elective local office	55	46	22	5
State legislature	47	30	17	3
Appointive state office	12	10	20	7
Governor	16	9	5	4

The congressional leaders of 1963, moreover, were more often professional politicians than the congressional leaders of 1903: in 1903 only 5 per cent of the congressional leaders had no major occupation outside politics, while in 1963, 22 per cent of the congressional leaders had spent almost all their lives in electoral politics.

The typical congressman may have gone away to college, but he then returned to his home state to pursue an electoral career, working his way up through local office, the state legislature, and eventually to Congress. The typical political executive, on the other hand, like the typical corporation executive, went away to college and then did not return home but instead pursued a career in a metropolitan center or worked in one or more national organizations with frequent changes of residence. As a result, political executives have become divorced from state and local politics, just as the congressional leaders have become isolated from national organizations. Congressional leaders, in short, come up through a "local politics" line while executives move up through a "national organization" line.

The differences in geographical mobility and career patterns reflect two different styles of life which cut across the usual occupational groupings. Businessmen, lawyers, and bankers are found in both Congress and the administration. But those in Congress are likely to be small businessmen, small-town lawyers, and small-town bankers. Among the sixty-six lawyers in the Senate in 1963, for instance, only two—Joseph Clark and Clifford Case—had been "prominent corporation counsel[s]" before go-

ing into politics.[8] Administration leaders, in contrast, are far more likely
to be affiliated with large national industrial corporations, with Wall
Street or State Street law firms, and with New York banks.

(7) *The provincialism of congressmen.* The absence of mobility between Congress and the executive branch and the differing backgrounds
of the leaders of the two branches of government stimulate different
policy attitudes. Congressmen tend to be oriented toward local needs
and small-town ways of thought. The leaders of the administration and
of the great private national institutions are more likely to think in
national terms. Analyzing consensus-building on foreign aid, James N.
Rosenau concluded that congressmen typically had "segmental" orientations while other national leaders had "continental" orientations. The
segmentally oriented leaders "give highest priority to the subnational
units which they head or represent" and are "not prepared to admit a
discrepancy between" the national welfare and "their subnational concerns." The congressman is part of a local consensus of local politicians,
local businessmen, local bankers, local trade union leaders, and local
newspaper editors who constitute the opinion-making elite of their
districts. As Senator Richard Neuberger noted: "If there is one maxim
which seems to prevail among many members of our national legislature,
it is that local matters must come first and global problems a poor second
—that is, if the member of Congress is to survive politically." As a
result, the members of Congress are "isolated" from other national leaders. At gatherings of national leaders, "members of Congress seem more
conspicuous by their absence than by their presence." One piece of evidence is fairly conclusive: of 623 national opinion-makers who attended
ten American Assembly sessions between 1956 and 1960, only nine (1.4
per cent) were members of Congress! [9]

The differences in attitude between segmentally oriented congressmen
and the other, continentally oriented national leaders are particularly
marked in those areas of foreign policy (such as foreign aid) which involve the commitment of tangible resources for intangible ends. But they
may also exist in domestic policy. The approaches of senators and corporation presidents to economic issues, Andrew Hacker found, are rooted
in "disparate images of society." Senators are provincially oriented; corporation presidents "metropolitan" in their thinking. Senators may be
sympathetic to business, but they think of business in small-town, small-
business terms. They may attempt to accommodate themselves to the
needs of the national corporations, but basically "they are faced with a
power they do not really understand and with demands about whose
legitimacy they are uneasy." As a result, Hacker suggests, "serious ten-

[8] Andrew Hacker, "Are There Too Many Lawyers in Congress?" *New York Times
Magazine,* January 5, 1964, 74.

[9] James N. Rosenau, *National Leadership and Foreign Policy* (Princeton: Princeton
University Press, 1963), pp. 30-31, 347-350.

sions exist between our major political and economic institutions . . . .
There is, at base, a real lack of understanding and a failure of communication between the two elites." [10]

"Segmental" or "provincial" attitudes are undoubtedly stronger in the
House than they are in the Senate. But they also exist in the Senate.
Despite the increased unity of the country caused by mass communications and the growth of "national as distinguished from local or sectional
industry," the Senate, according to an admiring portraitist, "is if anything progressively less national in its approach to most affairs" and "is
increasingly engaged upon the protection of what is primarily local or
sectional in economic life." [11]

Old ideas, old values, old beliefs die hard in Congress. The structure
of Congress encourages their perpetuation. The newcomer to Congress
is repeatedly warned that "to get along he must go along." To go along
means to adjust to the prevailing mores and attitudes of the Inner Club.
The more the young congressman desires a career in the House or Senate,
the more readily he makes the necessary adjustments. The country at
large has become urban, suburban, and metropolitan. Its economic, social, educational, and technological activities are increasingly performed
by huge national bureaucratic organizations. But on Capitol Hill the
nineteenth-century ethos of the small-town, the independent farmer, and
the small businessman is still entrenched behind the institutional defenses which have developed in this century to insulate Congress from
the new America.

*   *   *

The executive branch has thus grown in power vis-à-vis Congress for
precisely the same reason that the House of Representatives grew in
power vis-à-vis the Executive in the second and third decades of the
nineteenth century. It has become more powerful because it has become
more representative. Congress has lost power because it has had two
defects as a representative body. One, relatively minor and in part easily
remedied, deals with the representation of people as individuals; the
other, more serious and perhaps beyond remedy, concerns the representation of organized groups and interests.

Congress was originally designed to represent individuals in the House
and governmental units—the states—in the Senate. In the course of time
the significance of the states as organized interests declined, and popular
election of senators was introduced. In effect, both senators and representatives now represent relatively arbitrarily-defined territorial collec-
tions of individuals. This system of individual representation suffers from
two inequities. First, of course, is the constitutional equal representation

[10] Hacker, *op. cit.*, 547-49.
[11] William S. White, *Citadel* (New York: Harper & Bros., 1956), p. 136.

of states in the Senate irrespective of population. Second, in the House, congressional districts vary widely in size and may also be gerrymandered to benefit one party or group of voters. The net effect of these practices in recent years has been to place the urban and, even more importantly, the suburban voter at a disadvantage vis-à-vis the rural and small-town voter. In due course, however, the Supreme Court decision in *Wesberry* v. *Sanders* in February 1964 will correct much of this discrepancy.

The second and more significant deficiency of Congress as a representative body concerns its insulation from the interests which have emerged in the twentieth century's "organizational revolution." How can national institutions be represented in a locally-elected legislature? In the absence of any easy answer to this question, the administration has tended to emerge as the natural point of access to the government for these national organizations and the place where their interests and viewpoints are brought into the policy-making process. In effect, the American system of government is moving toward a three-way system of representation. Particular territorial interests are represented in Congress; particular functional interests are represented in the administration; and the national interest is represented territorially and functionally in the Presidency.

Every four years the American people choose a President, but they elect an administration. In this century the administration has acquired many of the traditional characteristics of a representative body that Congress has tended to lose. The Jacksonian principle of "rotation in office" and the classic concept of the Cincinnatus-like statesman are far more relevant now to the administration than they are to Congress. Administration officials, unlike congressmen, are more frequently mobile amateurs in government than career professionals in politics. The patterns of power in Congress are rigid. The patterns of power in the administration are flexible. The administration is thus a far more sensitive register of changing currents of opinion than is Congress. A continuous adjustment of power and authority takes place within each administration; major changes in the distribution of power take place at every change of administration. The Truman Administration represented one combination of men, interests, and experience, the Eisenhower Administration another, and the Kennedy Administration yet a third. Each time a new President takes office, the executive branch is invigorated in the same way that the House of Representatives was invigorated by Henry Clay and his western congressmen in 1811. A thousand new officials descend on Washington, coming fresh from the people, representing the diverse forces behind the new President, and bringing with them new demands, new ideas, and new power. Here truly is representative government along classic lines and of a sort which Congress has not known for decades. One key to the "decline" of Congress lies in the defects of Congress as a representative body.

STRUCTURE: THE DISPERSION OF POWER IN CONGRESS

The influence of Congress in our political system thus varies directly with its ties to the more dynamic and dominant groups in society. The power of Congress also varies directly, however, with the centralization of power in Congress. The corollary of these propositions is likewise true: centralization of authority within Congress usually goes with close connections between congressional leadership and major external forces and groups. The power of the House of Representatives was at a peak in the second decade of the nineteenth century, when power was centralized in the Speaker and when Henry Clay and his associates represented the dynamic new forces of trans-Appalachian nationalism. Another peak in the power of the House came during Reconstruction, when power was centralized in Speaker Colfax and the Joint Committee on Reconstruction as spokesmen for triumphant northern Radicalism. A third peak in the power of the House came between 1890 and 1910, when the authority of the Speaker reached its height and Speakers Reed and Cannon reflected the newly established forces of nationalist conservatism. The peak in Senate power came during the post-Reconstruction period of the 1870's and 1880's. Within Congress, power was centralized in the senatorial leaders who represented the booming forces of the rising industrial capitalism and the new party machines. These were the years, as Wilfred Binkley put it, of "the Hegemony of the Senate."

Since its first years, the twentieth century has seen no comparable centralization of power in Congress. Instead, the dominant tendency has been toward the dispersion of power. This leaves Congress only partially equipped to deal with the problems of modern society. In general, the complex modern environment requires in social and political institutions *both* a high degree of specialization and a high degree of centralized authority to coordinate and to integrate the activities of the specialized units. Specialization of function and centralization of authority have been the dominant trends of twentieth-century institutional development. Congress, however, has adjusted only half-way. Through its committees and subcommittees it has provided effectively for specialization, much more effectively, indeed, than the national legislature of any other country. But it has failed to combine increasing specialization of function with increasing centralization of authority. Instead the central leadership in Congress has been weakened, and as a result Congress lacks the central authority to integrate its specialized bodies. In a "rational" bureaucracy authority varies inversely with specialization. Within Congress authority usually varies directly with specialization.

The authority of the specialist is a distinctive feature of congressional behavior. "Specialization" is a key norm in both House and Senate. The man who makes a career in the House, one congressman has observed "is primarily a worker, a specialist, and a craftsman—someone who will concentrate his energies in a particular field and gain prestige and influence in that." "The members who are most successful," another congressman concurred, "are those who pick a specialty or an area and become real experts in it." [12] The emphasis on specialization as a norm, of course, complements the importance of the committee as an institution. It also leads to a great stress on reciprocity. In a bureaucracy, specialized units compete with each other for the support of less specialized officials. In Congress, however, reciprocity among specialists replaces coordination by generalists. When a committee bill comes to the floor, the non-specialists in that subject acquiesce in its passage with the unspoken but complete understanding that they will receive similar treatment. "The traditional deference to the authority of one of its committees overwhelms the main body," one congressman has observed. "The whole fabric of Congress is based on committee expertise. . . ." [13] Reciprocity thus substitutes for centralization and confirms the diffusion of power among the committees.

The current phase of dispersed power in Congress dates from the second decade of this century. The turning point in the House came with the revolt against Speaker Cannon in 1910, the removal of the Speaker from the Rules Committee, and the loss by the Speaker of his power to appoint standing committees. For a brief period, from 1911 to 1915, much of the Speaker's former power was assumed by Oscar Underwood in his capacities as majority floor leader and chairman of the Ways and Means Committee. In 1915, however, Underwood was elected to the Senate, and the dispersion of power which had begun with the overthrow of the Speaker rapidly accelerated.

During the first years of the Wilson Administration, authority in the Senate was concentrated in the floor leader, John Worth Kern, a junior senator first elected to the Senate in 1910. Under his leadership the seniority system was bypassed, and the Senate played an active and creative role in the remarkable legislative achievements of the Sixty-third Congress. Conceivably the long-entrenched position of seniority could have been broken at this point. "If the rule of 'seniority' was not destroyed in 1913," says Claude G. Bowers, "it was so badly shattered that it easily could have been given the finishing stroke." [14] Kern, however, was defeated for re-election in 1916, seniority was restored to its earlier position of eminence, and the power which Kern had temporarily centralized was again dispersed.

Thus since 1910 in the House and since 1915 in the Senate the overall tendency has been toward the weakening of central leadership and the strengthening of the committees. The restoration of seniority in the

[12] Clapp, *op. cit.*, pp. 23-24.
[13] Clem Miller, *Member of the House* (New York: Scribner's, 1962), p. 51.
[14] Claude G. Bowers, *The Life of John Worth Kern* (Indianapolis: Hollenback Press, 1918), p 240.

Senate and its development and rigidification in the House have contributed directly to this end. So also have most of the "reforms" which have been made in the procedures of Congress. "Since 1910," the historian of the House has observed, "the leadership of the House has been in commission. . . . The net effect of the various changes of the last thirty-five years in the power structure of the House of Representatives has been to diffuse the leadership, and to disperse its risks, among a numerous body of leaders." [15] The Budget and Accounting Act of 1921 strengthened the Appropriations Committees by giving them exclusive authority to report appropriations, but its primary effects were felt in the executive branch with the creation of the Bureau of the Budget. During the 1920s power was further dispersed among the Speaker, floor leaders, Rules, Appropriations, Ways and Means chairmen, and caucus chairman. In the following decade political development also contributed to the diffusion of influence when the conservative majority on the Rules Committee broke with the administration in 1937.

The dispersion of power to the committees of Congress was intensified by the Legislative Reorganization Act of 1946. In essence, this act was a "Committee reorganization act" making the committees stronger and more effective. The reduction in the number of standing committees from eighty-one to thirty-four increased the importance of the committee chairmanships. Committee consolidation led to the proliferation of subcommittees, now estimated to number over two hundred and fifty. Thus the functions of integration and coordination which, if performed at all, would previously have been performed by the central leadership of the two houses, have now devolved on the leadership of the standing committees. Before the reorganization, for instance, committee jurisdictions frequently overlapped, and the presiding officers of the House and Senate could often influence the fate of a bill by exercising their discretion in referring it to committee. While jurisdictional uncertainties have not been totally eliminated, the discretion of the presiding officers has been drastically curtailed. The committee chairman, on the other hand, can often influence the fate of legislation by manipulating the subcommittee structure of the committee and by exercising his discretion in referring bills to subcommittees. Similarly, the intention of the framers of the Reorganization Act to reduce, if not to eliminate, the use of special committees has had the effect of restricting the freedom of action of the central leadership in the two houses at the same time that it confirms the authority of the standing committees in their respective jurisdictions. The Reorganization Act also bolstered the committees by significantly expanding their staffs and by specifically authorizing them to exercise legislative overseeing functions with respect to the administrative agencies in their field of responsibility.

[15] Galloway, *op. cit.,* pp. 95, 98, 128.

The Act included few provisions strengthening the central leadership of Congress. Those which it did include usually have not operated successfully. A proposal for party policy committees in each house was defeated in the House of Representatives. The Senate subsequently authorized party policy committees in the Senate, but they have not been active or influential enough to affect the legislative process significantly. The Act's provision for a Joint Committee on the Budget which would set an appropriations ceiling by February 15th of each year was implemented twice and then abandoned. In 1950 the Appropriations Committees reported a consolidated supply bill which cut the presidential estimates by two billion dollars and was approved by Congress two months before the approval of the individual supply bills of 1949. Specialized interests within Congress, however, objected strenuously to this procedure, and it has not been attempted again. The net effect of the Reorganization Act was thus to further the dispersion of power, to strengthen and to institutionalize committee authority, and to circumscribe still more the influence of the central leadership.

In the years after the Legislative Reorganization Act, the issues which earlier had divided the central leadership and committee chairmen reappeared in each committee in struggles between committee chairmen and subcommittees. The chairmen attempted to maintain their own control and flexibility over the number, nature, staff, membership, and leadership of their subcommittees. Several of the most assertive chairmen either prevented the creation of subcommittees or created numbered subcommittees without distinct legislative jurisdictions, thereby reserving to themselves the assignment of legislation to the subcommittees. Those who wished to limit the power of the chairman, on the other hand, often invoked seniority as the rule to be followed in designating subcommittee chairmen. In 1961 thirty-one of the thirty-six standing committees of the House and Senate had subcommittees and in twenty-four the subcommittees had fixed jurisdictions and significant autonomy, thus playing a major role in the legislative process. In many committees the subcommittees go their independent way, jealously guarding their autonomy and prerogatives against other subcommittees and their own committee chairman. "Given an active subcommittee chairman working in a specialized field with a staff of his own," one congressional staff member observes, "the parent committee can do no more than change the grammar of a subcommittee report." [16] Specialization of function and dispersion of power, which once worked to the benefit of the committee chairmen, now work against them.

The Speaker and the majority floor leaders are, of course, the most powerful men in Congress, but their power is not markedly greater than

---

[16] George Goodwin, Jr., "Subcommittees: The Miniature Legislatures of Congress," *American Political Science Review*, 56 (September 1962), 596-601.

that of many other congressional leaders. In 1959, for instance, thirteen
of nineteen committee chairmen broke with the Speaker to support the
Landrum-Griffin bill. "This graphically illustrated the locus of power in
the House," one congressman commented. "The Speaker, unable to deliver votes, was revealed in outline against the chairmen. This fact was
not lost on Democratic Members." [17] The power base of the central leaders has tended to atrophy, caught between the expansion of presidential
authority and influence, on the one hand, and the institutionalization of
committee authority, on the other.

At times individual central leaders have built up impressive networks
of personal influence. These, however, have been individual, not institutional, phenomena. The ascendency of Rayburn and Johnson during the
1950s, for instance, tended to obscure the difference between personal
influence and institutional authority. With the departure of the Texas
coalition their personal networks collapsed. "Rayburn's personal power
and prestige," observed Representative Richard Bolling, "made the institution *appear* to work. When Rayburn died, the thing just fell
apart." [18] Similarly, Johnson's effectiveness as Senate leader, in the words
of one of his assistants, was "overwhelmingly a matter of personal influence. By all accounts, Johnson was the most personal among recent
leaders in his approach. For years it was said that he talked to every
Democratic senator every day. Persuasion ranged from the awesome pyro-
technics known as 'Treatment A' to the apparently casual but always pur-
poseful exchange as he roamed the floor and the cloakroom." [19] When
Johnson's successor was accused of failing to provide the necessary leadership to the Senate, he defended himself on the grounds that he was
Mansfield and not Johnson. His definition of the leader's role was largely
negative: "I am neither a circus ringmaster, the master of ceremonies of
a Senate nightclub, a tamer of Senate lions, or a wheeler and dealer
. . . ." [20] The majority leadership role was uninstitutionalized and the
kindly, gentlemanly, easygoing qualities which Mansfield had had as
Senator from Montana were not changed when he became majority
leader. The power of the President has been institutionalized; the powers
of the congressional committees and their chairmen have been institutionalized; but the power of the central leaders of Congress remains
personal, *ad hoc,* and transitory.

FUNCTION: THE SHIFT TO OVERSIGHT

The insulation of Congress from external social forces and the dispersion of power within Congress have stimulated significant changes

[17] Miller, *op. cit.,* p. 110.

[18] Quoted in Stewart Alsop, "The Failure of Congress," *Saturday Evening Post,* 236
(December 7, 1963), 24.

[19] Ralph K. Huitt, "Democratic Party Leadership in the Senate," *American Political
Science Review,* 55 (June 1961), 338.

[20] *Congressional Record* (November 27, 1963), p. 21, 758 (daily ed.).

in the functions of Congress. The congressional role in legislation has largely been reduced to delay and amendment; congressional activity in overseeing administration has expanded and diversified. During the nineteenth century Congress frequently took the legislative initiative in dealing with major national problems. Even when the original proposal came from the President, Congress usually played an active and positive role in reshaping the proposal into law. "The predominant and controlling force, the centre and source of all motive and of all regulative power," Woodrow Wilson observed in 1885, "is Congress. . . . The legislature is the aggressive spirit." [21] Since 1933, however, the initiative in formulating legislation, in assigning legislative priorities, in arousing support for legislation, and in determining the final content of the legislation enacted has clearly shifted to the executive branch. All three elements of the executive branch—President, administration, and bureaucracy—have gained legislative functions at the expense of Congress. Today's "aggressive spirit" is clearly the executive branch.

In 1908, it is reported, the Senate, in high dudgeon at the effrontery of the Secretary of the Interior, returned to him the draft of a bill which he had proposed, resolving to refuse any further communications from executive officers unless they were transmitted by the President himself.[22] Now, however, congressmen expect the executive departments to present them with bills. Eighty per cent of the bills enacted into law, one congressman has estimated, originate in the executive branch. Indeed, in most instances congressmen do not admit a responsibility to take legislative action except in response to executive requests. Congress, as one senator has complained, "has surrendered its rightful place in the leadership in the lawmaking process to the White House. No longer is Congress the source of major legislation. It now merely filters legislative proposals from the President, straining out some and reluctantly letting others pass through. These days no one expects Congress to devise the important bills." [23] The President now determines the legislative agenda of Congress almost as thoroughly as the British Cabinet sets the legislative agenda of Parliament. The institutionalization of this role was one of the more significant developments in presidential-congressional relations after World War II.[24]

Congress has conceded not only the initiative in originating legislation but—and perhaps inevitably as the result of losing the initiative—it has also lost the dominant influence it once had in shaping the final

---

[21] Woodrow Wilson, *Congressional Government* (Boston: Houghton Mifflin Company, 1885), pp. 11, 36.

[22] George B. Galloway, *The Legislative Process in Congress* (New York: Thomas Y. Crowell, 1955), p. 9.

[23] Abraham Ribicoff, "Doesn't Congress Have Ideas of Its Own?" *Saturday Evening Post*, 237 (March 21, 1964), 6.

[24] Richard E. Neustadt, "Presidency and Legislation: Planning the President's Program," *American Political Science Review*, 49 (December 1955), 980-1021.

content of legislation. Between 1882 and 1909 Congress had a preponderant influence in shaping the content of sixteen (55 per cent) out of twenty-nine major laws enacted during those years. It had a preponderant influence over seventeen (46 per cent) of thirty-seven major laws passed between 1910 and 1932. During the constitutional revolution of the New Deal, however, its influence declined markedly: only two (8 per cent) of twenty-four major laws passed between 1933 and 1940 were primarily the work of Congress.[25] Certainly its record after World War II was little better. The loss of congressional control over the substance of policy is most marked, of course, in the area of national defense and foreign policy. At one time Congress did not hesitate to legislate the size and weapons of the armed forces. Now this power—to raise and support armies, to provide and maintain a navy—is firmly in the hands of the executive. Is Congress, one congressional committee asked plaintively in 1962, to play simply "the passive role of supine acquiescence" in executive programs or is it to be "an active participant in the determination of the direction of our defense policy?" The committee, however, already knew the answer:

> To any student of government, it is eminently clear that the role of the Congress in determining national policy, defense or otherwise, has deteriorated over the years. More and more the role of Congress has come to be that of a sometimes querulous but essentially kindly uncle who complains while furiously puffing on his pipe but who finally, as everyone expects, gives in and hands over the allowance, grants the permission, or raises his hand in blessing, and then returns to the rocking chair for another year of somnolence broken only by an occasional anxious glance down the avenue and a muttered doubt as to whether he had done the right thing.[26]

In domestic legislation Congress's influence is undoubtedly greater, but even here its primary impact is on the timing and details of legislation, not on the subjects and content of legislation.

The decline in the legislative role of Congress has been accompanied by an increase in its administrative role. The modern state differs from the liberal state of the eighteenth and nineteenth centuries in terms of the greater control it exercises over society and the increase in the size, functions, and importance of its bureaucracy. Needed in the modern state are means to control, check, supplement, stimulate, and ameliorate this bureaucracy. The institutions and techniques available for this task vary from country to country: the Scandinavian countries have their *Ombudsmen;* Communist countries use party bureaucracy to check state bureaucracy. In the United States, Congress has come to play a major, if not the major, role in this regard. Indeed, many of the innovations in Congress in recent years have strengthened its control over the adminis-

[25] Lawrence H. Chamberlain, *The President, Congress, and Legislation* (New York: Columbia University Press, 1946), pp. 450-52.
[26] House Report 1406, Eighty-seventh Congress, Second Session (1962), p. 7.

trative processes of the executive branch. Congressional committees responded with alacrity to the mandate of the 1946 Reorganization Act that they "exercise continuous watchfulness" over the administration of laws. Congressional investigations of the bureaucracy have multiplied: each Congress during the period between 1950 and 1962 conducted more investigations than were conducted by *all* the Congresses during the nineteenth century.[27] Other mechanisms of committee control, such as the legislative veto and committee clearance of administrative decisions, have been increasingly employed. "Not legislation but control of administration," as Galloway remarks, "is becoming the primary function of the modern Congress." [28] In discharging this function, congressmen uncover waste and abuse, push particular projects and innovations, highlight inconsistencies, correct injustices, and compel exposition and defense of bureaucratic decisions.

In performing these activities, Congress is acting where it is most competent to act: it is dealing with particulars, not general policies. Unlike legislating, these concerns are perfectly compatible with the current patterns of insulation and dispersion. Committee specialization and committee power enhance rather than detract from the effectiveness of the committees as administrative overseers. In addition, as the great organized interests of society come to be represented more directly in the bureaucracy and administration, the role of Congress as representative of individual citizens becomes all the more important. The congressman more often serves their interests by representing them in the administrative process than in the legislative process. As has been recognized many times, the actual work of congressmen, in practice if not in theory, is directed toward mediation between constituents and government agencies. "The most pressing day-to-day demands for the time of Senators and Congressmen," Hubert Humphrey has written, "are not directly linked to legislative tasks. They come from constituents." [29] One representative has estimated that half of his own time and two-thirds of that of his staff are devoted to constituent service.[30] This appears to be average. In performing these services congressmen are both representing their constituents where they need to be represented and checking upon and ameliorating the impact of the federal bureaucracy. Constituent service and legislative oversight are two sides of the same coin. Increasingly divorced from the principal organized social forces of society, Congress has come to play a more and more significant role as spokesman for the interests of unorganized individuals.

[27] Galloway, *op. cit.*, p. 166.
[28] *Ibid.*, pp. 56-57.
[29] Hubert H. Humphrey, "To Move Congress Out of Its Ruts," *New York Times Magazine* (April 7, 1963), 39.
[30] Clarence D. Long, "Observations of a Freshman in Congress," *New York Times Magazine* (December 1, 1963), 73.

ADAPTATION OR REFORM

Insulation has made Congress unwilling to initiate laws. Dispersion has made Congress unable to aggregate individual bills into a coherent legislative program. Constituent service and administrative overseeing have eaten into the time and energy which congressmen give legislative matters. Congress is thus left in its legislative dilemma where the assertion of power is almost equivalent to the obstruction of action. What then are the possibilities for institutional adaptation or institutional reform?

Living with the dilemma. Conceivably neither adaptation nor reform is necessary. The present distribution of power and functions could continue indefinitely. Instead of escaping from its dilemma, Congress could learn to live with it. In each of the four institutional crises mentioned earlier, the issue of institutional adaptation came to a head over one issue: the presidential election of 1824, the House of Commons Reform Bill of 1832, the Lloyd George budget of 1910, and the Supreme Court reorganization plan of 1937. The adaptation crisis of Congress differs in that to date a constitutional crisis between the executive branch and Congress has been avoided. Congress has procrastinated, obstructed, and watered down executive legislative proposals, but it has also come close to the point where it no longer dares openly to veto them. Thus the challenge which Congress poses to the executive branch is less blatant and dramatic, but in many ways more complex, ambiguous, and irritating, than the challenge which the Lords posed to Asquith or the Supreme Court to Roosevelt. If Congress uses its powers to delay and to amend with prudence and circumspection, there is no necessary reason why it should not retain them for the indefinite future. In this case, the legislative process in the national government would continually appear to be on the verge of stalemate and breakdown which never quite materialize. The supporters of Congress would continue to bemoan its decline at the same time that its critics would continue to denounce its obstructionism. The system would work so long as Congress stretched but did not exhaust the patience of the executive branch and public. If Congress, however, did reject a major administration measure, like tax reduction or civil rights, the issue would be joined, the country would be thrown into a constitutional crisis, and the executive branch would mobilize its forces for a showdown over the authority of Congress to veto legislation.

Reform versus adaptation: restructuring power. The resumption by Congress of an active, positive role in the legislative process would require a drastic restructuring of power relationships, including reversal of the tendencies toward insulation, dispersion, and oversight. Fundamental "reforms" would thus be required. To date two general types of proposals have been advanced for the structural reform of Congress. Ironically, however, neither set of proposals is likely, if enacted, to achieve the results which its principal proponents desire. One set of reformers, "democratizers" like Senator Clark, attack the power of the Senate "Establishment" or "Inner Club" and urge an equalizing of power among congressmen so that a majority of each house can work its will. These reformers stand four-square in the Norris tradition. Dissolution of the Senate "Establishment" and other measures of democratization, however, would disperse power among still more people, multiply the opportunities for minority veto (by extending them to more minorities), and thus make timely legislative action still more difficult. The "party reformers" such as Professor James M. Burns, on the other hand, place their reliance on presidential leadership and urge the strengthening of the party organization in Congress to insure support by his own party for the President's measures. In actuality, however, the centralization of power within Congress in party committees and leadership bodies would also increase the power of Congress. It would tend to reconstitute Congress as an effective legislative body, deprive the President of his monopoly of the "national interest," and force him to come to terms with the centralized congressional leadership, much as Theodore Roosevelt had to come to terms with Speaker Cannon. Instead of strengthening presidential leadership, the proposals of the party reformers would weaken it.

The dispersion of power in Congress has created a situation in which the internal problem of Congress is not dictatorship but oligarchy. The only effective alternative to oligarchy is centralized authority. Oligarchies, however, are unlikely to reform themselves. In most political systems centralized power is a necessary although not sufficient condition for reform and adaptation to environmental change. At present the central leaders of Congress are, with rare exceptions, products of and closely identified with the committee oligarchy. Reform of Congress would depend upon the central leaders' breaking with the oligarchy, mobilizing majorities from younger and less influential congressmen, and employing these majorities to expand and to institutionalize their own power.

Centralization of power within Congress would also, in some measure, help solve the problem of insulation. Some of Congress's insulation has been defensive in nature, a compensation for its declining role in the legislative process as well as a cause of that decline. Seniority, which is largely responsible for the insulation, is a symptom of more basic institutional needs and fears. Greater authority for the central leaders of Congress would necessarily involve a modification of the seniority system. Conversely, in the absence of strong central leadership, recourse to seniority is virtually inevitable. Election of committee chairmen by the committees themselves, by party caucuses, or by each house would stimulate antagonisms among members and multiply the opportunities for outside forces from the executive branch or from interest groups to influence the proceedings. Selection by seniority is, in effect, selection by heredity: power goes not to the oldest son of the king but to the oldest child of the institution. It protects Congress against divisive and external influences. It does this, however, through a purely arbitrary method which offers no assurance that the distribution of authority in the Congress will bear any relation to the distribution of opinion in the country, in the rest of the government, or within Congress itself. It purchases institutional integrity at a high price in terms of institutional isolation. The nineteenth-century assignment of committee positions and chairmanships by the Speaker, on the other hand, permitted flexibility and a balancing of viewpoints from within and without the House. External influences, however nefarious (as the earlier remark about Blaine suggests they might be at times), all came to bear on the Speaker, and yet the authority which he possessed enabled him to play a creative political role in balancing these external influences against the claims and viewpoints arising from within the House and against his own personal and policy preferences. The process by which the Speaker selected committee chairmen was not too different from the process by which a President selects a cabinet, and it resembled rather closely the process by which a British Prime Minister appoints a ministry from among his colleagues in Parliament. The resumption of this power by the Speaker in the House and its acquisition by the majority leader in the Senate would restore to Congress a more positive role in the legislative process and strengthen it vis-à-vis the executive branch. Paradoxically, however, the most ardent congressional critics of executive power are also the most strenuous opponents of centralized power in Congress.

Congressional insulation may also be weakened in other ways. The decline in mobility between congressional leadership positions and administration leadership positions has been counterbalanced, in some measure, by the rise of the Senate as a source of Presidents. This is due to several causes. The almost insoluble problems confronting state governments tarnish the glamor and limit the tenure of their governors. The nationalization of communications has helped senators play a role in the news media which is exceeded only by the President. In addition, senators, unlike governors, can usually claim some familiarity with the overriding problems of domestic and foreign policy.

Senatorial insulation may also be weakened to the extent that individuals who have made their reputations on the national scene find it feasible and desirable to run for the Senate. It is normally assumed that too much attention to national problems and too much neglect of state and constituency issues complicate election or reelection to the Senate. Lucas, McFarland, George, and Connally are cited as cases in point. Given the nationalization of communications, however, a political leader may be able to develop greater appeal in a local area by action on the national level than by action on the local level. Salinger's California and Robert Kennedy's New York Senate candidacies could mark the beginning of a new trend in American politics. It is effective testimonial to the extent to which the President dominates the national scene and the na-

tional scene dominates the news that in 1964 Robert Kennedy would probably have been the strongest candidate in any one of a dozen northeastern
industrial states.

Recruitment of senators from the national scene rather than from local
politics would significantly narrow the gap between Congress and the
other elements of national leadership. The "local politics" ladder to the
Senate would be replaced or supplemented by a "national politics" line
in which mobile individuals might move from the establishment to the
administration to the Senate. This would be one important step toward
breaking congressional insulation. The end of insulation, however, would
only occur if at a later date these same individuals could freely move
back from the Senate to the administration. Mobility between Congress
and the administration similar to that which now exists between the
establishment and the administration would bring about drastic changes
in American politics, not the least of which would be a great increase in
the attractiveness of running for Congress. Opening up this possibility,
however, depends upon the modification of seniority, and that, in turn,
depends upon the centralization of power in Congress.

Adaptation and reform: redefining function. A politically easier, although psychologically more difficult, way out of Congress's dilemma
involves not the reversal but the intensification of the recent trends of
congressional evolution. Congress is in a legislative dilemma because
opinion conceives of it as a legislature. If it gave up the effort to play
even a delaying role in the legislative process, it could, quite conceivably,
play a much more positive and influential role in the political system as
a whole. Representative assemblies have not always been legislatures.
They had their origins in medieval times as courts and as councils. An
assembly need not legislate to exist and to be important. Indeed, some
would argue that assemblies should not legislate. "[A] numerous assembly," John Stuart Mill contended, "is as little fitted for the direct business of legislation as for that of administration." [31] Representative assemblies acquired their legislative functions in the 17th and 18th centuries;
there is no necessary reason why liberty, democracy, or constitutional government depends upon their exercising those functions in the twentieth
century. Legislation has become much too complex politically to be
effectively handled by a representative assembly. The primary work of
legislation must be done, and increasingly is being done, by the three
"houses" of the executive branch: the bureaucracy, the administration,
and the President.

Far more important than the preservation of Congress as a legislative
institution is the preservation of Congress as an autonomous institution.
When the performance of one function becomes "dysfunctional" to the
workings of an institution, the sensible course is to abandon it for other

[31] John Stuart Mill, "On Representative Government," *Utilitarianism, Liberty, and
Representative Government* (London: J. M. Dent), p. 235.

functions. In the 1930s the Supreme Court was forced to surrender its function of disallowing national and state social legislation. Since then it has wielded its veto on federal legislation only rarely and with the greatest of discretion. This loss of power, however, has been more than compensated for by its new role in protecting civil rights and civil liberties against state action. This is a role which neither its supporters nor its opponents in the 1930s would have thought possible. In effect, the Court is using the great conservative weapon of the 1930s to promote the great liberal ends of the 1960s. Such is the way skillful leaders and great institutions adapt to changing circumstances.

The redefinition of Congress's functions away from legislation would involve, in the first instance, a restriction of the power of Congress to delay indefinitely presidential legislative requests. Constitutionally, Congress would still retain its authority to approve legislation. Practically, Congress could, as Walter Lippmann and others have suggested, bind itself to approve or disapprove urgent Presidential proposals within a time limit of, say, three or six months. If thus compelled to choose openly, Congress, it may be supposed, would almost invariably approve presidential requests. Its veto power would become a reserve power like that of the Supreme Court if not like that of the British Crown. On these "urgent" measures it would perform a legitimizing function rather than a legislative function. At the same time, the requirement that Congress pass or reject presidential requests would also presumably induce executive leaders to consult with congressional leaders in drafting such legislation. Congress would also, of course, continue to amend and to vote freely on "non-urgent" executive requests.

Explicit acceptance of the idea that legislation was not its primary function would, in large part, simply be recognition of the direction which change has already been taking. It would legitimize and expand the functions of constituent service and administrative oversight which, in practice, already constitute the principal work of most congressmen. Increasingly isolated as it is from the dominant social forces in society, Congress would capitalize on its position as the representative of the unorganized interests of individuals. It would become a proponent of popular demands against the bureaucracy rather than the opponent of popular demands for legislation. It would thus continue to play a major although different role in the constitutional system of checks and balances.

A recent survey of the functioning of legislative bodies in forty-one countries concludes that parliaments are in general losing their initiative and power in legislation. At the same time, however, they are gaining power in the "control of government activity." [32] Most legislatures,

[32] Inter-Parliamentary Union, *Parliaments: A Comparative Study on Structure and Functioning of Representative Institutions in Forty-One Countries* (New York: Frederick A. Praeger, 1963), p. 398.

however, are much less autonomous and powerful than Congress. Congress has lost less power over legislation and gained more power over administration than other parliaments. It is precisely this fact which gives rise to its legislative dilemma. If Congress can generate the leadership and the will to make the drastic changes required to reverse the trends toward insulation, dispersion, and overseeing, it could still resume a positive role in the legislative process. If this is impossible, an alternative path is to abandon the legislative effort and to focus upon those functions of constituent service and bureaucratic control which insulation and dispersion do enable it to play in the national government.

H. Douglas Price

2

The Electoral Arena

The conditions of entry into a legislative body and of survival through successive terms are a major factor in the behavior of aspirants and incumbents. In turn the career perspectives and ambitions of House and Senate members go a long way toward giving structure to those bodies. Looked at the other way, proposals for changes in the structure or procedure of Congress are likely to have a direct impact on the careers of individual members. Some types of changes in the institution are likely only when changes are made in the risks and rewards of the legislative career, either in Congress or in the constituencies. An understanding of the risks of the electoral arena is important for an understanding of Congress, not because local pressures are always decisive on particular votes but because the local basis of election tends to promote a local orientation toward issues in general. Specific local pressures may only infrequently be decisive, but they constitute the pervasive milieu within which congressmen and senators operate.

Two basic and divergent trends have shaped the pattern of election to the House and Senate over the past half century. The first has been the *democratization of the Senate,* brought about by the adoption of direct election of senators, the spread of the direct primary, and the growth of effective two-party competition in the great majority of states.[1] In the late nineteenth and early twentieth centuries the Senate was a bastion of conservatism, something of a "rich man's club," and highly resistant to liberal or progressive sentiment. Since World War II the Senate has

HUGH DOUGLAS PRICE *is Associate Professor of Political Science at Syracuse University. He is the author of* The Negro and Southern Politics *and "Race, Religion, and the Rules Committee," in Alan F. Westin, ed.,* The Uses of Power.

[1] The direct election of senators was not a sudden constitutional change, but the result of a long previous evolution brilliantly analyzed by William Riker, "The Senate and American Federalism," *American Political Science Review* (1955), 452-69.

been the more liberal half of the Congress on most issues and has been highly responsive to the legislative demands of various marginal voting groups.

Just as the critics and defenders of the Supreme Court have more or less exchanged positions, and arguments, since 1937, so have the critics and defenders of the Senate. Where progressives once blasted "the treason of the Senate," liberals now praise its responsiveness to the problems of industrialism and urbanism. Some liberals—such as Senator Joseph Clark of Pennsylvania—would like to see further changes, especially in regard to the filibuster, but sophisticated conservatives now tend to write the Senate off and look for hope to the more conservative House.

Thus in 1962 a writer in *Fortune* magazine, which is widely read in the business community, summarized the impact of direct senatorial election (under conditions of close party competition) as follows:

> There emerged then one significant difference between Senators and Representatives: Senators' constituencies were entire states; Representatives' were fractionalized districts. In time this difference switched the bias of the Senate from conservative to liberal, for it made Senators subject to a twentieth-century phenomenon, the 'bullet vote' of the activist political minorities—labor unions, racial groups, and religious-ethnic organizations. These minorities, usually concentrated in cities, can make their influence felt only on those Representatives in the House who come from urban districts. In the Senate, however, they hold a power beyond their actual numbers. In a closely contested state their votes, cast preponderantly for one candidate or the other, can frequently make the difference between victory and defeat. Senatorial candidates, as a result, have given greater and greater consideration to these city voters, who tend to be highly in favor of public housing, medical care, higher minimum wages, and the general liberal program . . . . No Senator from a state with heavily unionized industry willingly gets himself classified as 'antilabor.' No Senator from a state with politically effective racial groups dares oppose their wishes.[2]

A spokesman from Americans for Democratic Action would phrase the matter somewhat differently but hardly would disagree as to the basic point.

While the Senate has become more liberal and more subject to close competition, the House has become more conservative and less subject to competition in the great majority of congressional districts. Thus a second major trend, resulting from the combined effects of safe districts plus the seniority system, has been the *professionalization of the House career*. The "activist political minorities" which are so important for the statewide politics of the Senate (and the Presidency) are important for only a few House districts. At least three-quarters of all House districts are relatively "safe" year after year. This lack of effective party competition at the congressional district level has made reelection to the House

[2] Neil MacNeil, "The House Confronts Mr. Kennedy," *Fortune* (January 1962), 71-73.

generally possible. And the twentieth-century emphasis on the seniority system—which was *not* the standard practice in the nineteenth century —has made repeated reelection desirable and indeed necessary for the member who wants to have an impact on what the House does.

The Formal Rules of the Game

The structural differences between the House and Senate can be dealt with briefly. The six-year term for senators removes them somewhat from the pressure of imminent reelection campaigns. The two-year term for representatives means that a member from a relatively competitive district is almost perpetually campaigning. House members from "safe" districts, however, may face serious challenge even less frequently than does the typical senator.

A four-year term for House members is often suggested but is an exceedingly unlikely change. Its advocates argue that it would permit representatives to devote more time and attention to their legislative duties for at least three years out of four, and that abolition of the mid-term elections might help to strengthen presidential leadership in legislation. Critics of the change suggest that most members actually find that they get in their most effective "campaigning" by appearances during the non-election year, when their activities are not discounted as "mere politics." They also argue that the mid-term election provides a useful chance for the electorate to clarify the mandate given in a presidential election: Thus the Democratic victories in 1954 and 1958 indicated that Eisenhower's election victories of 1952 and 1956 were not a clear call for orthodox Republicanism. The issue of the four-year term is, however, largely academic. Its most direct effect, as Charles Clapp points out, is that it would be a virtual invitation for sitting House members to run against incumbent senators who would come up for reelection in the off years.[3] As it is, a House member generally must give up running for his own seat in order to run against a senator—and that seems to be the way most senators intend to keep it.

The equal representation of states in the Senate makes that body technically unrepresentative of sheer population, but there are very few issues which tend to pit small states as such against the states with a large population. And most major sections of the country include states with both large and small populations. The most concentrated sectional over-representation in the Senate is of the Rocky Mountain West (including the Southwest). The eight mountain states elect sixteen senators, but on a population basis are entitled to only 17 of the 435 House members (which tells a lot about why the Senate has been more responsive than the House to silver miners and sheep herders).

The apportionment of House seats among the states has, since 1929,

[3] Charles L. Clapp, *The Congressman: His Work as He Sees It* (Washington: Brookings Institution, 1963), p. 330.

been put on an automatic basis. But the drawing of individual district lines within a state has long been a problem. Incumbent representatives often oppose upsetting established district lines, and state legislatures controlled by one party have opposed changes that might improve the electoral chances of the other party. States gaining an additional House seat have frequently resorted to electing the additional member at large. Opportunities for such vagaries were finally narrowed, however, by the Supreme Court's 1964 decision (*Wesberry* v. *Sanders*) requiring that House districts be of substantially equal population. This still leaves some room for judicious gerrymandering, but only within the confines of districts with substantially equal population. It should also be noted that a House district may be especially designed, modified, or expressly left unchanged for the specific benefit of a particular representative's career.

The Constitution plus long-standing informal and statutory arrangements thus provide for the direct election of 100 members of the Senate and the 435 members of the House of Representatives. In consequence the local constituencies—states and districts—are provided "representation" through at least three separate processes. First, there is a kind of automatic representation which is roughly achieved by taking almost any individual from a given state or local district. Senator Eastland of Mississippi and Harlem's Congressman Adam Clayton Powell take sharply contrasting stands on civil rights and integration, and the chances are that most white Mississippi residents and almost any Harlem Negro would do likewise. On such basic issues a legislator himself is likely to share the basic views of his effective constituency and to be in no need of a poll on the subject.

A second process of representation occurs through the election system itself. On issues where the local constituency is not so overwhelmingly in agreement, or where a legislator gets widely out of line with the grass-roots view, then the electoral process provides a means for a popular test. Theoretically, at least, an incumbent may be defeated by an opponent of the opposite party or in a primary contest. This possibility of dumping one man and replacing him with another remains the ultimate sanction in a democratic system, but it is something of a blunderbuss weapon. Elections are infrequent, at times set by law rather than by the rise and fall of popular issues, and there may be a great many issues but only two candidates.

The *possibility* of opposition, however, remains a powerful factor in attuning the incumbent to the third process of representation. This is the more subtle process by which constituents can express opinions and exert influence in such a manner that the politically sophisticated legislator can, if he desires, make an estimate of the amount of local backing (in terms of influence, not of counting noses) and adapt his position accordingly. Thus the incumbent can often adjust to changes in the make-up of his constituency, to shifts in the national climate, or to new and urgent demands from individuals or groups that are important to him or to his district. To the extent that the representative can, and is willing, to perform this third type of delicate representation, then the probability of the electorate resorting to the second type (throwing the rascal out) is reduced. But the possibility of defeat remains, and in the case of a major electoral landslide it often falls equally on the just and the unjust.

Each of these processes of representation depends upon a variety of institutional arrangements. Operation of the first form is guaranteed through residence requirements. The sharp contrast between the American emphasis on local residence and the British practice of assigning parliamentary candidates to seats anywhere in the country has often been noted. In point of fact, however, the American practice is largely *informal;* the Constitution requires only that a member "when elected, be an inhabitant of that state" in which he is chosen. As the nomination of Pierre Salinger for the Senate in California and the election of Robert Kennedy in New York show, this is a nominal requiremnt. But the *informal* emphasis on a "local man," who knows, appreciates, and is responsive to the local scene, is still the norm. The customary length of local residence necessary for political acceptance, however, may vary from several generations (in parts of the South) to barely a decade (in Southern California or peninsular Florida).

The legislator's job is unique, in large part because of the unusual risks which are built into the role. These risks or occupational hazards are of two general types. On the one hand, there is the double hurdle of winning both the nomination and general election in order to become, or remain, a member of the House or Senate. But there also are, or at least can be, serious risks to the member's position and influence resulting from changes within the legislative chamber itself. The two sorts of risks are closely linked, and changes in either one are likely to have effects on the other. Thus if House committee assignments and appointment of chairmen were made with no regard to seniority or continuity, but rather on the basis of factional contests for the leadership (as is the case with some state legislatures), then the incentives for repeatedly facing the hazards of the electoral arena would be substantially reduced.

The operation of the electoral process and the leeway it often leaves for the functioning of other channels of influence are worth examining in some detail. The first major hurdle is the nominating process, and it is to that we now turn.

MAKING PARTY NOMINATIONS: THE RISE OF THE DIRECT PRIMARY

Iowa's Senator Jonathan P. Dolliver is best remembered today for his aphorism that Iowa would go Democratic when Hell freezes over. But Dolliver is also interesting as one of the last generation of politicians who came to Congress via the old path of nomination by a delegate convention rather than by winning a primary election contest. In his particular case he first won the Republican nomination to the House, which was tantamount to election, on the 110th ballot of a district convention. He had home-country support but also proved to be the most acceptable second choice for a majority of other delegates. In more recent times would-be congressmen or senators in most states have had to win their nominations in a primary election.

Nomination by primary election is a peculiarly American phenomenon. Just as the delegate convention had replaced the old practice of nomination by legislative caucus as a more direct and more democratic procedure, so the same reasons led to the primary election replacing the convention. The holding of statewide primaries spread rapidly throughout the South during the decade of the 1890's and was adopted by many Northern and Western states, beginning with Wisconsin in 1903. By 1960 every state had *some* sort of primary election system, although a few states—New York, Indiana, Connecticut, and Delaware—still make their senatorial and gubernatorial nominations by convention.[4] But there has been some tendency since World War II for primary states with complex ethnic or nationality mixes to adopt a pre-primary convention which can endorse a ticket—usually a "balanced" one—in the party primary.

At the turn of the century two major factors combined to generate unusual enthusiasm for the adoption of the primary, and for the related issue of direct election of senators. On the one hand, there was widespread and in many cases justifiable dissatisfaction with the manipulation and control of conventions (and state legislatures) by patronage-based bosses and by various special interests. It was a bit optimistic to hope that a shift to nomination by primaries would remove entirely the influence of party bosses or special interests, but it did change the rules of the game. This change reduced the advantages of some types of candidates and some sorts of interests, while improving the position of other candidates and other interests.

The abuses of conventions and of legislative choice of senators were most marked in one-party areas where the general election contest did not constitute a restraining influence. The second factor behind the rapid spread of the primary was the sharp decline in general election competition which occurred in the 1890s. By 1900 so much of the country was one-party Democratic or one-party Republican that if people were to be provided a meaningful vote between rivals it would have to be in the primary. In the South the Negro had been finally removed as a political factor, and the Republican party reduced to a nullity. In much of the

---

[4] Since 1955 Connecticut has authorized a "challenge" primary in which the loser in the convention can force the winner into a primary, but the procedure has generally been avoided.

North the nomination of William Jennings Bryan in 1896 had brought catastrophe to the Democrats. Hence the primary afforded the people a means of having at least some sort of election contest, and this seemed all the more important since the decline of general election competition severely lessened the restraints on the potential abuses of the largely un-regulated convention process. As E. E. Schattschneider has noted, in the period prior to 1896 "the two major parties were able to compete on re-markably even terms throughout the country." As he puts it:

> Thus the crisis of 1896 destroyed the balance of the party system. In 1892 there were thirty-six states in which a competitive party situation existed. By 1904 there remained only six states in which the parties were evenly matched, while there were twenty-nine states in which the parties were so unbalanced that the situation could no longer be described as competitive.[5]

Under such circumstances the nomination became, for all practical pur-poses, the decisive step in the electoral contest in most states.

By and large the primary proved to be a poor substitute for general election competition, but in the absence of such competition the primary doubtless had substantial advantages over the convention system. The very flexibility of the primary system, however, seems to have worked so as to further weaken the local minority party. Voters and candidates who might have helped to develop the opposition party tended to register and to enter politics in the ranks of the dominant majority. And within the majority party lines were fluid, participation was less than in general elections and incumbents could usually count on reelection. Except in states with sharp factional cleavage, there was no continuing base of support or group of organizers to advance candidates to challenge the incumbent.

For congressmen and senators the operation of the primary has tended to emphasize the highly decentralized nature of the American party sys-tem. At the nominating stage of the process the national party hardly exists. Rather it provides a label that automatically goes to any and all those local candidates who happen to win in the party's local primaries. The candidate may win solely because of his name or because he vigor-ously opposes the national party on some major local issue, such as segregation in the Deep South. Thus in each state and in most congres-sional districts the party nomination is up for grabs. Or at least it is when the incumbent is not a candidate for renomination.

Sociologists have found it useful to distinguish between educational systems which operate along lines of *sponsored* mobility (such as the British preparatory schools for the upper classes) as contrasted with a more open system of *contest* mobility (such as American public schools

---

[5] E. E. Schattschneider, "United States: The Functional Approach to Party Govern-ment," in Sigmund Neumann, *Modern Political Parties* (Chicago: University of Chicago Press, 1956), p. 203.

and low-tuition state universities).[6] Much the same distinction can be made in regard to party nominating systems—British parties sponsor candidates and assign them constituencies in order to bring them into the national political scene. In American parties the local primary is generally an open contest, to be won by a local candidate campaigning on local issues.

The tendency for incumbents to win renomination is a tribute both to the material advantages which accrue to the incumbent and to the skill with which most incumbents work to keep their local fences mended. In 1960 only six House members failed in their renomination campaigns. Charles L. Clapp, summarizing a series of round-table sessions held with both Republican and Democratic members, puts the matter this way:

> Although members of Congress are inclined to talk about re-election campaigns in terms of the problems involved, they agree that as incumbents they possess extraordinary advantages over their opponents. There is a tendency to believe that, aside from isolated instances where an overriding issue is present, there is little excuse for defeat.[7]

This is even more true of the primary than of the general election, in which the fate of the incumbent is at least somewhat linked with that of his party and, especially in presidential years, with the national ticket.

On occasion an incumbent's performance may provide a potent issue. In the South, especially since the Supreme Court's 1954 school desegregation decision, the race issue has been the most dangerous subject. The 1950 defeats of Senators Claude Pepper (Florida) and Frank P. Graham (North Carolina) were generally attributed to their being "soft" on the race question. Several House members have been ousted on the same grounds, and in the 1960s Negro voters may help to retire some pro-segregationists. In 1956 two of the three North Carolina congressmen who refused to sign the "Southern Manifesto" (protesting the Court's decision) were defeated in primaries. In 1958 Brooks Hays was upset by an organized write-in campaign launched after the primary and amid the Little Rock, Arkansas, school crisis. In 1964 the more liberal northern Alabama congressmen found themselves in trouble because of having to run statewide, rather than in their regular districts. Carl Elliott was defeated, and Albert Rains had previously announced that he was retiring. In the Atlanta, Georgia, district, however, a moderate candidate—with considerable Negro support—ousted a staunch supporter of segregation. With rapid changes in the intensity of racial conflict, shifts in the control of state government, and a gradual increase in the number of Negro voters there may be an increase in the number of primary upsets in the South.

[6] Ralph Turner, "Modes of Social Ascent through Education: Sponsored and Contest Mobility," in H. A. Halsey, Jean Floud, and C. A. Anderson, eds., *Education, Economy, and Society* (New York: Free Press of Glencoe, 1961), especially pp. 122-25.

[7] Clapp, *op. cit.*, p. 331.

In most parts of the country there is no effective party organization which can sponsor a candidate and advance him to Congress because of his potential for national politics. And in those few areas where a party organization still does control the nominating process, a seat in the House is more likely to be regarded as a step up the career ladder within a city organization or as a sinecure. Still, there are some areas, usually major cities, where it is difficult or impossible for a member to develop his own independent base of strength. Chicago is perhaps the most obvious example of organization control of the nomination process. There candidates for the House are slated for nomination by, and most depend for renomination upon, the Cook County Democratic organization. And in some parts of Pennsylvania the Republican organization has an almost equal control over Republican incumbents. Thus in 1964 the "retirement" of a Pennsylvania Republican and of a Chicago Democrat were announced under circumstances where the "retirement" seemed to come as much as a surprise to the member as to his colleagues. More typical, however, was the unsuccessful 1964 effort of the once-powerful Kansas City Democratic organization to defeat Congressman Richard Bolling. After a vigorous campaign Bolling was renominated by a two-to-one margin.

Where no incumbent is in the primary race there is usually a scramble for the nomination, especially in the party which is in the majority locally. In this situation the norm is against open presidential intervention, but campaign contributors and expert advisers can be steered in the direction of a favored contender.

The most difficult problem for a President is to influence the outcome of a primary where an anti-administration incumbent is faced by a challenger. Aided perhaps by wartime enthusiasm, Woodrow Wilson was successful in intervening in several Southern primaries in 1918. But Franklin D. Roosevelt was generally unsuccessful in his 1938 "purge" efforts, which were undertaken without much advance planning.[8] Except in unusual circumstances, it would appear that national party leaders are more likely to be effective by quietly searching out a strong local candidate, or a national figure with a local connection, than by public denunciation of the incumbent.

Like the common cold, a primary is seldom fatal but it is almost always an unpleasant disruption. Time, funds, and energy which could otherwise be channeled in other directions have to be diverted to the local scene. Small wonder that most legislators find it advantageous to cultivate the home state or district on a continuous basis, and especially in non-election years, in the hope of deterring opposition. In some states

[8] On Presidential intervention in primaries see Austin Ranney and Willmoore Kendall, *Democracy and the American Party System* (New York: Harcourt, Brace and World, 1956), pp. 286-89, and William Riker, *Democracy in the United States* (New York: Macmillan, 1953), pp. 285-93.

and in a good many House districts the same tactic can be used to reduce the risks of the general election.

Prior political experience and an existing base of support are important in capturing nomination to the House and a virtual necessity in running for the Senate. Thus House nominations often go to members of a state legislature or of local government, especially in the case of the local majority party. The minority party's nomination, often regarded as a useless honor, is more easily captured by a political neophyte. In turn, the members of the House constitute the single largest source of successful Senate candidates—a point of some dismay to many House leaders. In his study of the 180 members serving in the Senate from 1947 to 1957, D. R. Matthews found that almost half had been elected to *some* public office prior to reaching age 30, and that less than 10 per cent came to the Senate without previously holding some public office.[9] He reports the last public office held immediately prior to election to the Senate as indicated in Table I, below.

Table I

ROADS TO THE SENATE—LAST PREVIOUS OFFICE HELD BY SENATORS
WITH PRIOR EXPERIENCE IN OFFICE, 1947 THROUGH 1957
(EXCLUDES PARTY OFFICE AND UNSUCCESSFUL CAMPAIGNS)

Last Previous Office Held	*Percentage of Senators*
State Governor	22%
U.S. Representative	28
State Legislator	10
Statewide Elective Office	2
Local Elective Office	6
Law-Enforcement Office	15
Administrative Office	17
Congressional Staff	1

Adapted from Matthews, *op. cit.*, p. 55. (Figures are rounded off and hence do not total 100 per cent.)

Nominations are thus generally on a do-it-yourself basis. Most candidates and most voters do not consider the nomination to be a national matter in which local preferences receive some consideration, but rather as strictly local matters in which any national intervention or even outside comment may backfire. A popular President may lend substantial strength to his party's ticket, but he finds it extraordinarily difficult to influence the make-up of that ticket. Administration leverage comes easiest in providing aid and comfort to an incumbent who faces opposition. In this case either public endorsement or timely action on long-

[9] Donald R. Matthews, *U.S. Senators and Their World* (Chapel Hill: University of North Carolina Press, 1960), p. 50.

awaited local appointments or projects can be of at least marginal assistance.

GENERAL ELECTION COMPETITION: DIVERGING PATTERNS

The decentralizing tendencies of the nominating process are too strong to be overcome by the few centralizing features of the general election. In November traditional party loyalties, national issues, and the strength of the presidential candidates (in presidential election years) play an important role. But they can only affect the margin between the two major-party nominees on the ballot, and they are only likely to affect the outcome in states or districts where the party balance is relatively close.

It is well known that a majority of the national electorate have some sort of enduring attachment to one or the other major party. Most voters do not have to stop and "decide" every two years which party they are going to favor; they have a standing decision in favor of one or the other. Much the same thing is true of most congressional districts—and used to be the case with a majority of states. The most marked differences in the incidence of close two-party competition are between the state-level Senate contests and the individual congressional district contests. This in turn is due to the marked increase in the number of competitive states, which reflects the steady erosion of sectionalism in the nation.

Evidence for the change toward greater competition at the state level is available on every side. It is indicated in registration figures, in presidential voting patterns, and in the sharp increase in the number of senators elected by narrow margins. The change in the fundamental geographical basis of partisanship can be seen by comparing the presidential vote of 1900 and 1960: In 1900 there were 18 states in which the Democrats polled less than 40 or more than 60 per cent, and only 15 states in which the Democratic percentage of the vote ranged from 45 to 55 per cent. In 1960, in contrast, there were 34 states in which the Democratic vote ranged between 45 and 55, and only 6 states in which it was under 40 or over 60 per cent. Figure 1 presents in graphic form the contrast between states and congressional districts in the partisan division of the vote.

Although the presidential vote is somewhat more volatile than voting for Senate or House members, the same trend is clearly evident in regard to Senate elections. Thus of all senators elected in 1960 and 1962 almost half won by margins of less than 55 per cent, and over two-thirds won by less than 60 per cent. But the various population and economic trends which are working toward producing two-party competition in virtually every state are *not* producing such competition within the more restricted confines of the individual House district. In six of the seven elections held from 1950 through 1962 less than 100 of the 435 House seats were won by under 55 per cent. The "swing" district, like the highly rational "independent" voter, is an exception to the rule and not the usual thing.

In the five elections from 1952 through 1960 there was only one House district in the whole country which changed in party control in each election—this was the 19th district of Pennsylvania. Over the same decade —which included two Eisenhower landslides and the Democratic sweep

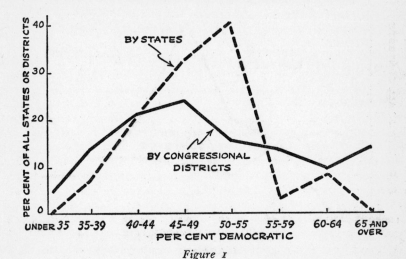

Figure 1

PARTY COMPETITION: DEMOCRATIC PERCENTAGE OF 1960 VOTE FOR PRESIDENT, BY STATES AND BY CONGRESSIONAL DISTRICTS

of 1958—over two hundred House districts remained unswervingly Democratic, and over one hundred and thirty remained unswervingly Republican. Party turnover was limited to the remaining ninety-odd districts: a limited political "no-man's land." Indeed, Professor Charles O. Jones, in a detailed study of party turnover in the twentieth-century House of Representatives, points out that the trend has been downward for half a century.[10]

The "safe" one-party House seats are to be found in every part of the country, including the big, industrialized states which are very closely balanced at the statewide level. Thus in 1962 Pennsylvania voters reelected Senator Joseph Clark with 51.2 per cent of the vote. But at the same election the same voters elected 23 of the 27 Pennsylvania congressmen by margins of greater than ten per cent. Much the same thing holds for New York or Illinois or any of the large states. Thus Figure 2 compares the margin of House and Senate victories in the eight most populous states, which elect all told almost half of the House (211 of 435 seats) and which generally dominate the electoral college. There are

[10] Charles O. Jones, "Inter-Party Competition for Congressional Seats," *Western Political Quarterly* (September 1964), 461-76.

roughly as many "safe" districts in these eight competitive states as in
the eleven states of the South!

That the ordinary tides of political change lap only into relatively
competitive states and districts has been amply demonstrated for both

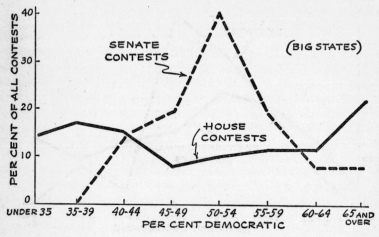

Figure 2

PARTY COMPETITION IN THE EIGHT MOST POPULOUS STATES: PERCENTAGE DEMO-
CRATIC FOR HOUSE CANDIDATES IN 1962 AND FOR ALL SENATE CANDIDATES, 1958-62
(INCLUDES NEW YORK, CALIFORNIA, PENNSYLVANIA, ILLINOIS, OHIO, TEXAS, MICH-
IGAN, AND NEW JERSEY)

House and Senate by V. O. Key.[11] Thus after the 1958 election Key
found that over 90 per cent of the districts voting Democratic by 50 to
55 per cent were represented by freshman members, although for the
whole House freshmen accounted for only 8.1 per cent of the seats.[12] In
areas where the minority party lacks a substantial number of partisan
supporters, even the most vigorous efforts by the minority party's nominees are generally unavailing. In the absence of a major error by the incumbents, such challengers just do not have the ordinary baseline of
partisan support to work from that a candidate has in a competitive
district and that is necessary for a chance to win. What needs to be
emphasized here is not the increasing number of statewide electorates
which *are* becoming susceptible to party change, but the small—and
dwindling—number of competitive House districts. These changes in the
incidence of competition, in turn, have major consequences for the respective chambers.

[11] See chapter 20 of Key, *Politics, Parties, and Pressure Groups* (New York: Thomas
Y. Crowell Co., Inc., 1964).

[12] *Ibid.*, p. 559.

After the 1962 elections the authoritative *Congressional Quarterly* summarized the evidence for what it termed "a remarkable and growing stability" in House membership.[13] Thus the average number of new members elected to the House dropped from 96 per election in the period from 1940 to 1948 to 68 per election from 1950 to 1958, and was even lower for both 1960 and 1962. The increased ability of incumbents to win reelection has been accompanied by the reduced effectiveness of "Presidential coattails." In both 1956 and 1960 the party winning the Presidency actually *lost* seats in the House, and even in 1952 the Republicans gained only 22 seats. According to *CQ*, the *average* gain for the party winning the Presidency over the period from 1890 to 1948 was 32.4 seats, and the average mid-term loss was 46.5 seats. From 1950 to 1964 the average gain in presidential years was 9.5, and the average mid-term loss only 24.5 seats.[14]

All of which suggests that for the House the general election—given a better educated, more literate electorate, able to view the candidates on television—may become even less a party battle and put more emphasis on "the man" and his record. Close party competition may be increasingly limited to the handful of "swing" districts plus those districts where an incumbent has retired or died. Incumbents have found it increasingly easy to win reelection so long as they make a good impression and do not become involved in scandal (such as financial involvement with Billie Sol Estes or Bobby Baker, excessive drinking in public, or highly publicized marital problems). Their chances are also improved by the many ways in which an incumbent provides assistance or information to constituents, and by the difficulties which a challenger must face in raising adequate campaign funds.

CAMPAIGN FINANCE: THE HIGH COST OF POLITICS

"It costs too much to run for office." On this incumbents and challengers, Republicans and Democrats all agree. In most parts of the country it does cost a great deal to wage an effective campaign for the House or Senate. Moreover, most of the money has to be raised locally by the candidate and his supporters. The national parties can supply only limited funds plus some research materials and advice to their nominees —and sometimes they may furnish nothing more than a telegram of congratulations.

In a few states, such as heavily industrialized Massachusetts or Ohio or Michigan, the state Republican organization may carry out a "united fund" type of drive for the benefit of the entire party ticket. The Democrats, lacking a natural financial base such as the business community, are less likely to be able to carry out such a coordinated fund-raising operation. Except for areas with unusually active labor unions, as in

---

[13] See *Congressional Quarterly* "Weekly Report" No. 49 (December 7, 1962), 2225-2230.
[14] *Ibid.*, 2227.

Michigan, or a powerful city organization, as in Chicago, Democratic nominees are likely to have to scrounge for funds on their own. The local emphasis on fund raising thus constitutes another decentralizing feature of the electoral process.

Precise accounts of the amounts spent in campaigns are hard to come by. Because of unrealistic state and federal limits, many candidates make it a point *not* to know in detail how much is being spent in their behalf. But the general order of magnitude is well known. Thus in 1962 Indiana Democrats allocated $520,000 to Birch Bayh's campaign against Senator Capehart, and in the closing days of the campaign Bayh was in desperate need of an additional $25,000 to go on television with his views on the Cuban crisis.[15] In a very large state, expenditure of a full million dollars in a Senate race is regarded as regrettable but necessary. Costs for a House campaign vary widely. An incumbent from a safe district may need only to pay his filing fee, but in a closely contested urban district a figure of forty or fifty thousand dollars is not unusual. Much of course depends upon the amount of use made of television, and whether the House candidate conducts a separate campaign or the party runs a joint one.

Something of the scale of the problem can be seen from experience in Massachusetts, a state with relatively complete reporting of expenditures.[16] Thus when John F. Kennedy ran against Henry Cabot Lodge, Jr., for the Senate in 1952 various Kennedy-for-Senator committees reported net expenditures of $350,292.37. Lodge and his campaign reported only $58,266.63 in net expenditures, but were among the chief beneficiaries of the Republican State Committee's spending of $1,058,501.08 for the overall ticket. In the Democratic primary contest for the House seat that Kennedy was vacating, the committe backing Thomas P. O'Neill raised $28,125 as compared with $9,900 for the group backing his unsuccessful primary opponent.

When measured against the magnitude of the task, the amounts made available to House and Senate candidates by the national campaign committees are very limited. And even these amounts are not under the control of the party's national committee but are doled out in each party by independent House and Senate campaign committees. These groups have their own staff, their own offices (in the Capitol Hill area), and their own customary sources of funds. The allocation of funds by national-level committees has been analyzed by Herbert E. Alexander, who reports the following patterns for the 1960 campaign:[17]

[15] See the account in Michael J. Kirwan, *How to Succeed in Politics* (New York: Macfadden Books, 1964), pp. 86-99.

[16] Figures in this paragraph are from H. D. Price, "Campaign Finance in Massachusetts in 1952," in *Public Policy*, Vol. VI (1955), 25-46.

[17] Alexander, *Financing the 1960 Election* (Princeton: Citizens' Research Foundation, 1962), pp. 45-47.

Table II

NATIONAL COMMITTEE FUNDS GRANTED FOR STATE CAMPAIGNS

Congressional Campaign Committees	*Amounts Granted*
Republican Senatorial Campaign Committee	$185,000
Republican Congressional Campaign Committee	656,800
Democratic Senatorial Campaign Committee	201,458
Democratic Congressional Campaign Committee	195,200

To round out the national picture, it should be noted that in 1960 labor committees contributed $444,482 to Democratic candidates (about evenly divided between House and Senate), but only $12,250 to various Republicans.

Only a very few of the most hard-pressed Senate candidates of either party can expect to receive more than ten thousand dollars from their senatorial campaign committee; most Senate candidates receive less than that. Candidates for the House generally receive only one or two thousand dollars from the Democratic campaign committee, or two to three thousand from the Republican group. Five thousand is usually the absolute top granted a House candidate by either national campaign committee. And even this assistance is available only after the candidate has officially received the party nomination.

The increasing cost of campaigning and the paucity of national party assistance probably works to the advantage of the incumbent, and may mean better access for those local interests which do help foot the bill. In 1962 James A. Michener, the well-known novelist, waged a determined but unsuccessful campaign in a strong Republican district north of Philadelphia. He notes:

> I have come upon quite a few facts I have [*sic*] not known before. The incumbent has an overwhelming advantage . . . . He mails his letters free. You pay for yours. For him to send a piece of literature to each family in his district costs about $6,000 paid for by the taxpayers. You cough up your own $6,000, in cash.
>
> He has at his command a staff of about five secretaries and helpers with a total yearly salary of around $45,000 paid for by the taxpayers. You find one girl and pay her yourself.[18]

Perhaps most important of all, incumbents have myriads of opportunities to establish contacts and perform services for constituents year in and year out. Careful attention to this "errand boy" aspect of the legislative role can strengthen an incumbent's position to the point that opposition may seem hopeless.

[18] Quoted by Kirwan, *op. cit.*, p. 20.

Care and Feeding of Constituents:
the Legislator as Ombudsman

A visitor to the House or Senate Office Buildings is likely to be impressed by the clatter of electric typewriters, the whir of mimeograph machines, and the stacks of outgoing mail. Most of this blur of activity has little or nothing to do with pending legislation or public policy, but a great deal to do with the reelection possibilities of the members of the House and Senate. Prompt attention to mail, careful follow-up on individual "case" work, and maximum cultivation of district (or state) contacts and media add up to the secret weapon by which the modern incumbent hopes to remain in office.

Several Scandinavian countries have a special official, the *Ombudsman,* who receives complaints and tries to help the average citizen in his contacts with the bureaucracy. But a general complaint bureau is one agency which the New Deal did not get around to establishing. In its stead the United States has 535 legislators who serve—with amazing effectiveness—as "ombudsmen" for their local constituents. As various federal agencies came to have more, and more complicated, contacts with individual citizens, it was inevitable that some bureaucratic errors would be made and that many people would not know what to do about a missing social security check or getting an emergency furlough for a serviceman overseas. The simple solution was to "write your congressman" and hope he could help. Within a generation the flow of requests for help or advice has grown from a tiny trickle into a massive daily tide of mail. And in the process modern senators and congressmen have come to perform functions—and enjoy a continued tenure—undreamed of by their nineteenth-century predecessors.

In most congressional offices there are secretaries who specialize in the various types of "case work" and know the appropriate liaison personnel in the various downtown departments. On the Senate side the volume of work for a single senator may be so great that various secretaries will deal exclusively with cases involving Veterans Affairs, or Social Security, or the Department of Defense. This provides a helpful function for the citizen and also can give the legislator some rough idea of some of the problem areas and weak spots of bureaucratic operation. And its political value is beyond question. It was providing assistance in an hour of need which helped cement the immigrant's loyalty to the big-city machines of bygone years. In an up-dated, white-collar sort of way today's legislators perform a similar—but much more technical—function. And it is appreciated.

Not all "cases" are small matters. There are "big" problems too, involving disposition of federal land or property, status of urban renewal requests, the location of proposed projects and installations, complex contract negotiations, and all the rest of the contacts between federal agencies and local citizens, local business firms, or even local governmental units. Here again the assistance of the local congressman or senator may be of vital importance. But the dividing line between proper and improper involvement is hard to define, and problems of "conflict of interest" may arise. But in general the level of congressional ethics, despite occasional lapses, seems to be far above that of most state legislatures. And it may not be much below that of the federal bureaucracy or the world of private business.

Since World War II congressmen and senators have also taken on an added role in promoting the growth of the local economy. They are expected to do everything within their power to oppose any move which would destroy local employment or buying power, whether the closing of an ancient naval ropewalk or the curtailing of an obsolescent navy yard. In an age when the federal government is heavily involved in spending not only for defense but for research and for natural resource development, the legislator's local prestige may rise or fall with the curve of federal investment and spending in his state or district. And the member who can land a major plum—such as the NASA Headquarters which went to Houston, Texas—is likely to be regarded as a civic benefactor and local hero.

Finally, a member's name and good works need to be made known to his constituents. Brief radio or television reports may be taped (at cost) and sent to local stations for broadcast, except during campaigns, as a public service. The great majority of members put out some sort of newsletter, and some send out periodic questionnaires. Special letters of congratulations may go to all graduating high school seniors or to newly wed couples. Many members maintain a year-round office in the district or home state. With the increased length of congressional sessions frequent trips home become even more important. Once Congress adjourns the members from thinly populated areas may cover the local by-ways in a mobile trailer office, or in a small airplane.[19] As Congressman Michael J. Kirwan, Chairman of the Democratic Congressional Campaign Committee, puts it: "No Congressman who gets elected and who minds his business should ever be beaten. Everything is there for him to use if he'll only keep his nose to the grindstone and use what is offered." [20]

THE CONGRESSIONAL VIEW: LOCAL OR COSMOPOLITAN?

The analysis up to this point might be taken to suggest that the legislator is caught up in a web of local influence that dictates his every move.

---

[19] The unusual amount of travel required is one of the little-noted hazards of serving in Congress. Thus California Congressman Clem Miller, author of *Member of the House*, was killed in a private airplane crash while campaigning for reelection in 1962; two years later Senator Edward Kennedy was seriously injured in a crash while flying to Massachusetts to speak to the Democratic State Convention.

[20] Kirwan, *op. cit.*, p. 20.

Actually this is far from being the case. As one influential House member put it to Lewis Anthony Dexter: "You know I am sure you will find out a Congressman can do pretty much what he decides to do, and he doesn't have to bother too much about criticism." [21] In the very multiplicity of demands and pressures, from within the legislative chamber as well as from the constituency, the legislator finds a significant degree of freedom of maneuver.

In this day and age no senator or representative can hope to please everyone in regard to everything that he does. Rather, he must pick and choose among specific stands so that his over-all pattern of performance —or the voters' image of his performance—is not outrageously out of line with the expectations of his constituents. As Dexter puts the matter:

> Within the limits of the morally and sociologically conceivable (no congressman from Alabama in 1942 could have advocated racial integration, for instance!), a congressman has a very wide range of choices on any given issue, *so far as his constituency is concerned*. His relationships in the House or Senate and with party leadership, of course, limit these choices severely. It is a fact, however, that there is no district viewpoint *as such* to be represented on the overwhelming majority of issues.[22]

And this relative freedom is reinforced by the fact that a member's activities as "errand boy" or "ombudsman" can build up a significant cushion of support entirely aside from his legislative record.

Why, then, the strong local emphasis in Congress? It is not simply a matter of irresistible constituent pressures. Often it seems to be the result of differences in the way the members look at their roles as congressmen. Some, to borrow Robert K. Merton's famous distinction,[23] are "locals" in orientation and interest—they read local newspapers, recruit their staff from the home district, and look at issues in terms of local impact. Others, however, are much more "cosmopolitan"—they follow national newspapers as well as local, hire staff in Washington, and are more sensitive to national or international problems. Thus the late "Cotton Ed" Smith, long-time senator from South Carolina, was assuredly a "local," just as a Fulbright of Arkansas is, on most issues, a "cosmopolitan."

The workings of the electoral process in the United States tend to require a certain degree of commitment to a "local" orientation, but impose little penalty for a lack of "cosmopolitan" interests. The politician with a "cosmopolitan" outlook, however, can hardly hope to survive long

---

[21] Dexter, "The Representative and His District," in Nelson W. Polsby, *et al., Politics and Social Life* (Boston: Houghton Mifflin Company, 1963), p. 498.

[22] *Ibid.,* pp. 498-99.

[23] Merton, "Patterns of Influence: A Study of Interpersonal Influence and Communications Behavior in a Local Community," in Paul Lazarsfeld and Frank Stanton, eds., *Communications Research, 1948-49* (New York: Harper, 1949), pp. 180-219. The application to congressmen has been suggested by Professor Nelson W. Polsby.

in Congress without also developing many "local" preoccupations. This would seem to be even more true of the House than of the Senate.

Close exposure to the "grass roots" can be a broadening experience—as with John F. Kennedy's discovery of real poverty while campaigning in West Virginia. But this is more likely to be the case where the constituency is large and diverse. Within the confines of a typical House district the range of dominant interests is likely to be rather limited. Moreover, the congressional emphasis upon seniority may make the legislative career less attractive to the policy-oriented "cosmopolitan." As Nelson Polsby has noted: "To that large fraction of members for whom the House is a career and a vocation, the longevity of members above them in the many hierarchies of the House—not the entirely predictable congressional election returns in their home districts—is the key to the political future." [24] Those politicians desiring to have a more immediate impact upon policy may prefer to seek elective executive office or to accept appointive posts. And to the extent that this occurs the tendency toward a "local" orientation in Congress is reinforced.

The decentralized structure of the nomination and election process thus has both a direct impact on congressional behavior and an indirect affect on the types of candidates who are drawn to Capitol Hill. Once elected, however, they all face new and additional problems. For both chambers have developed into complex institutions whose internal norms and procedures are often of as much importance as outside influences.

[24] Polsby, "Two Strategies of Influence: Choosing a Majority Leader, 1962," in Robert Peabody and Nelson Polsby, *New Perspectives on the House of Representatives* (Chicago: Rand McNally and Co., 1963), p. 244.

Richard F. Fenno, Jr.

3

The Internal Distribution
of Influence: The House

Every action taken in the House of Representatives is shaped by that body's structure of influence. That structure, in turn, has emerged as a response to two very basic problems of organization. The first is the problem of decision-making. That is, who shall be given influence over what, and how should he (or they) exercise that influence? Influence can be defined simply as a share in the making of House decisions. The House's first problem, then, involves the distribution of these shares among its members and, hence, the creation of a decision-making structure.

The second organizational problem is that of holding the decision-making structure together so that the House can be maintained as an on-going institution. This is the problem of maintenance. How, in other words, should the members be made to work together so as to minimize disruptive internal conflicts? The House must be capable of making decisions, but it must not tear itself apart in the process. It is in response to these twin problems—decision-making and maintenance—that the House's internal structure of influence has developed. And it is by focusing on these two problems that the structure can best be understood.

DECISION-MAKING

Shares in the making of House decisions are not distributed equally among the 435 members. Two sets of formal leadership positions have emerged: the decision-making positions, such as those on the com-

RICHARD F. FENNO, JR. *is Professor of Political Science at the University of Rochester. Among his publications are* The President's Cabinet *and* National Politics *and* Federal Aid to Education (*co-author*).

mittees, which have been established and maintained by the entire membership of the House, and those positions, such as majority leader and minority leader, which have been established and maintained by the members of the two congressional parties. These two structures of influence, the House structure and the party structure, do overlap—the position of the Speaker, for example, fits into both. But they are distinguishable. Those House members who occupy leadership positions in either structure or both possess the greatest potential for influence in the chamber. Some may not be able to capitalize on that potential; and it is wrong to assume that every man occupying a leadership position is, in fact, a leader. On the other hand, few members of the House become very influential without first occupying a formal leadership position in the House or party structures. Decision-making in the chamber must be described primarily in terms of these two interrelated structures.

House structure

In 1963, 9,565 bills and 1,731 resolutions were introduced in the House, each calling for a decision. In that same year, one individual member alone reported having received 10,000 letters, kept 900 appointments in his office and attended 650 meetings, nearly all of which carried requests that he take action of some sort. Individually and collectively, House members are called upon to make decisions, sometimes within the space of a few hours, on matters ranging from national security to constituency service. In short, a body of 435 men must process a work load that is enormous, enormously complicated and enormously consequential. And they must do so under conditions in which their most precious resources, time and information, are in chronically short supply. The need for internal organization is obvious.

Committees, division of labor and specialization. To assist them in making their constituency-related decisions, members hire an office staff and distribute them between Washington and "the district." To meet the more general problems the House has developed a division of labor—a system of standing committees. To this they have added a few *ad hoc* select committees and, in conjunction with the Senate, a few joint committees. The 20 standing committees plus the Joint Committee on Atomic Energy provide the backbone of the House's decision-making structure. They screen out most of the bills and resolutions introduced in the House—10,412 out of 11,296 in 1963. On a small fraction, they hold hearings. In fewer cases still the committee will send a modified bill out to the floor of the House for final action. With a few important exceptions, the full House accepts the version of the bill produced by the committee. Decisions of the House for the most part are the decisions of its committees.

The authority of the committees in the chamber rests on the belief that the members of a committee devote more time and possess more information on the subjects within their jurisdiction than do the other congressmen. Specialization is believed to produce expertise. For the non-committee member, reliance on the judgment of the experts on the committee is a useful short-cut in making his decisions. For the committee member, the deference of others is a source of influence. A man of whom it can be said that "he does his homework," "he knows what he's talking about," and "he knows more about that executive bureau than they do themselves" is a prestigeful figure in the House. Members pride themselves on producing, through specialization, a home-grown body of legislative experts to guide them in making their decisions and to serve as a counterweight to the experts of the executive branch. Carl Vinson, George Mahon, and Gerald Ford on military affairs, Wilbur Mills and John Byrnes on taxes, and John Fogarty on medical research are a few such men.

The conditions of committee influence vary. Members are likely to defer to a committee, for example, when the issues are technical and complicated, when large numbers do not feel personally involved, or when all committee members unite in support of the committee's proposal. Some or all of these conditions obtain for committees such as Armed Services and Appropriations, and doubtless help to account for the fact that their recommendations are seldom altered on the floor. Conversely, members are less likely to defer to the judgment of a committee when the issue is of a broad ideological sort, where national controversy has been stirred, or where the committee is not unanimous. These latter conditions frequently mark the work of the Committees on Education and Labor and on Agriculture. Under such circumstances committee influence may be displaced by the influence of party, of constituency, or of a member's social philosophy. Yet even here the committee can determine the framework for later decision-making, and members not on the committee may still be influenced by the factional alignments within the committee.

Committee claims to expertise stem not only from the individual talents of their leaders, but from the abilities of their professional staffs. One of the goals of the Legislative Reorganization Act of 1946 was to strengthen committee staffs. Within the limits of this law, and within budgetary limits voted each year by the House, staff selection is one of the important prerogatives of the committee chairman. Staff size, partisan composition, professional capacity, and duties will reflect his desires. Staff influence varies with the confidence which committee members, and especially the chairman, place in their abilities and their judgment. Where the desire to use a staff and confidence in it exists, staff members constitute a linchpin of internal committee decision-making. When these conditions are not present, it does not make much difference what kind of staff a committee has. Such staff influence as does exist in the House exists here—in the committees. One committee, the Joint Committee on Internal Revenue Taxation, functions primarily as the formal "holding company" for an expert staff which dominates decision-making in that field. In only a few cases does any member of a congressman's personal office staff enter the mainstream of legislative decision-making—in marked contrast to the situation in the Senate. Thus, to advocate larger staff in the House is to argue in favor of the division of labor, of subject-matter specialization, and of an increase in the influence of the twenty standing committees.

Committee leadership and its conditions. Acceptance of the division of labor as a necessity by House members makes it likely that committee leaders will have major shares in the making of House decisions. Who, then, are the committee leaders and how do their shares vary? In describing the committee-based leaders, it is easy to mistake form for substance. The most common pitfalls are to assume that invariably the most influential committee leaders are the chairmen and to infer that the vital statistics of these twenty individuals characterize committee leadership. Each committee chairman does have a formidable set of prerogatives—over procedure, agenda, hearings, subcommittee creation, subcommittee membership, subcommittee jurisdiction, staff membership, staff functions —which gives him a potential for influence. His actual influence in the House, however, will depend not only upon the prestige of his committee, but also upon his ability to capitalize on his potential and to control his committee. Consequently, many important committee leaders do not hold the position of chairman. They may be subcommittee chairmen, ranking minority members of committees or subcommittees, and occasionally members who hold no formal committee position.

Because House committees differ tremendously in power and prestige, committees like Ways and Means, Rules and Appropriations necessarily are more influential than committees like Post Office and Civil Service, House Administration, and District of Columbia. These differentials in influence are demonstrated by the House members themselves when, in seeking to change their committee assignments, they regularly trade the possibility of a chairmanship on a low-influence committee for a low-ranking position on a high-influence committee. Circumstance may, of course, alter the relative importance of committees, but at any point in time influential House leaders must be sought among the most influential House committees.

House leaders must be sought, too, among the subcommittee leaders of important House committees. The Committee on Appropriations, for example, divides its tasks among thirteen largely autonomous subcommittees, whose chairmen have as large a share in House decision-making as all but a few full committee chairmen. Thus the chairman of the Appropriations Subcommittee on Foreign Aid exercises more influence over that program than does the chairman of the Foreign Affairs Committee. And the equivalent statement can be made about a half-dozen other Appropriations subcommittee chairmen. When the Reorganization Act of 1946 reduced the number of standing committees from forty-eight to nineteen, it stimulated the growth and the importance of subcommittees. This outcome has obscured the realities of committee-based influence. Analyses of committee leadership which exclude the 123 (as of 1964) subcommittees can be but caricatures of the influence patterns in the House.

The influence of a committee leader in the House depends not only upon the relative power of his committee, but also upon how each committee or subcommittee makes its decisions. To be influential in the House a committee leader must first be influential in his committee. The patterns vary from autocracy to democracy. A chairman who is the acknowledged expert in his field, whose skill in political maneuver is at least as great as that of his colleagues, and who exploits his prerogatives to the fullest can dominate his committee or subcommittee. But his dominance may well proceed with the acquiescence of a majority of the committee. They may, and usually do, expect him to lead. Since a majority of any committee can make its rules, it is impossible for a chairman to dictate committee decisions against the wishes of a cohesive and determined majority of its members—at least in the long run. The aquiescence of his subcommittee chairmen will be especially crucial. On the other hand, since timing is of the essence in legislative maneuver, a short-run autocracy may be decisive in shaping House decisions. A successful chairman, however, must retain the support of his committee, and most chairmen are sensitive to pressures which may arise inside the committee for a wider distribution of internal influence. Long-term resistance to such pressures may bring about a revolt inside the committee which permanently weakens the influence of its chairman. Such revolts occurred, for instance, in the Committee on Government Operations in 1953 and in the Committee on Education and Labor from 1959 to 1961.

It is wrong to assume that most chairmen—even if they could—would monopolize decision-making in their committees. In most cases the creation of subcommittees means a sharing of influence inside the committee. Sharing can be kept to a minimum by designating subcommittees (sometimes simply by numbers) and giving them no permanent jurisdiction of any kind—as has been tried by chairmen of the committees on Armed Services and on the District of Columbia. Or the same result can be produced by withholding jurisdiction over certain bills for the full committee, as is sometimes done by the chairmen of the Armed Services and the Interstate and Foreign Commerce Committees. But where subcommittees are allowed a maximum of autonomy (Government Operations, Public Works, Appropriations, for example) the chairmen may willingly provide leaders of his subcommittees with a base of influence in the House. In the Committee on Government Operations John Moss's Subcommittee on Foreign Operations and Government Information, and in the Committee on Public Works John Blatnik's Subcommittee on Rivers and Harbors come readily to mind. Although the former chairman of the Banking and Currency Committee used the system of numbered subcommittees without permanent jurisdiction as a method of controlling committee activity, he gave to Albert Rains a subcommittee with permanent jurisdiction over housing, thereby enabling Rains to become an influential subject-matter expert. In some cases committee or subcommittee chairmen who work harmoniously with their opposite numbers in the minority party invest the latter with a potential for House influence.

Characteristics of committee leaders. The chairmen and ranking minority members of the standing committees attain their formal leadership positions through seniority. A variety of rules exist for determining seniority in the case of simultaneous appointments to a committee, but the rules of advancement from that time on are simple to understand and can be applied automatically. A chairman or ranking minority member who retains his party designation and gets re-elected is not removed from his leadership position.

Seniority, however, only partially governs the selection of subcommittee leaders. These positions are filled by the committee chairman (and by the ranking minority member for his side), and he retains sufficient authority over the subcommittee structure to modify the impact of seniority if he so desires. Once a committee member has been appointed to a subcommittee, he usually rises via seniority to become its chairman or ranking minority member. But the original assignment to subcommittees may not be made in accordance with seniority on the parent committee. It may be made on the basis of constituency interests (as is the case with the crop-oriented Agriculture subcommittees), on the basis of prior experience, or on the basis of the chairman's design for influencing subcommittee decisions.

Since the chairman may control subcommittee leadership by his power to determine their jurisdiction and to create or abolish subcommittees, his actions may infuse an important element of flexibility into the rigidities created by strict adherence to seniority. Thus chairmen of the Armed Services and the Post Office and Civil Service Committees have often operated with *ad hoc* subcommittees, hand-picked to consider a particular piece of legislation. The number of Appropriations subcommittees has varied from nine to fifteen since the Reorganization Act, and many of these changes resulted in giving or taking away a subcommittee chairmanship without regard for the claims of seniority.

Normal adherence to the rule of seniority means that by and large committee leaders have had long experience in dealing with their subject matter. Committee-based leadership is founded on subject-matter specialization, and committee-based influence in the House operates within subject-matter areas. Along with information and knowledge, the accumulated experience of committee leaders normally produces practical political wisdom on such matters as how to retain the support of a committee, when to compromise on the contents of a bill, when to take a bill to the floor, how to maneuver in debate, and how to bargain with the Senate in conference—all in a special subject-matter area.

Seniority practices also mean that formal committee leaders represent the traditional areas of party strength—especially the rural South and the rural Midwest and East. In 1964 the twenty Democratic chairmen represented primarily the party strongholds in the South (twelve) and to a smaller degree districts in the urban North (four). The ranking Republicans came in like proportions from rural districts in the Midwest and East (twelve) and from suburban constituencies (four). If one includes the formal subcommittee leaders from the half-dozen most prestigeful committees which have subcommittees (Appropriations, Armed Services, Foreign Affairs, Agriculture, Judiciary and Interstate and Foreign Commerce), the picture is similar.

What difference does it make to draw committee leaders from safe constituencies? Clearly such interests as can be identified with these areas of the country are advantaged by the makeup of committee leadership. The safest general description of those social interests is that they tend to be conservative, but even this is a gross oversimplification. The important question concerns how the committee chairmen in fact act on those matters which come before their particular committees. By itself the fact that leaders come from safe constituencies tells us only that they will respond to district sentiment that is clear and intense. In all other instances, however, such men remain freer than most other members to use their own judgment in legislative matters without fear of reprisal at the polls. All things being equal, a member who has flexibility of maneuver in the House will be more influential there than one whose constituency obligations leave him without elbow room.

Committee leaders, moreover, defy any easy typology. Representative Howard Smith, Chairman of the Rules Committee, is a prime example of the advantage given to conservative interests by a rural Southern chairman of a key committee. On the other hand, Carl Vinson of Georgia, Chairman of the Armed Services Committee and also a rural Southerner, wielded a critical influence on behalf of President Kennedy's New Frontier proposals. Wilbur Mills, Chairman of the Ways and Means Committee, who represents a rural Arkansas district, followed a pattern of action between these two—steering the Trade Act and the tax cut through his Committee and the House, but blocking Medicare legislation.

The committee structure is a decentralized decision-making system. A fully accurate description of who it is that benefits from the committee structure almost requires, therefore, a committee-by-committee, subcommittee-by-subcommittee, and leader-by-leader analysis.

Rules and the distribution of influence. What we have called the

House structure of influence (as distinguished from the party structure) results not only from the division of labor by committees but also from the body of formal rules which superintend decision-making. One obvious requirement for the House is a body of rules sufficiently restrictive to prevent unlimited delay and to permit the members to take positive action. Such a set of rules must recognize both a majority's right to govern and a minority's right to criticize. Each is necessary if the rules are to be accepted by both. The accomplishment of this kind of balance is best evidenced by the extraordinary devotion to established rules and to procedural regularity which characterize every aspect of House action.

Increments of influence accrue to those leaders who understand House rules and can put them to use in their behalf. As they exist in the Constitution, in Jefferson's Manual, in the eleven volumes of Hinds's and Cannon's precedents, and in the forty-two Rules of the House, the procedures of the chamber represent as technical and complex a body of knowledge as any subject-matter area. Influence inside a committee may carry over to the House floor, but success on the floor requires additional skills. Primary among these are the ability to sense the temper of the House and the ability to use the Rules of the House to advantage. A Clarence Cannon, a Howard Smith, or an Albert Rains is a procedural specialist, quite apart from any subject-matter competence he may possess.

The official with the greatest potential for influence in the House, especially in matters of procedure, is the Speaker. Although his importance stems primarily from his position as leader of the majority party, he derives considerable influence from his position as the presiding officer of the House. In this capacity, he exercises a series of procedural controls over House activity. And some of these, in turn, provide opportunities to affect the substance of House decisions. He must recognize any member who wishes to speak on the floor; he rules on the appropriateness of parliamentary procedures; he determines the presence of a quorum; he selects the Chairman of the Committee of the Whole; he votes in case of a tie; he counts and announces votes; he decides in doubtful cases to which standing committee a bill will be assigned; he appoints special or select committees; he appoints the House members to each conference committee; and he maintains decorum in the chamber. The small element of discretion involved in any of these prerogatives occasionally affects legislation. The refusal, for example, of Speaker Sam Rayburn to entertain dilatory tactics before announcing the 203-202 vote extending the draft in 1941 may have prevented a different outcome.

Because the procedural controls of the Speaker extend fairly broadly across the stages through which legislative proposals must pass before they emerge as law, the scope of his procedural influence is probably more important than its weight at any one point. For most House leaders, however, the various decision-making stages represent boundaries which contain their influence. Committee leaders dominate the initial stage of review, reformulation and recommendation; the Committee on Rules and a few party leaders control the agenda stage; committee leaders, party leaders and a cluster of other interested members combine to dominate the floor debate and amending stage; a very few committee leaders speak for the House in the conference committee. At each stage a few members normally dominate decision-making. But from stage to stage and from bill to bill, dispersion, not concentration, of influence is the dominant pattern.

The Committee on Rules. No better illustration of these generalizations about influence—its concentration within stages and its dispersion across stages—exists than the Committee on Rules. This Committee owes its great influence in the chamber to the fact that it stands athwart the flow of legislation at one stage—the agenda stage. Since bills flow out of the standing committees and onto the various House calendars in considerable profusion, some mechanism is necessary for sending them to the floor in an orderly fashion. For most important bills these agenda decisions are made by the Rules Committee. By "granting a rule" to a bill the Committee takes it from a calendar, where action is uncertain, and sends it to the floor, where final action is assured. The rule for a bill specifies the length of the debate and the number and kinds of floor amendments to be allowed, and it may remove from challenge provisions which otherwise would violate standing House rules, such as the prohibition against legislation in an appropriation bill.

Commonly referred to as a toll gate or a traffic cop, the Committee obviously functions in the interest of an orderly and efficient flow of business. Just as obviously, however, the Rules Committee functions as a second substantive, policy-making committee for each bill which passes its way. Its fifteen members can exact concessions from the bill's sponsors as their price for granting a rule. Or, as they do on about a dozen bills each year, they can refuse to grant a rule altogether. The Committee thus can wield and threaten to wield a virtual veto over the decision-making process. The veto power is not absolute. Money bills from the Appropriations Committee do not require a rule. A number of bypasses, such as the discharge petition and Calendar Wednesday are available; but they are clumsy and hence are rarely attempted and hardly ever succeed. The members' devotion to procedural regularity contributes an essential underpinning to Rules Committee influence.

Since House decision is a composite of several formal (and countless informal) decisions, and since at each stage in decision-making a different cluster of House leaders may prevail, supporters of a given bill must build a series of majorities—in the substantive committee, in the Rules Committee, on the floor, and in conference—if they are to be successful. Opponents of a bill, however, need to build but a single majority—at any one stage in the process—to achieve their ends. The Committee on

Rules in particular has lent itself to such defensive action. Thus in 1960, when for the first time in history both houses of Congress had passed a federal-aid-to-education bill and the Rules Committee refused to grant a rule so that the bill could go to conference, it was the only place in the entire Congress where opponents of Federal aid could block a majority vote. But it was enough. The consequence, therefore, of the series of stages when accompanied by a corresponding dispersion of influence is to confer a substantial advantage on those interests in society that wish to preserve the *status quo.* House rules make it easier to stop a bill than to pass one.

Party structure

The complex processes of majority-building involve a party structure of influence which is both different from and yet closely interwoven with the House structure of influence. Considered by itself, the House structure of influence is markedly decentralized—substantively in accordance with committee specialization and procedurally in accordance with a sequence of stages. The party groups organize decision-making across committees and across stages, thereby functioning as a centralizing force in the making of House decisions. Specifically, they organize to elect their own members to the formal leadership positions of the House, to superintend the flow of legislation within and across the various stages, and to determine the substance of policy. Generally, they organize to give some element of central direction to the process of majority building.

The parties as centralizers. On the record, such centralization as does occur in House decision-making comes about largely as a result of action taken by the party groups. On the other hand, the centralizing capacity of the parties is distinctly limited—so much so that in some ways the net of their activity is to add yet another decentralizing force to that of the House structure. It is a well-established fact that the voting patterns of House members can be explained better by knowing their party affiliation than by knowing anything else about them. On the other hand, it is an equally well-established fact that on many of the most controversial decisions House majorities must be made up of members of both parties. As organizing, centralizing forces inside the House, the parties have inherent strengths and inherent weaknesses.

Their strength rests in the fact that they are the most comprehensive groups in the House and in the fact that for most members the party is a meaningful source of identification, support, and loyalty. For most of its members, a party label stands for some things which they share in common—an emotional attachment, an interest in getting and keeping power, some perceptions of the political world and, perhaps, certain broad policy orientations. But the unitary party label also masks a pluralism of geographic, social, ideological, and organizational sources of identification, support, and loyalty. The roots of this pluralism lie outside the chamber, in the disparity of conditions under which the members are elected and in the decentralized organization of the parties nationally. As electoral organizations, the two parties are coalitions of diverse social interests and party organizations formed to elect governmental officials—especially the President. No national party hierarchy exists to control the nomination and election of House members or to control their decision-making activity once they are elected. Different House members owe their election to different elements in the party coalition, and they can be expected, in the interests of survival, to respond to their own special local sources of support. Each party label therefore papers over disparate factional blocs and conflicting policy viewpoints. Inside the House as well as outside, the parties remain loose coalitions of social interests and local party organizations.

Majority party leadership. Since its members constitute an automatic majority in the House, the larger of the two parties has the greater potential for influence. If the members of the majority party could be brought into perfect agreement, they could produce majorities at every stage of decision-making and transform every party decision into a decision of the House. The fact is, of course, that they cannot. But they do come much closer to the goal than does the minority party. Their successes and failures at maintaining their internal unity and at organizing decision-making provide, therefore, the best insights into the strengths and weaknesses of the party groups in the House.

The majority party achieves its maximum degree of unity and, hence, its greatest success, in filling the leadership positions of the House with its own members. Technically, the whole House elects its Speaker, the chairmen of its standing committees, and the members of each committee. But so long as the majority party prefers to vote its own members into these positions in preference to members of the other party, the decisions are made within the majority party and are only ratified on the House floor. On few, if any, other votes can the majority party achieve unanimity.

The leaders selected inside the majority party—in the Democratic caucus or the Republican conference as the case may be—become leaders in the House. The Speaker, of course, is the prime example and represents the complete interweaving of House and party structure. His dual role gives him a centralizing potential far greater than that of any other member. His effectiveness, however, has varied with the formal authority vested in him by the House and the informal authority he could amass through political skill.

The most successful imposition of party influence upon the House has occurred under strong Speakers—men like Thomas Reed and Joseph Cannon. And the basis of their strength lay in the fact that their formal authority extended into critical areas of personnel and procedure.

Speaker Cannon, for example, controlled the Rules Committee by sitting as its chairman. He controlled the substantive committees by selecting their chairmen and members—with or without regard to seniority as he saw fit. Given these and other controls, the majority party leader was able to dominate policy making in the House and become a party leader co-equal with the President. Since 1910, however, the Speaker's formal authority has been modest; and his centralizing influence has been more informal and interstitial than formal and comprehensive. Sam Rayburn's success as Speaker was a triumph of personal skill and only served to obscure the essential modesty of his formal powers.

The majority party elects another leader for the purpose of bringing party influence to bear on the making of House decisions, the majority floor leader. Both he and his counterpart in the minority party remain outside the official House structure. The fact that each of the last eight Speakers served previously as his party's floor leader suggests not only a close working relationship but also some similarity of personal qualifications. In the post-Cannon era, these qualifications have been those of the negotiator. Prime among them has been the recognized ability to command the trust, respect, and confidence of various party factions to the end that the tasks of informal negotiation among them will be facilitated. Successful Speakers and majority leaders are men who appeal personally to their fellow House members and not men whose main appeal is to party elements outside the House. They have been men whose devotion to the House was considered greater than any devotion to ideological causes. These characteristics improve the likelihood that formal party leaders can influence House decision-making. The Speaker and the majority floor leader constitute the nucleus of that somewhat amorphous group in the majority party known as "the leadership." Such centralization as the majority party is able to bring to House decision-making springs from them.

In barest organizational terms, the job of the majority floor leader is to manage the legislative schedule of the House by programming the day-to-day business on the floor. In so doing, he avails himself of the full range of the Speaker's procedural controls. He also avails himself of the party whip and his assistants who inform members of the schedule, take polls to assess party sentiment, round up members when a vote is to be taken, and generally channel communications between leaders and followers. In their execution, obviously, these scheduling and communications functions shade into the most crucial kinds of procedural concerns —setting legislative priorities, determining strategies of timing, planning parliamentary maneuver. And these functions, in turn, bring opportunities to affect the substance of decisions. The success of many a bill depends more upon when it is called up than on anything else. The effectiveness of the majority party in centralizing House decision-making depends upon its ability to control the procedural flow of legislation. Such success depends in turn upon the ability of the speaker, the majority leader, and the whips to pool their resources to this end.

Party leadership and committee personnel. Whether viewed as a control over personnel, procedure, or policy, one fundamental limitation on majority party influence in the House is the inability of its leaders to select committee chairmen. All committee chairmen do, of course, come from the majority party; but the only action which that party takes is to ratify the workings of seniority. More than anything else, this practice perpetuates the separation of House and party structures of influence. The subject-matter committees dominate policy making in their areas of specialization. The Rules Committee exercises a crucial influence over the flow of legislation. But to the degree that the majority party leaders cannot select the chairmen of these committees, their control over procedure and policy is restricted. When the leaders of the party and the committee leaders are in basic disagreement, centralized control is impossible. If in such circumstances unity between members of the same party is to be achieved at all, it must be brought about by the subtle processes of negotiation, bargaining, and compromise.

Lacking influence over the selection of committee chairmen, the most important control over committee personnel which remains within the purview of elective party leaders is that of filling committee vacancies. On the Democratic side, committee assignments are made by action of the Democratic members of the Ways and Means Committee. The selection of Democrats for that Committee, by the entire caucus, is among the most important decisions made in that party. Accordingly, Speaker Rayburn kept tight control over that process, screened the candidates carefully, and maintained his influence in all their subsequent deliberations. Committee assignments on the Republican side are made by a committee comprised of one member from each state which has a Republican congressman—with each member having as many votes as there are Republicans in his state's delegation. The party leader is the chairman of the group; he also chooses and then chairs the subcommittee which actually does the work. Thus Joseph Martin and Charles Halleck have exercised a direct influence on committee assignments.

These personnel decisions can have important consequences for House decision-making. If there are enough vacancies on a given committee, the impact of committee assignments on committee policy may be immediate—as happened in the filling of six vacancies on the Education and Labor Committee in 1959. In this case, a new majority was created which pushed a new set of rules through the committee, overrode the chairman, and got the first general aid-to-education bill in history through the House. If the policy balance is close, a single appointment may be decisive. Those Democrats who in 1962 defeated Representative Landrum's bid for a seat on the Ways and Means Committee, in caucus and against the wishes of Speaker McCormack, believed that the fate of President Kennedy's trade program, of his tax program, and of the Medicare bill might be at stake in that single assignment. But even if no short-run effect can be foreseen, changes in committee leadership and policy may be effected. So reasoned the Democrats with their five "liberal" appointments to the Appropriations Committee and the Republicans with their five "conservative" appointments to the Foreign Affairs Committee in 1963. It is important to understand that seniority is but one among a large number of criteria that custom prescribes for filling vacancies. Party leaders are not at all bound by it, and the process, therefore, has great potential as a means for impressing party influence on the House.

Typically, a formal party leader does not dictate to his "Committee on Committees." Rather he negotiates with them in making committee assignments. The reason for this is simply that the members of these important committees represent the various elements in the party coalition and, as such, may be important party leaders in their own right. Among the Democrats on the Ways and Means Committee are customarily found representatives of the big-city delegations (New York, Philadelphia, Chicago, Detroit), of key state delegations (California, Texas), and of regional groupings (New England, Southeastern, and Border states). The membership of the key Republican subcommittee will include representatives from all the large state delegations—New York, Pennsylvania, Ohio, California and Illinois. The most influential members of these committees—men like the late Thomas O'Brien, dean of the Illinois Democratic delegation, and Clarence Brown, veteran leader of the Ohio Republican delegation—are the leaders of party factions. These factions represent important sources of electoral strength and they are the building blocks of the party inside the House as well. In making party decisions, the Speaker and majority leader must always negotiate with the leaders of such coalition elements—thus, in effect, broadening "the leadership" itself into a kind of coalition.

Party leadership and policy making. Further evidence of the fragmentation of party groups can be found in the attempts by each to organize for the making of policy. Formally the Democratic caucus can make such decisions and bind all House Democrats to vote as directed. But the exceptions are kept sufficiently broad so that no one is, in effect, under any constraint. Furthermore, so deep has been the cleavage between the northern and the southern factions of the party in recent years that the caucus never meets to discuss policy. To do so, say the leaders, would only heat up factional division and make their task of negotiation among the elements of the coalition more difficult. The Democrats also have a steering committee, a smaller group containing representatives of all factions—also designed to discuss and recommend policy positions. But for fear that it, too, might exacerbate disunities, it has not met in recent years.

The Republicans have a representative Policy Committee which has been active and whose chairman, at least, is recognized as a member of the Republican "leadership." Typically, however, its main function is one of facilitating communication among various Republican factions—East and Midwest, suburban and rural, young and old, liberal and conservative. Where a policy consensus already exists, the Policy Committee will state the party position. Where disagreement exists, the Policy Committee is powerless to make a statement of party policy—much less enforce one on its members. If dissident party members refuse to be bound by policy pronouncements worked out within the chamber, they are of course far less willing to listen to the counsels of party groups outside Congress, whether the national committees or such *ad hoc* groups as the Democratic Advisory Council and the All-Republican Conference.

Nothing makes clearer the decentralized nature of policy making by the congressional parties than an examination of certain other policy-oriented groups which exist within (and between) the parties. The most elaborate of these is the Democratic Study Group. These 125 northern and western liberals have concerted their efforts by settling policy positions, by organizing their own whip system to deliver the vote, and by looking even to the financing of House campaigns for like-minded individuals. Conservative southern Democrats also meet (now under the leadership of Omar Burleson of Texas) to discuss issues and strategy on matters of regional concern. Across the two parties, linked by the informal communications of their leaders, a coalition of Democrats and Republicans has operated off and on since 1938 as an informal policy alliance. Similarly the party delegations from each state meet to discuss and seek unity on policies of interest to them. In the Republican party especially, each "class" of first-term party members forms a group in whose meetings party policy is discussed. Smaller discussion groups—the Marching and Chowder Society, the Acorns—persist as forums in which sympathetic party members can talk shop. And, even more informally, members talk policy at regular coffee hours, during workouts in the gym, at poker games, in visits along the same corridor in the office buildings or between nearby Washington residences. The communication networks of congressmen are infinitely complex and, in the absence of two party hierarchies capable of making policy, all of these less formal sources of consultation become consequential for policy making.

Such policy leadership as comes to the party group comes most importantly from the President. To the members of his party in the House, his program provides a unifying, centralizing influence. It reduces the necessity for any active policy-making organ for his party. To the members of the other party, presidential initiatives furnish targets to shoot at. Activity is stirred among the minority party's policy-making organs in an attempt to put together some coherent opposition. But, on the evidence, factionalism in the party which cannot claim the President remains more pronounced than in the party which can. The optimum conditions for policy leadership by the majority party in Congress occur when the President is of the same party. Under other conditions fragmentation is harder to check. Even under the best of circumstances, however, the limitations on the President, not in proposing but in disposing of his program, must be recognized. Since he does not control the electoral fortunes or the House careers of most of his own party members, he may not be able to give them what they most want or discipline them if they fail to follow him. He too, therefore, is normally cast in the role of a negotiator with the elements of his party coalition and, when necessary, with elements of the other party coalition.

Majority building by the majority party. The decisions with which the party groups are concerned thus are made by processes of negotiation and bargaining. Through these processes party leaders try to build and maintain the majorities they need to control House personnel, House procedure, and House policy. In the era since Speaker Cannon, the success of the majority party leaders has depended more on a mixed bag of resources than on any massive concentration of formal authority. Typically, in any effort at any stage, "the leadership" of either party can depend on a hard core of support within the party, based on a sympathy of views and overlaid with a sense of party loyalty. Members have, as well, as ingrained respect for the constituted authority of their party leader. All things being equal, party members feel more comfortable when they find it possible to be "with" the party leadership rather than against it. The negotiations of "the leadership" center on making this support possible for a majority of members.

A successful leader of the majority party will put his experience and his political intuition to work in assessing what is possible for key individuals on the committees and in factional blocs. At any point in time, he must make a judgment as to the "temper of the House," what its dominant sentiments are and what things it can or cannot accept. And the same is true for committees, for blocs, or for individuals. In making these assessments and then negotiating for support the effective Speaker avails himself of his own good personal relations with members, his reputation for fairness, for integrity, for trustworthiness, and for political judgment. He extends his own capacities by using the talents of those friends and protegés whom he locates in every House group. Through them he maintains a line into every committee, every bloc, and every informal group. With them, "the Speaker's boys," he shares his party leadership and, in return, secures a broader base of support than he might otherwise get. Through personal friendship—such as that which existed between Sam Rayburn and Joseph Martin—he maintains a line into the opposition party. Through these networks he identifies the views of others and calculates what concessions he can make before the costs exceed the benefits. He learns whether he can build a majority with his own party or must rely upon negotiations with the other party as well. He decides how partisan a tone he wishes to give to the contest. By adding up support in terms of large blocs, he can determine whether the policy he supports has a fighting chance. If it does not, he is likely to wait, for he will not willingly commit his prestige in a losing cause.

If the large bases of support have been secured and the task of majority building boils down to persuading a few waverers, the knowledge which the party leaders possess of individual idiosyncrasies plus the availability of rewards and punishments may then come into play. The leaders do, after all, influence committee assignments. Through the Congressional Campaign Committee they influence the distribution of campaign money often in small amounts but badly needed nonetheless. Through the Congressional Patronage Committee they influence the distribution of a few jobs. Through their procedural controls they may influence the disposition of bills on the Private Bill Calendar, the Consent Calendar, and bills passed by a suspension of the rules. Through their contact with the President they may be able to influence the disposition of a "pet project" of a given member—a dam, a post office, a research laboratory, a federal building. By manipulating rewards and punishments like these, the leaders can bargain for increments of support—in the committees or on the floor.

Majority party leaders negotiate in order to overcome the decentralizing tendencies of party factionalism and the committee system. It follows, then, that the sternest challenge to the centralizing capacities of "the leadership" arises when they confront a dissident party faction in control of an important committee. And, since "the leadership" is normally trying to construct a majority on behalf of some positive action, the greatest test of all occurs when an entrenched party faction uses the advantages of the rules to defend the *status quo*. In recent years the classic contests of this sort have occurred between the leadership of the majority Democratic party and the bipartisan coalition of Southern Democrats and Republicans operating from the bastion of the Committee on Rules.

Since the mid-1930s the party leadership has had to fight for its view that the Rules Committee is an arm of the majority party leadership. The Committee has alternately acceded to this view and fought to retain an autonomous role in the making of House decisions.

Over the past twenty years factional splits in the Democratic party have made the Democratic leadership's relation to the Rules Committee an unstable one. In 1949 the leadership sought and gained by House vote a twenty-one day rule, which proved a procedure by which the chairman of a committee might gain recognition by the Speaker and bring a bill to the floor if the Rules Committee refused to act favorably upon it within twenty-one days of its referral. While it was in force, eight rather important bills were moved to the floor via this route. After a two-year trial and aided by gains in the 1950 elections, however, the Southern

Democrats and Republicans in the House repealed the twenty-one day rule and restored the coalition to its position of dominance inside the Committee.

In some respects the twenty-one day rule increased the influence of the Speaker; but it also increased the influence of committee chairmen. Speaker Rayburn regarded it as a very mixed blessing. In any case, during most of the 1940s and 1950s, when it was not in effect, Rayburn frequently had to rely on Republican leader Joseph Martin to provide him with the margin of victory on the Committee.

In 1961, in the wake of a number of defeats in the Rules Committee, in the presence of a new and less cooperative Republican leader, and faced with the prospect of implementing the new Democratic President's program, Speaker Rayburn decided to challenge Chairman Howard Smith for control of the Rules Committee. It was a contest that neither man wanted; and it could only have come about, as did the revolt against Speaker Cannon in 1910, under conditions of serious and irreconcilable differences over policy. The Speaker employed the full range of his authority and skills in this contest and pushed his influence to its outermost limits. He succeeded in enlarging the membership of the Committee from twelve to fifteen—from eight to ten for the majority-party Democrats and from four to five for the minority. Then he added two personal choices to the Democratic side. With eight dependable Democratic votes, the task of majority-building has subsequently been much easier. Still, it should be noted that the Speaker could not have won his 217-to-212 victory without the votes of twenty-two Republicans, most of whom were sympathetic to his policy goals. And it should also be noted that a single defection among the "dependable" eight can still thwart majority building by the majority party—as it did on federal aid to education and on the urban affairs bill in 1961.

Clashes between the majority-party leadership and the Rules Committee go to the heart of the structural separation between House and party. Proposed changes in that larger relationship thus almost inescapably must center on Rules Committee activity.

The relations between the Democratic party leadership and the Rules Committee illustrate something about the social interests served by the majority party leadership. When the same party "controls" both the Presidency and Congress, the majority party leadership is more likely than the committee chairmen to be a vehicle through which interests in society opposed to the *status quo* can assert themselves. Given the fact that presidential programs are likely to be pointed more toward change than many committee chairmen desire, the majority party leadership will most often operate against the influence of the committees. From the perspective of conservatively and liberally oriented groups outside Congress, the twenty-one-day rule and the Rayburn-Smith contests involved the distribution of real advantages and disadvantages.

This identification of the majority party leadership and liberal interests is only approximate, however. Majority leaders are by no means obedient to every presidential desire. Since majority party leaders are chosen for their ability to communicate across party factions, they may work hand in glove with a conservatively oriented committee to preserve the *status quo*. By blocking legislation the Rules Committee, for example, can and often does serve the interests of the leadership. (In some cases it keeps off the floor legislation on which members do not want to have to vote and then provides a whipping boy for them to blame for the resultant inaction.) Neither conservative nor liberal social interests bear a one-to-one relationship to particular elements of the House structure.

Maintenance

Decentralized and yet distributing influence unequally among the 435 members, the decision-making structure of the House is essentially a semi-oligarchy. This semi-oligarchical structure has been in existence since shortly after the revolution of 1910. In order fully to understand that structure it is necessary finally to understand those internal processes by which it has maintained itself. Structural stability is the result, in brief, of internal processes which have served to keep the institution from tearing itself apart while engaged in the business of decision-making.

The disruption of the influence structure of the House is prevented through the existence of certain general norms of conduct which are widely held and widely observed by House members and which function to minimize internal conflicts. Foremost among these is the norm that members be devoted to the House as an institution, that they do not pursue internal conflicts to the point where the effectiveness of the House is impaired. Immediately after he is elected and sworn in, the Speaker customarily voices this norm and his total allegiance to it. Similarly, the minority party leader graciously accepts the results of the election, thereby symbolizing the minority commitment to the House as an institution. From this over-arching rule of conduct follows the norm that all formal rules and informal traditions of the House should be observed.

Two distinguishable clusters of such rules and traditions are of special importance to the preservation of the existing structure. One cluster functions to maintain harmony between those who hold leadership positions in the House and those who do not. It is the seniority-protégé-apprentice system of norms. A second cluster functions to maintain harmony among those members who hold leadership positions. This is the negotiation and bargaining system of norms. Together the two systems maintain the degree of centralization-decentralization which gives to the House its semioligarchical characteristics.

These clusters of norms represent what most members regard as proper behavior. By word and by example they are taught to the newcomers of the House in the earliest years of their tenure. Members who learn them well and whose behavior demonstrates an attachment to them are rewarded with increased influence. Conversely, members who seriously and persistently deviate from them are punished by diminution of their influence. Members may be denied or given the potential for leadership that goes with such formal positions as subcommittee leader or party leader. Or, if they are committee chairmen, rewards and punishments may affect their capacity to maximize the potential for influence. But for these socializing and sanctioning mechanisms, the structure of influence would be quite different from the one just described.

The seniority-protegé-apprentice system

The seniority rules which govern the selection of committee chairmen draw a great deal of attention in commentaries on Congress. What does not draw attention is the fact that these rules are only the most visible ones out of a large and complex body of norms which superintend the House career of every member. Seniority governs ultimate leadership selection; but for all those who do not hold leadership positions, the rules which count represent the other side of the coin. Seniority rules rest on the basic assumption that a man must first spend time learning to be a representative, just as he learns any other occupation. Seniority signifies experience, and experience brings that combination of subject-matter knowledge and political wisdom which alone is held to qualify a man for leadership in the House. Before a member can be certified as an experienced senior member, he must first be an apprentice and a protegé.

Every new member of the House is expected to observe an apprenticeship—to work hard, tend to his constituency, learn his committee work, specialize in an area of public policy, appear often but speak very seldom on the floor, and cooperate with the leaders of his committee and of his party. Naturally, this is the time in their careers when House members are most critical of the system which denies them influence. The proportion of newcomers to non-newcomers is, therefore, a key index of potential conflict in the House influence structure. It was, for example, the extraordinarily large number of new Republicans that made possible the overthrow of Charles Hoeven, the Chairman of the Republican Conference, in 1963. Normally, however, the number of newcomers is sufficiently small so that they have difficulty in organizing to combat the existing leadership structure.

House members believe there is no better judge of a man's worth than the institutional judgment of the House. The assessment and reassessment of one's colleagues—the calculation of each members "Dow Jones average"—goes on without end. Indeed, this searching scrutiny of one another is an occupational necessity for men whose business is majority-building. After a term or two or three of apprenticeship, men on whom the judgment of the formal leaders is favorable will be rewarded—with an assignment to a more prestigeful committee or with an assignment to one of the committees of his party. The more promising among the newcomers will become the protegés of committee and party leaders. Protegés of a committee chairman may turn up as a special confidants, as subcommittee chairmen, or as floor managers of minor bills. Protegés of the Speaker turn up as Chairmen of the Committee of the Whole, as participants in strategy meetings, or as "a leadership man" on various committees. No mark of preferment, however slight, escapes the notice of the membership. These protegés, with three or four terms of service, have reached an intermediate stage in their House careers. They will have demonstrated their ability, their devotion to the House, and their willingness to cooperate with its leaders. They will be expected to assume the grinding responsibilities of House decision-making and to exercise an independent influence in the chamber. As other members see them, they have gained in stature and are marked as the future leaders in the chamber. As the protegés see it, they have been rewarded for their apprenticeship with a gratifying measure of influence. They have been given, too, time in which to ponder and prepare for the eventualities of formal leadership.

The seniority-protegé-apprentice system emphasizes a gradual and well-modulated ascent to positions of formal leadership. In its early stages this process of leadership selection is affected by the behavior of the individual member and by the reaction of the leaders to him. The idea of a ladder is basic; but members are sorted out and placed on different career ladders. By their third term most members will be embarked on a House and party career that will follow a fairly predictable path. And in its climactic stage, the process is totally predictable, automatic, and quick. Custom has made this nearly as true for the succession from majority leader to Speaker as is has for the succession to committee chairmanships. The seniority-protegé-apprentice system is basically a system for minimizing conflict among members over who shall exercise influence and who shall not. Its apprentice norms damp down a potential conflict over leadership between newcomers and the more experienced members. Its rules for rewarding the newcomer with a predictable degree of influence keep most of those in mid-career reasonably satisfied with their prospects. Finally, at the point where conflict would be greatest, namely, where formal leadership positions are at stake, the system proscribes conflict entirely.

The seniority-protegé-apprenticeship system is a regulator of many relationships in the chamber—not merely a way of picking committee chairmen. The system must be considered in its entirety as it functions to stabilize the internal structure of influence. It must be considered, too, as a system which touches almost every activity of the House. Consequently, proposed changes in the seniority-protegé-apprentice system cannot be considered as minor. They would produce a new distribution of influence in the House.

The negotiation and bargaining system

An organization like the House, in which influence is distributed among forty or fifty different leaders, risks the danger of irreconcilable conflict among them. And it is to prevent such internecine struggle from destroying the institution that a system of norms has developed to govern the business of majority-building.

The negotiation and bargaining system of norms defines for the members how majority building should proceed. The over-arching norm of this system is that compromise through negotiation be accepted as the proper way of making decisions in the chamber. No individual or group ought to expect to get exactly what it wants from the process. Each must "give a little and take a little" if majorities are to be built and the institution is to survive. A corollary of this norm is that all conflicts should be de-personalized as possible and that policy disagreement should not produce personal animosities. Members should "disagree without being disagreeable." Only thus will it be possible to negotiate and bargain with one's colleagues on a continuing basis and construct new alliances with former opponents. From these basic norms of conduct flow other rules to govern those interactions between specific leaders or specific groups where conflict might be expected to arise.

Working back through the structure as we have described it, one obvious point of conflict is that between committees or between a committee and the rest of the House. One source of such conflict was reduced considerably by the elaboration of committee jurisdictions in the Reorganization Act of 1946. Committees which authorize programs still conflict, however, with the Appropriations Committee, which must act on the money for those programs. Between the two, however, there normally exists a mutual recognition that the Appropriations Committee should not define programs, i.e., legislate, in an appropriation bill and that the authorizing committee must accept the dollar figure set by the appropriating committee. To keep this conflict to a minimum, informal consultation between the two committees frequently occurs so as to exchange information and to negotiate outstanding differences of opinion. In general, it is the acceptance of the norm of specialization that minimizes inter-committee conflict. On this basis, committees negotiate treaties of reciprocity ranging from "I will stay out of your specialty if you will stay out of mine" to "I'll support your bill if you will support mine." Committee leaders share the desire to preserve their autonomy within the House and will come to each other's aid when they perceive a threat to the committee system in general. The survival of them all demands, and produces, a norm of mutual respect one for another.

Inside the various committees, conflict is frequently held down by

similar norms of negotiation. Where influential subcommittees exist, as
on the Appropriations Committee, the rules of specialization and reciprocity underpin a system of mutual subcommittee support. To the degree that the committee leaders share their influence and bargain with
other members of the committee in working over a piece of legislation,
internal committee conflict may be minimized. Also inside the committee,
conflict may be averted by obedience to norms which stress a minimum of
partisanship—as they do on the Armed Services Committee—and which
produce a close working relationship between chairman and ranking
minority member and their respective party groups.

One especially delicate relationship involves that between the majority
party leadership and the committee chairmen—the sore point of House
and party structure. The disruptive potentialities of this kind of conflict
are well illustrated by the struggle between Speaker Rayburn and Chairman Smith of the Rules Committee, causing damage that took Speaker
McCormack much of his first year to repair. But this case is an extraordinary one precisely because actions taken in accordance with the usual
norms of negotiation and bargaining failed. Most of the time the two
kinds of leaders cooperate—sometimes on the basis of a policy agreement,
but always on the basis of a mutual need. The party leaders need the
support of the committee leaders if they want any bill at all to get to
the floor; the committee leaders need the support of the party leaders if
they want procedural assistance and sufficient supporting votes on the
floor. So committee leaders remain amenable to the wishes of the party
leaders; but the party leaders by and large defer to and support the
specialized committees. Sanctions and the threat of sanctions are, of
course, available on both sides and may be used. But knock-down, drag-
out battles within the majority party are events to be avoided at nearly
any cost. The committee leaders risk a loss of influence inside and outside their committees; and the party leaders risk the permanent loss of
sources of support which they may need on later issues.

Given the fact that partisanship runs deep in the structure of influence,
the norms which keep inter-party conflict at a minimum are perhaps the
most important of all. Without them the House could not survive as we
know it. The existence and the observance of such rules were symbolized
in the trust, the friendship, the consultation, the exchange of information, and the mutual assistance between Sam Rayburn and Joseph Martin
and, similarly, between Nicholas Longworth and John Garner before
them.

Most basic to inter-party relations are the continuous consultations
between the respective leaders on the legislative program. The rule that
the majority should schedule the business of the House is accompanied
by the rule that the minority should be apprised of that schedule in advance and that minority objections or suggestions should be entertained
where possible. Here again, there is mutual need. For the majority, speed

and order may be of the essence. The minority cannot obstruct indefinitely, but it can surely disrupt the smooth flow of House business. On the other hand, for the minority, predictability is critically important. They do not want to live under constant threat of parliamentary tricks, snap roll call votes, or unscheduled sessions. Informal working agreements and trust between majority and minority lubricate House decision-making. Similar agreements as to the size and party ratio of each committee, together with the agreement not to interfere in each other's committee assignment processes, undergird the committee system.

The fact that all-out conflict between the parties is subject to certain limiting norms at every stage in decision-making means that when a majority is built, its decision is more likely to be accepted as legitimate and supported as such by the minority. This is doubly essential in a system where much of today's majority may be found in tomorrow's minority.

Since the divisions within each party make intra-party conflict likely, some note should be made of those norms which help to keep such conflict from disrupting the party altogether. Foremost, perhaps, is the rule that no man is required to show complete party loyalty. A great many reasons are acceptable as excuses for going "off the reservation" and against "the leadership." Constituency and conscience are recognized as taking precedence over party, and a vote cast on these grounds will not be held against a member. On the other hand, in return for this degree of freedom, party leaders do expect that when a man is importuned specifically and directly on a vote, he will do everything he can to "go along." Party members who seek immunity even from this degree of give and take will receive no rewards at the hands of the leadership. But, as we have seen, the leaders must take the party coalition as they find it. Thus they preside over negotiations which take place among the elements of the coalition and preserve its loose unity. Such negotiations dominate internal party organs. Committee assignments are negotiated among party blocs in accordance with formulas that give proportionate representation to party factions. Similarly, all factions will be represented on party policy organs. And party leaders, as we have noted, will be chosen from those most able to communicate on a basis of trust and respect with all factions.

Conflict is the very life blood of a decision-making body in a free society. Yet it is amazing how much of the time and energy of House members is devoted to the business of avoiding conflict. The reason for this is simple. Excessive conflict will disrupt and disable the entire internal structure. In the interests of stability, therefore, a cluster of norms calling for negotiation and bargaining is operative at every point where conflict might destroy the institution. In view of the criticisms frequently pointed at bargaining techniques—"back scratching," "log rolling," "pork barrelling," "vote trading"—it should be noted that these techniques are designed to make majority-building possible. Negotiations in which exchanges of trust or exchanges of tangible benefits minimize conflict pervade every attempt to exercise influence in the chamber. If they were replaced with new rules of conduct, a wholly new structure for decision-making would have to be inaugurated in the House.

CONCLUSION

This essay has attempted to describe the existing structure of influence inside the House of Representatives. And it has used the problems of decision-making and maintenance as the vehicles for that description. The reader has been invited to view influence relationships in the House as they function to solve these two basic organizational problems. Present relations within and between committees and party units have been treated as one solution to the problem of decision-making. Seniority and bargaining norms have been considered in terms of their contribution to maintenance. Obviously, many other structural arrangements can be devised to deal with these same problems. The pre-1910 Speaker-centered structure comes most readily to mind. This essay, however, offers neither blueprints nor prescriptions. To those who may be concerned with alternative arrangements, the suggestion here is simply that they focus their attention on the twin problems of decision-making and maintenance.

In choosing to highlight decision-making and maintenance as crucial *internal* problems, the essay declares a bias in favor of an influential House of Representatives. If one believes that the House should be dominated either by a powerful President or by a national party organization, then neither decision-making nor maintenance are significant internal problems. They will have to be solved—but the solution will come from outside the chamber. And the internal structure of influence will be a mere shadow of the external structure of influence. To those, therefore, who would prefer a weaker House of Representatives, this essay will miss the mark and, hence, have little to offer. To those who wish to preserve or strengthen the influence of the House of Representatives within the American political system, this analysis of one kind of internal structure may help in assessing the likely consequences of another.

Ralph K. Huitt

4

The Internal Distribution
of Influence: The Senate

The Senate of the United States is a small and special world. The chamber is quiet. It must be, because there is no public address system and business is conducted in conversational tones. It is dignified: somber-suited men, a few quite old, move in the perpetual twilight of its high ceiling lights. There is a feeling of continuity; in the bottom drawer of the Victorian desks the men who sat there have signed their names and some, at least, must stir the least imaginative newcomer.

It is the place of the states, as the Founding Fathers meant it to be. No teeming state may override the constitutional guarantee of perfect numerical equality, and no man is bigger simply because he comes from a big state. Indeed, men from small states have walked this floor with a heavy tread: Borah of Idaho, Norris of Nebraska, LaFollette of Wisconsin. It is the place of the individual; most business is done by unanimous consent, and one man with ruffled feelings must be pacified, if he knows the rules.

It is a small world, ingrown and not wholly immune from narcissism, yet its nerve ends are in the great world outside, and its reaction to events can be instantaneous. It does not forget, nor does it let the Executive forget, that it has unique powers over and responsibilities for the conduct of foreign policy.

RALPH K. HUITT *is Professor of Political Science at the University of Wisconsin. Director of the Wisconsin Center for Education and Politics since 1955, he has written extensively for political science journals and contributed to numerous policy studies. Professor Huitt has had direct experience with the workings of the United States Senate, having served on the staffs of Lyndon B. Johnson, and William Proxmire. In 1964 he was appointed to direct a study of Congress for the American Political Science Association.*

Its members are accustomed to deference; their elevators carry them where *they* want to go while the public waits. Nevertheless all of them must return, sooner or later, to account to the people who sent them, and not one may be absolutely sure he will come back.

The small and special world of the Senate is not easy for the outsider —nor all the insiders—to understand. Prestige outside and inside the body are not necessarily equated, and prestige both outside and inside does not necessarily mean influence inside. Formal powers are less important than the brains and self-confidence to assume a large role, tempered by the sensitivity to internal controls necessary not to overplay it. The tranquil outer surface is deceptively simple; the complex and largely unstated rules of its inner life may be missed or misunderstood even by men who live with them a long time.

Sober and sophisticated men have fallen in love with the Senate, and some of them have betrayed their infatuation in print. Others, including some members of the body, have excoriated it in harsh despair.

All this seems worth saying, or trying to say, at the beginning of what is intended as a dispassionate analysis of some of the elements of power in the Senate. It is a way of saying that the Senate is not easy to write about with confidence. Some familiarity with senators and their world brings with it a hesitancy to say very much with certainty. Nevertheless the Senate *does* have a public life, and some insights may be gained from it.

FORMAL PARTY LEADERSHIP

In the House of Representatives the chair is more than a symbol of authority; it is the seat of the most powerful man in the body, the Speaker. He is there when great business is afoot and many other times besides. Not so in the Senate. The Constitution says the Vice-President (a man of prestige if not much power) should preside and sometimes he does—during the opening prayer, perhaps, or when a tie vote (which he can break) seems likely. His surrogate technically is the President *pro tempore*, a venerable majority member who may spend more time in the chauffeured limousine the office provides than in the chair itself. Presiding is the special burden of the freshman senators of the majority party, who among them do it most of the time. Their staff people like to send constituents over to the gallery (with a pardonably deceitful hint of pride in his quick success) "to see our senator preside." It is a good joke but a small one—poor pay indeed for hours spent at the most tedious and least influential job in the Senate. Nevertheless their chore underlines a basic truth about the Senate, that power is not where rules say or appearances suggest it should be, but where it is found.

The men who sit in the front seat on either side of the aisle, the floor leaders of the respective parties, have much influence, as have the chairmen of the standing committees in varying degrees. Besides these incumbents of formal positions there are senators who exercise influence in informal groups which set the tone and shape the norms of the body. The relative effectiveness of these extra-constitutional power-wielders depends upon a combination of personal aggressiveness and sensitivity to the climate of the Senate, of time and circumstance and external influences, which makes generalization hazardous indeed. Generalizations must be tried just the same. Political power of the magnitude of that exercised by and within the Senate demands that repeated attempts at analysis be made.

The floor leaders: some stable elements

There are elements of the floor leader's power in the Senate which are relatively stable and permanent, others which are variable; among the variable elements there are some about which he personally can do much and others about which he can do little.

The most important stable element by far is the character of the American political system. Governmental power is divided between the national government and the fifty states, and at the national level it is shared in a shifting balance by the Executive, Congress, and the courts. These are basic constitutional arrangements about which the leader can do almost literally nothing. He can do little more to change the kind of political parties these arrangements have helped to produce. The leader is the principal officer in the Senate of a national political party. What does this mean? If his party has captured the White House, he can expect some policy guidance from the President; but if he is in the minority, he would be hard put to it to find anyone with a claim to national party leadership superior to his own. "National" party in America is an ambiguous concept: ideologically, it is a cluster of ideas, symbols and associations which its "members" share more or less; operationally, it is an agglomeration of state and local parties, interest groups, and temporary associations which want for one reason or another to elect a President. Its quadrennial platform, compounded of principle and expediency, may be ignored or even denounced by the presidential candidate himself. The most astonishing thing about this remarkable organization, the party, is that it *does* command considerable loyalty from its members, inside and outside public office.

But it is not a loyalty which binds a congressman to a party line, no matter who enunciates it, when it goes contrary to his own convictions or strongly held wishes his constituents appear to hold. Party identification may be the strongest influence on voters without meaning the same thing to all voters; so a high score on party votes will not necessarily get a campaigning senator in free. Survival in office rests ultimately on his relations with his own constituency. The leadership cannot help him or hurt him very much, and he knows it. Great careers have been built on party dissidence, and he has seen party giants go down. The leader understands this, too, because his party office gives him no immunity. What leader did more than John Worth Kern, who put Woodrow Wilson's massive legislative program through the Senate virtually intact? And what was his reward but to be retired by Indiana voters in 1916? What else happened to Scott Lucas in Illinois and Ernest McFarland in Arizona, both Democratic leaders, in successive elections? For each man defeat closed his senatorial career; there is no device in American life by which a party may restore a defeated leader to office. Moreover, congressmen know that a trip to the party woodshed may smart but is seldom fatal; not even Franklin Roosevelt could purge intransigent Democrats. No member of Congress can escape the lonely awareness that he is essentially on his own. This explains a basic fact of life in the Senate: no one finally can make anyone else do anything.

A second element affecting the leader's situation which changes little is the relative paucity of formal powers attached to this position. He is not a national officer in the government. He is not a national officer in his party. He is not even an officer in his house, as the Speaker is in the House of Representatives. He must put together "fragments of power," as David Truman has said, combining them with great personal skill and tenacity, if he is to succeed.[1] The majority leader has, for instance, the right to be recognized first when he pleases, which gives him substantial parliamentary advantage. Through the Policy Committee he may control the scheduling of floor consideration of bills; through the committee on Committees (or the Democrats' Steering Committee) he may influence his party's committee assignments. If he is a Democrat both are made easier, because he is also chairman of the two committees. Because he is the center of the senatorial party's communications network and has access to the President if they are of the same party, the leader knows more than other senators and can share what he knows as he chooses. He may use these advantages, with some small favors he can bestow, to help other senators get what they want and expect them, in return, to help him. Democratic leader Mike Mansfield certainly was too modest when he said he had no more power than any other senator. On the other hand, there is no reading of these formal powers which will support the notion that they amount to much.

The converse of the leader's powers is the very considerable freedom of action reserved to the members themselves. This freedom is tenable only because it is exercised in the main with moderation and good sense. The Senate transacts most of its business through unanimous consent; debate is limited, schedules agreed to, rules set aside without objection because leaders respect the rights and interests of individual senators, who in turn go along with reasonable arrangements proposed by their

[1] David B. Truman, *The Congressional Party: A Case Study* (New York, 1959), p. 115.

leaders. But nothing is surrendered. One man may object and slow business to a halt. The ultimate expression of a latent institutionalized anarchy in the Senate is, as everyone knows, the filibuster—the privilege of unlimited talk—which permits a determined minority, and under certain circumstances a single member, to impose a negative on the entire body.

The Senate has never been entirely easy with its rule of "unlimited debate." Henry Clay tried unsuccessfully in 1841 to get adoption of a one-hour rule to limit debate. Nearly a century later the Senate accepted a cloture rule after a "little group of willful men" had, in Woodrow Wilson's opinion, "rendered the great government of the United States helpless and contemptible" by successfully filibustering his proposal to arm merchant ships. Cloture has gone through several variations since then, but it has always been hard to invoke and slow to take effect. Sixteen senators must sign a petition for limitation of debate, which brings the question to a vote two days later. At times the votes of two-thirds of the whole membership have been required to adopt cloture, but in 1959 this was reduced to two-thirds of those present and voting. After adoption of cloture each senator still may talk an hour on the measure.

Cloture undoubtedly is difficult to achieve. It has been employed successfully only six times since 1917, and four of these came in the first ten years of the rule's existence. Perhaps it will be easier in the future; the last two times have come close together. In 1962 a cloture motion was adopted 63-27 to overcome a liberal filibuster against the creation of a private corporation to develop and manage communications satellites such as Telstar. In 1964 every member of the Senate was present to adopt cloture 71-29 on a civil rights bill. But this is a relative matter; there is no prospect that the present rule ever will make it simple to terminate debate on a fiercely controverted matter, and the filibuster (or the threat of it) will remain a potent weapon.

Should cloture be made substantially easier to attain? The question seems to be one of the relative importance of majority will and minority rights. The argument for a more liberal rule is that the majority always should be able, finally, to prevail. After extended debate—long enough to correct imperfections, effect all possible compromises, and provide catharsis for the losers—the majority should work its will. The defenders of the conservative rule point out that the majority can in fact have its way; what is required is the mustering of more than a simple majority. They argue that a special majority should be required to over-ride a determined minority which is not open to being converted by debate. Otherwise resistance and nullification are encouraged and enforcement is made more difficult. The rule of the special majority is a familiar one in the Constitution; it is required for approval of treaties, impeachments, constitutional amendments, expulsion of members, and overriding presidential vetoes.

What is more important than the leader's powers—and more will be said about this later—the leader cannot control the vast delegations of power parceled out by the Senate to those feudal chieftains, the chairmen of the standing committees. Nor is there any prospect that the delegations can be recalled; the Constitution has seen to that. The separation of powers means that to the Executive and the legislature the other must always be "they." The British House of Commons may rely upon the bureaucracy for assessments as well as facts; the departments are controlled by ministers who also sit as leaders of Parliament. If they do not like what they get, the Honourable Members have sanctions which ministers heed. Not so Congress; vigilance in the committees is the alternative to the forfeit of that equal status to which Congress is entitled and may, in the rough fashion in which such sums must be calculated, actually have.

The leader is a man of great influence nevertheless. The basic reason is that the Senate must be led, and the need will grow more compelling, not less. It is significant that when the senatorial party chooses a man to bring a measure of coordination to this body of specialists, it often abandons the strict seniority principle. Election by his peers is a mark of confidence in him which is bound to strengthen his hand.

The floor leaders: important variables

Some elements of the leader's power potential are variable; of these the situational probably is the most crucial. Perhaps some illustrations will support the point.

The two most productive bursts of congressional energy in this century came in the early years of the administrations of Woodrow Wilson and Franklin Roosevelt. Congress worked continuously the first 567 days of Wilson's first term (April 7, 1913 to October 24, 1914) and was *not* in session only eleven months in four years. Working through Washington summers without air conditioning, Congress passed the most impressive array of constructive legislation perhaps in its history. The New Deal's beginning, with its fabulous "hundred days," needs no retelling; why labor a legend? The two periods, in many ways dissimilar, had this in common: Congress felt the hot breath of the country. Wilson's Democrats had been long out of power; his progressivism had brought them back. They bent willingly to his imperious leadership—so much so that Senate Democrats allowed themselves to be dominated by twenty progressives with no more than two years' seniority (including their leader, Kern), eleven of whom were newly elected! Kern, serving his only term, failed to muster his majority on only one bill Wilson really wanted.[2] Twenty years later, Roosevelt's legions were as eager to go along. Joseph T. Robinson put the emergency banking bill through the Senate in seven hours—including committee and floor consideration—using the

[2] Claude G. Bowers, *The Life of John Worth Kern* (Indianapolis, 1918). See Chapters Fourteen, Seventeen for Kern's record as leader.

only copy of the bill in existence. (The House of Representatives had passed a folded newspaper, accepting the fiction that it was the bill.[3])

It is not necessary to define "normal" times to say that these were not normal, nor that Kennedy's years were more nearly so. When a newsmagazine asked majority leader Mike Mansfield in 1962 "why Kennedy's program is in trouble with Congress," Mansfield replied that Congress responds to sentiment in the country; he believed the country would support the President but there was no sense of urgency yet.[4]

Lucas and McFarland had a Democratic President with a program; they shattered the senatorial party trying to enact the Fair Deal. Johnson had two precious years in the minority to put it together again; he literally sought issues on which the Democrats could be got to vote together. Taft and Knowland, his opposite numbers, could do little with their bare majority and small help from the White House. Johnson's six years as majority leader with Eisenhower raise the question: what difference would a Democratic President have made? Mansfield faced a reaction to Johnson's demanding leadership; a respite of some duration was in order.

The list could go on, but the point is clear: a leader is not free to be any kind of leader he pleases. His alternatives are framed for him by the situation in which he must operate.

At the same time he is not the creature of his situation. The second variable is his own perception of the role of leader. The sharp contrast between Johnson and his successor, Mansfield, is in point. Because he did not drive the Senate as Johnson did, Mansfield was accused (even publicly by a colleague) of being a weak leader. The charge missed the mark: Mansfield had not failed to be like Johnson, he did not *want* to be like Johnson. He was not a weak leader but a deliberately different kind of leader. This is made obvious by interviews held by *U.S. News* with Johnson, in 1960, and with Mansfield in 1962.[5] The men agreed that the majority leader has few real powers, but that is superficial. Johnson made it plain that he meant to use his "only real power," persuasion (by which he meant the employment of every resource he had), to the utmost. Mansfield called Johnson "the best majority leader the Senate ever had," but Johnson would not recognize Mansfield's description of the job. Mansfield did not want the leadership; he was drafted. He was "one among my peers." He had no instruments of authority. He would not use legislative scheduling for leverage nor influence a committee assignment. He would not "think" of telling a senator how to vote. Implicit in his com-

[3] Joseph Alsop, Jr. and Turner Catledge, "Joe Robinson, the New Deal's Old Reliable," *Saturday Evening Post* (September 26, 1936).

[4] "Why Kennedy's Program is in Trouble with Congress," *U.S. News and World Report* (September 17, 1962).

[5] "Leadership: An Interview with Senate Leader Lyndon Johnson," *U.S. News and World Report* (June 27, 1960). The Mansfield interview is cited in note 4.

ments was his basic philosophy that all senators are equal, that there is
none, not even the leader, who is "more equal" than the others.

How does the leader perceive his relationship with the President? This
is bound to affect his performance. There is the President's man; Robinson is an example. Unquestioning fidelity to Roosevelt came easy. He had
been successively an ardent Wilsonian, a conservative vice-presidential
candidate with Al Smith, an "Old Guardsman" in Congress, a gubernatorial candidate in Arkansas on a strict economy platform. He took the
New Deal in stride; party loyalty bridged all ideological chasms. Then
there is the man who represents each—the Senate and the President—
to the other, but places high value on loyalty to the President. This is
the Mansfield view; he said it was easy to follow Kennedy's leadership
because they saw eye-to-eye, but he would resign if there was a serious
difference. Kern, Barkley, and Lucas felt much the same way. Other
leaders have regarded themselves primarily as the Senate's agent to the
White House. This was McFarland's view. Taft seemed to regard his
relationship with the President as something like a partnership; and
Knowland drew a sharp distinction between the leadership and senatorial
roles, stepping back several rows to speak in support of the Bricker
amendment, which Eisenhower opposed. Again, it is tempting to specu-
late how Johnson would have worked with a Democratic President. No
man ever had more pride in the Senate, but he venerated the Presidency
and correctly assessed its unique importance to the successful working
of the American system. Despite criticism from the liberal wing of his
party, he would not oppose Eisenhower just to make issues nor encourage
his Democratic majority to attack the President.[6]

Still another aspect of the leader's perception of his role involves the
relations between majority and minority leaders. Ideally, there should
be two points of view at a time, which complement each other. Sometimes a leader thinks he must fight all the time; this seems to have been
the general notion of Kenneth Wherry, who apparently behaved more as
a senator from Nebraska than as the minority spokesman, even siding
consistently with a minority bloc in his own party. Other opposing leaders have seen their respectives roles much as might contending trial
lawyers whose professional obligation is to expedite the business of the
court. More than that, some pairs of leaders have been able to make
clear distinctions between their partisan roles and their partnership in
promoting the general welfare, and these relationships make attractive
chapters in the history of the Senate. Johnson with Taft, with Knowland,
and with Dirksen, as well as Mansfield with Dirksen, fit this pattern.

Perhaps the variable in the leader role which is easiest to identify and
hardest to assess is leadership style. The range of behavior has been

[6] Ralph K. Huitt, "Democratic Party Leadership in the Senate," *American Political
Science Review*, 55 (June 1961), 333-344; William S. White, *The Professional: Lyndon
B. Johnson* (Boston, 1964), pp. 171-177.

broad indeed. The contrast between the highly successful leaders of the New Freedom and the New Deal, whom we mentioned earlier, is relevant. Kern was modest, conciliatory, a man of "infinite patience and never-failing tact." A colleague said of him: "He was a strong partisan, but there was a kindliness about him that turned aside all feelings of ill will or animosity. [7] Of his New Deal counterpart, contemporary observers said "President Roosevelt uses him to push and pull, butt and bludgeon his ideas into legal existence. . . ." Robinson was a man who

> . . . loves a fight, and when it is necessary to make enemies, he never exhibits the usual politician's soft unwillingness to offend. He cheerfully steps on toes that require to be stepped on, and sometimes on some that don't, and he can read the riot act with complete authority.[8]

If these are extremes, Johnson might occupy a middle ground. His determination to "persuade" included everyone who might be got to go Johnson's way. The tactics ranged from the casual but pointed remark in his restless roaming of floor and cloakroom to the saturation bombardment known as "Treatment A," in which the whole gamut of emotions—patriotism, loyalty, selfishness, fear, pride—might be played upon. Johnson's persuasive talents were universally respected but not invariably loved.

Wise leaders have used other men for jobs not quite in their own line. Robinson was not a man for a sensitive situation; when persuasion was needed he called on "fixers" like James Byrnes and Pat Harrison; or at the second level, Vice-President Garner; or as a court of last resort, Jim Farley. One of Johnson's prime skills was his manipulation of the versatile Democratic "bench," fitting men to precise jobs he wanted them to do.

Much has been said here about the leader, particularly the majority leader, because he is the most influential and promising figure in the strongest centralizing agency in the Senate, the party. In his study of party operations in the Eighty-first Congress, Truman found the majority leader in both houses to be a middleman ideologically who sought positions on which a majority could be put together. He worked with the committee chairmen and tended to support committee bills, but when he and the chairman were in opposition on a committee bill the leader tended to carry with him a majority of the committee and the party as well.[9]

There is a limit to what party in the Senate can carry, but it is not a negligible force. Truman has said that the congressional party is "mediate and supplementary rather than immediate and inclusive in function," meaning by "mediate" that "its members' fortunes are not identical with those of the legislative party, but at the same time they are not com-

[7] Bowers, *op. cit.*, p. 374.
[8] Alsop and Catledge, *op. cit.*, p. 7.
[9] Truman, *op. cit.*, pp. 140, 242.

pletely independent of it." [10] The party emerges as the most often-heeded cue-giver in the Senate. A senator may vote with it because there are no competing cues; that is, on an issue he may hear no clear voice from home and may have no strong sentiments of his own. But it goes farther than that: on administration measures in the Eighty-first Congress even the dissident Southern wing voted with the Democratic majority more than the Republicans most likely to vote with the administration. This unifying tendency is more evident in the majority party. Lacking the recognized leadership furnished the majority by the President, the minority may lack the capacity to organize a stable majority of its members around a program of opposition.[11]

Other party agencies

Some students and practitioners of American politics have had a dream —an oft-recurring dream—about how the American political system might work. The dream is called responsible party government. There are variations in its details, but the basic notion is always the same, that the parties will perfect machinery through which they will keep the promises they make. The solemn pledges would be made in frequent conventions. The President and his congressional majorities would work together closely. The elected leaders in the two houses would formulate programs through policy committees made up of the chairmen of the standing committees and ratify them in conferences of all the members of the party in the respective houses. Members would be bound, formally or in honor, to support the party position. The chairmen of the standing committees would push through their groups the bills they agreed to in the policy committee. The minority in turn would provide a constructive and loyal opposition through similar party machinery. The majority would bear responsibility for its program, the minority would offer a genuine alternative, and the voter would have a chance to make an intelligent choice.

This is not an idle dream. All the parts of it exist in real life. Some of them are old and some relatively new. All of them work, more or less, but not quite the way the dream would have it.

The conference (or caucus, as it was called) is as old as the republic. Congressional caucuses nominated presidential candidates before there were conventions. The conference can indeed be an effective party instrument; Kern used it regularly in the enactment of Wilson's legislation. Members were bound and loyalty was expected. It is significant, however, that a substantial bloc of Kern's Democrats were themselves progressives, deeply committed to Wilsonian pledges which they also made. But ideological dedication is not the norm in Congress. Most members chafe

[10] *Ibid.*, p. 95.
[11] *Ibid.*, p. 192.

at efforts to bind them. They seek that blend of policy positions which they individually can comfortably defend at home. Johnson was bitterly criticized for not holding more conferences, but his critics made clear they did not mean to be bound by conference decisions; they wanted only to advise and be informed. Johnson responded with some conferences, and Mansfield began his tenure with several. Both parties have found them useful in recent times primarily as means to pass the word.

Policy committees by that designation are relatively new. The Joint Committee on the Organization of Congress recommended in 1946 that policy committees be created to formulate legislative policy of the parties, but the House struck them from the Reorganization Act passed that year. The next year the Senate independently established its own policy committees. The two committees have proved useful without having much effect on policy. They have developed differently in each party.

The Republican committee began with nine members but grew until, in 1955, all Republican senators up for reelection were made members. In the Eighty-eighth Congress the number was fourteen, eight of them *ex officio* as party officers, the other six elected by the conference. (The Republicans have a different man for every party job; the Democratic leader is also chairman of the conference, policy committee, and a committee on committees called the Steering Committee.) The practice of inviting other Republican senators interested in issues under discussion was expanded in the late years of the Eisenhower Administration to an open invitation to a weekly luncheon meeting where all members could be informed of the President's views. The practice has persisted, although attendance dropped off with the loss of the White House. In the Eighty-eighth Congress, nevertheless, the Republicans still could go from committee meeting to conference simply by switching chairmen, making the meeting a convenient platform for anouncing a Republican consensus on an issue.

The real utility of the Policy Committee to the Republicans has been the research staff it has made available to them. In the Eighty-eighth Congress there were generally eighteen staff members, about a dozen of them professional. Their importance was magnified by the fact that the rich professional resources of standing committee staffs were largely the possession of the majority, while the parties divided equally the policy committees' appropriation. The staff resources of the Policy Committee were available to individual Republicans as well as the leaders, and most took advantage of them. Sometimes work done for a single member later was distributed to all, along with a series of position papers of general usefulness.

The Democratic Policy Committee has been what the successive leaders have chosen to make it. There are nine members, three *ex officio* and six chosen by the leader—but the latter serve as long as they are in the

Senate. Barkley chose this mode of selection. Some effort has been made to keep an ideological and geographical balance on the committee, but there are liberal Northerners who would say it has been unsuccessful. The principal test in filling a vacancy is whether the leader *wants* him. Johnson made regular use of the committee to counsel with him. He liked to put friends on it who were men of power in their own right. No announcement of decisions was ever made except for tactical reasons. Mansfield apparently made small use of the committee except for legislative scheduling, which seems reasonable in light of his perception of the leader's role. The staff has also done useful research, but this is less crucial to the Democrats, who have controlled the committee staffs.

The other party agencies of importance are the committees on committees and the campaign committees. The Republican committee takes its committee selections to the conference, where consideration may be heated and prolonged. The Democratic leader may have critical influence over committee assignments if he wants it; he chairs the committee and the conference usually goes along. Johnson used his power deliberately and frankly. One of his first acts as leader was to give all Democrats at least one good committee, a revolution which won the support of freshmen members. He arranged shifts which would put members facing re-election on committees advantageous to them. Mansfield said that he let the Steering Committee freely decide committee assignments, but the makeup of the committee itself came under attack. The most vocal critic was Senator Joseph Clark of Pennsylvania, who charged that the "Establishment"—those senior members who "control the institutional machinery of Congress" (about whom more will be said)—dominates it, to the benefit primarily of the southern minority. He has contended that in 1963 new assignments and transfers went heavily against senators who had voted to liberalize the cloture rule.[12] It is not necessary to decide whether he is right to say that the matter is crucially important. The work of the Senate is done in committees; the careers of senators turn on committee assignments. The ability to control committee appointments is power indeed.

The senatorial campaign committees are designed to help senators of their party who are in close races with a chance to win. The committees are in continuous existence, with staff help and substantial assistance to give. They are mentioned here only because of occasional charges that the money and other help at their disposal are dispensed unfairly to penalize partisan colleagues with whom the committee majority are not sympathetic. Whether the charges are true or are merely attempts to get leverage with the committee, an outsider cannot decide.

[12] Joseph S. Clark, *Congress: The Sapless Branch* (New York, 1964), pp. 125-127, and *The Senate Establishment* (New York, 1963), pp. 40 *ff.*, 100-103.

THE LITTLE GOVERNMENTS OF THE STANDING COMMITTEES

The ultimate check on party government in the United States is the system of standing committees in Congress. This is another way to say that the ultimate check is the coordinate status of the legislature and the executive branches, so long as Congress is able roughly to hold its own. Because a coordinate legislature must have some way to gather and assess information on its own, if it is not to be a ward of the bureaucracy, the most efficient, practical way is to divide up in committees which specialize and develop a measure of expertise. Committees which specialize and have exclusive jurisdiction over certain kinds of legislation become little legislatures themselves, with power largely independent of the elected leadership of the parent body. Centralized power and dispersed power are contradictions; to the degree that the latter exists the former is limited.

It is necessary, therefore, to see the committees both as organs of investigation and deliberation, indispensable to Congress, and as subsystems of power, crucial both to the interests which seek access to government and to the work satisfactions and career aspirations of their members.

Internal life of the committees

The chairman of a major standing committee in the Senate is an influential and important man indeed. He usually is in virtual control of his committee. He calls committee meetings, decides what bills will be considered, appoints subcommittee chairmen, controls the selection of witnesses, and, excepting bills of overriding importance, determines which bills favorably reported by his committee really will be pressed for floor consideration. He probably will lead the floor fight for it or designate the man who will. In practice, he chooses committee members who will go to conference with the House on committee bills and may choose to lead the group himself. The chairman decides whether the staff will be as large and expert as money will buy or funds will be returned to the Treasury; whether the staff will be encouraged to be aggressive or passive; and whether a real fight will be made to carry the bill through floor and conference as the committee wrote it or the effort will be half-hearted.

That is why the mode of selection of the chairman is so important. Certainly the seniority system, which moves the ranking member of the majority on the committee automatically to the chairmanship, provokes hot debate. The principal points are clear. Seniority is good because it settles out-of-hand the most disruptive organizational problem Congress ever faced, which sometimes took months to settle. Seniority is bad because it gives a margin of influence to those states and sections which regularly return the same men—if one happens not to like their point of view. These obvious aspects of seniority obscure others as important, on which not much is known. What is the effect on committee operations and policy when a new chairman drastically different in style or ideology takes over—such as happened to the Senate Judiciary Committee when liberals Kilgore and Langer served as chairmen between conservatives McCarran and Eastland? Are there institutional devices for cushioning the change? What can committees do when the chairman becomes incompetent, perhaps from senility or especially if he has enough wit and obstinacy to hold on to the committee reins? Occasionally the leadership is forced to intervene, as the Democrats had to do with the Foreign Relations Committee chairmanship in Johnson's tenure as a leader, but there must be cases which have not been pushed that far. When a seniority chairman is out of step with a majority of his committee, what happens? Can he tyrannize over them and does he, or are reasonable accommodations made? These are questions to be answered if an intelligent assessment of the seniority system is to be made.

These questions lead to more basic ones. What are the patterns of relationships between chairmen and their committees? Or put somewhat differently, how do individual incumbents perceive the chairman's role? It should be obvious that elements discussed earlier which affect the floor leader's performance should be equally pertinent here. A chairman assumes a job that is fairly narrowly defined by the institutional history of his house. He confronts certain situational aspects: the size of his majority and its temper, the urgency at the moment of his committee's business, the attitudes and demeanor of his party's congressional and executive leaders. But within the limits of this institutional and situational frame he surely is as free as the floor leader to try to behave as he pleases.

Unfortunately, the behavior of chairmen has not been subjected to much scholarly or even journalistic scrutiny. It is not safe or fair, therefore, to try to offer examples. Even so, some "ideal types" of chairmen can be suggested. There is the chairman who successfully dominates his committee. He may use his dominion to make an empire, grasping all the legislative business he can claim title to, or he may suppress committee activity because he is out of sympathy with the majority; either way, he is the boss. A different kind of chairman may not be especially interested in his committee's subject matter, but may see his job as a facilitator of whatever its members want to do. He is a genuine chairman, the servant of the group's goals. Still another may be unsympathetic with what the majority wants but conscientiously helps them; he is a "service" chairman, reinforcing the majority sentiment with assistance only a chairman can give. Still another may regard his committee as a stage for his own performance, an extension of his own personality. He is not so much concerned with what it does as he is with the setting it provides for him. Undoubtedly the list could be extended. What matters, of course, is to discover through comparative studies the *range* of behavior open to chairmen, the patterns it commonly falls into.

The chairman's notion of his own role will probably determine how he reacts to that grievous problem, the need for subcommittees. The Legislative Reorganization Act of 1946 reduced the number of Senate committees from thirty-three to fifteen. What it did not and could not do was reduce the volume of committee business. The result was a steady proliferation of subcommittees, each of which tends to carve out for itself some specialized part of the full committee's jurisdiction. The subcommittee chairmen thus parcel out to a degree the chairman's power, as he and his colleagues have parceled out the power of the leadership. Some chairmen we have described do not care; at least one has given a subcommittee to every majority member of his committee (although he *did* later abolish one because he did not like what its chairman did with it). But to the man who hoards the power he has waited so long to get there must be other alternatives. He may eschew subcommittees entirely, putting the whole burden on the full committee. He may make himself chairman of every subcommittee. He may try to prevent specialization by the subcommittees, numbering instead of naming them and referring bills of all kinds to each of them. Needless to say, the subcommittee chairmen understand the game; they trade bills around until they have established *de facto* jurisdictions.

A problem faced by every member is what to do about transferring from one committee to another. Not many senators can at once get the committee they most want, and there definitely is a status system among committees. Donald Matthews studied gains and losses of membership on Senate committees over a period of a decade (1947-57) and found a discernible pecking order, with committees tending to lose members to committees above them and to gain from those below.[13] Foreign Relations, Appropriations, Finance, and Armed Services headed the list; the District of Columbia Committee was a predictable last. A transfer, regardless of his *Senate* seniority, is last in *committee* seniority; the agonizing question then is: better junior on a good committee or senior on a less prestigious one? The problem is complicated by the impossibility of calculating the rate at which senior members will die or retire.

Like other institutionalized human groups, committees tend to become small social systems in their own right, reflecting the norms of the larger system but developing nevertheless a group life of their own. Richard Fenno's study of the House Committee on Appropriations is a brilliant pioneering effort to explore the life of one such small system.[14]

[13] Donald R. Matthews, *U.S. Senators and Their World* (Chapel Hill, 1960), pp. 148-152.

[14] Richard F. Fenno, Jr., "The House Appropriations Committee as a Political System: The Problem of Integration," *American Political Science Review*, 56 (June 1962), 372.

He found the principal norms to be a dedication to work and a passion for protecting the Treasury. Junior members were socialized to respect these norms, and those who conformed best gained committee status earliest. It is probable that committees with great turnover do not develop a highly integrated group life, but the stable groups with great prestige surely must. If so, the character of that internal life, the norms that shape it, should be of great concern to bureaucrats, interest groups, and party leaders whose success may turn on their ability to placate and influence the committee.

But the balance must be kept: a committee is an institution of Congress; it exists to serve the purposes of congressmen. These are individual purposes as often as they are institutional or partisan. No one who has ever looked seriously at the committee's public activity, the hearing, can doubt that. David Truman has said that there are three functions or purposes of public hearings.[15] The first is to provide "a means of transmitting information, both technical and political, from various actual and potential interest groups to the committee." The second function "is as a propaganda channel through which a public may be extended and its segments partially consolidated or reinforced." The third is "to provide a quasi-ritualistic means of adjusting group conflicts and relieving disturbances through a safety valve." These purposes or functions relate to the performance of the committee as a working unit of the legislature, carrying its share of the work load, representing groups and reconciling their conflicts, reinforcing the authority of the political system. But the committee also affords the member a chance to get *his* job done. He may wish to make himself a national leader, build a reputation as a subject-matter expert, advertise himself to the constituency, do a favor for a supporter, discharge some of his own aggressions—the list could be a long one.[16] What is important is to see that in every aspect of congressional life it is necessary to satisfy both the system needs and the largely personal needs of the member who must keep himself solvent in a free-enterprise politics.

External relations of committees

Like every other human group, the Senate committee lives in an environment which affects and is affected by it, with which it must somehow get along. Its environment is both congressional and noncongressional—and the latter may extend around the globe. In the congressional environment there are the other committees. The relationship seems to be largely live and let live, which the party leadership, overlapping memberships, frequent transfers, the smallness of the body and the frequent testimony of members before committees not their own, all make easier.

[15] David B. Truman, *The Governmental Process* (New York, 1953), p. 372.
[16] Ralph K. Huitt, "The Congressional Committee: A Case Study," *American Political Science Review*, 48 (June 1954), 340-365.

Some tension between the legislative committees and the Appropriations Committee seems to exist beneath the surface, because what the former authorizes the latter may reduce or even deny, but this seems less sharp in the Senate than in the House. Undoubtedly friction is lessened by the Senate Committee's practice of inviting senior members of the legislative committee to participate when appropriations for their programs are discussed. Apparently little attempt is made generally for committees with the same jurisdictions in the two houses to work together; sometimes their staffs collaborate a bit, but the committees seem to work independently and meet in conference. The two taxing committees are an exception. Their senior members belong to the Joint Committee on Internal Revenue Taxation, through which they share an expert staff and collaborate effectively.[17] The separateness of the parallel committees reflects the separateness of the two houses, whose majority leaders probably meet only at the White House unless they are personal friends, as Johnson and Rayburn were. It is indeed true that "two houses do not make a home."

In the non-congressional environment, the most frequent and immediate relations of senatorial committees are with the administrative agencies. This usually is called "legislative oversight of administration," a term which is more misleading than not because it suggests a clear legislative mandate to the agency which the committee is determined to see carried out. Undoubtedly there is some of this in the relationship, and committees are directed in the Legislative Reorganization Act of 1946 to supervise the work of the agencies which fall within their jurisdiction. But unfortunately the mandate often is left unclear, sometimes deliberately so, and problems come up not dreamed of when the legislation was passed. Again, the relationship between committee and agency sometimes more nearly resembles a partnership than master and servant.

If oversight is the relationship the committee *does* want, there are traditional tools available to it. The appropriations committees in either house can guide and direct, under the threat of reduced funds. The committee may investigate the stewardship of the agency. The principal agency officers have to come before the committee before confirmation by the Senate. Congress can legislate in detail, telling the agency precisely what is desired. These formidable-seeming tools should be enough, but in practice they raise questions. Can the spending committees actually get to the heart of the matter in the enormous budgets they report, or are they limited to granting an increment, more or less, over last year? After the committee has terrorized the agency, does anything change or do the bureaucrats go back to business as usual? Is confirmation before assumption of office much of a check? How much effect on actual agency operations does the political officer have anyway? How can Congress effectively legislate in detail when the last century of administrative history has been that of increasingly large delegations of legislative power because of the legislature's inability to cope with the bewildering details of modern industrial life?

Moreover, despite a dearth of analysis of the oversight exercised by individual committees, there is enough to show that it varies widely from committee to committee. One may interfere with administrative detail outrageously, another may simply try to keep informed through its professional staff, and a third may decline to supervise at all. A single committee may bear down hard on one agency and be indifferent to another, and its militancy may wax and wane over time. Some variables might be suggested. The first, obviously, is the chairman: one aggressively suspicious of bureaucrats may be succeeded by another who thinks they should be let alone. A second is the character of the agency: a senator who would be horrified at the thought of congressional interference with the Federal Reserve Board may attempt to retry a National Labor Relations Board case in committee. Still another is the character of the program: one with wide interest and visibility will get more attention than other requiring expertise and secrecy. Again there is the closeness to the constituency: the State Department obviously does not affect as many people directly as the Department of Agriculture does. Finally, there is the quality and size of the professional staff: this may in fact be an *index* to the intentions of the chairman. What matters once again are *patterns* of recurring relationships, the *range* of behavior open to committee and staff.

These considerations are not unrelated to the question of power structure within the Senate; far from it. When committee and agency can work out something resembling a partnership, there is advantage in it for both sides. The committee adopts the agency; it protects the agency from other agencies and from executive control to the limit of its (perhaps considerable) ability. On the other hand, if the agency controls what senators (and their constituents) want, the senator with preferred access to the agency has far less need to get legislation. As a man with access to scarce services, he is in a bargaining position with legislator and bureaucrat alike. He can perform services which may make him unbeatable. These are power relationships—perhaps the most important of all and the least understood by outsiders.

THE INFORMAL SYSTEM

It is unlikely that there is an absolute correspondence in any institutionalized human organization between the formal structure of authority and the actual distribution of influence. Human groups develop "norms"—cultural "oughts" which prescribe proper behavior for their members on which there is a high degree of consensus. The most influential and effective members usually conform most closely to the norms; in their own behavior they represent, in effect, what the group values. Perhaps the formal leaders are these persons, but they may not be; they may instead be members without official power ascriptions who nevertheless exercise a measure of control over what the group decides and does. This is recognized in many groups by the labels attached to this informal influence structure—the "inner clique," the "old guard," the "king-makers."

It would seem highly probable, therefore, that such an informal structure exists in the Senate—but who are they, what do they control, and how do they exercise their influence? Two commentators on the Senate have confidently asserted the existence of such an influence group without agreeing on any of these questions. One is William S. White, an experienced journalist and sympathetic observer of the Senate.[18] The other is Joseph S. Clark, a senator who is, it may fairly be said, an unsympathetic participant-observer. White calls his influentials the "Inner Club," Clark his dynasts the "Establishment." [19]

White asserts that "the inner life of the Senate . . . is controlled by the Inner Club." Its members are the "Senate type" (or the "Senate man"). The Senate type is a prudent man. He serves a long apprenticeship before he begins to talk but even then speaks little. He is courteous and forbearing, never allowing the business of the body to affect personal relations. He is helpful to other senators and expects reciprocity. More than anything else he is devoted to the institution; he "speaks to the Senate," not to the country or the world or anyone outside. It does not matter what his political views are; wealth, popularity, social status, intellectual power, party affiliation, or national reputation are not determinants. "At the core of the Inner Club stand the Southerners . . ." but it is not a matter of geography; others may and do belong. Southerners are in because they "express, consciously or unconsciously, the deepest instincts of the 'Senate type' . . ." who is "a man for whom the institution is a career in itself, a life in itself and an end in itself." He is a man who has "tolerance toward his fellows, intolerance toward any who would in any real way change the Senate, its customs or its way of life." How do they operate? Certainly not in conventional ways: ". . . one day the perceptive onlooker will discover a kind of aura from the Inner Club that informs him of what the Senate is later going to do about such and such." In 1956 a proposal to establish a joint committee to oversee the work of the Central Intelligence Agency failed. "Under

[18] *Citadel: The Story of the U.S. Senate* (New York, 1956). All the quotations used here are taken from Chapter Seven.
[19] Clark, *Congress: The Sapless Branch.* The quotations are taken from Chapter Six.

their bleak and languid frowns the whole project simply died; a wind had blown upon it from the Inner Club and its erstwhile sponsors simply left it." But White admits that the Inner Club members may not have nearly so much influence on what the Senate does that affects the outside world as men who are not truly Senate types at all; they are guardians of the "inner life."

Senator Clark is not talking about that kind of thing at all. His "Establishment" consists of "those Democratic chairmen and ranking Republican members of the important legislative committees who, through seniority and pressures exerted on junior colleagues, control the institutional machinery of Congress." The official leadership group "are usually captives of the Establishment, although they can sometimes be found looking out over the walls of their prison, plotting escape." "Establishment" members have specific ideological commitments: the bonds which unite them are "white supremacy; a stronger devotion to property than human rights; support of the military establishment; belligerence in foreign affairs; and a determination to prevent Congressional reform." Clark gives names; among seventeen Democrats, only two are not Southerners; among eleven Republicans, only two or three would not be included among hard-core conservatives. This informal structure therefore *is* selected by ideology: Clark's ultimate tests are these: "So long as a Democrat stands firm against civil rights and cloture, or a Republican against cloture only, his (or her) Establishment status remains unquestionable." Clark clearly is not talking about White's Inner Club; Hubert Humphrey was specifically named as a member of it, but he could only be a captive of the "Establishment." Clark is a liberal and the "Establishment" is the conservative opposition. They are the people who oppose the President's program. Yet the record adduced by Clark does not make them seem so formidable; on three important record votes mentioned, the "Establishment" lost 80-19, 57-35, and 61-26.

For the student of influence in the Senate these formulations are not much help. White's empathy for the Senate is uniquely his; how does one learn how to discover an aura, to interpret a frown? How does one translate the influence of the inner life of the Senate on the public discharge of its constitutional responsibilities? Clark's "Establishment" certainly is concretely conceived, but how seriously can one take a senatorial power elite which would not include Johnson, Humphrey, or Mansfield? Moreover, the strength of the "Establishment" comes largely from certain advantages they hold under the rules, a condition Clark devoutly wishes to change. The informal structure of power in the Senate remains a legitimate problem of research, but it seems reasonable to agree with Truman and Matthews "that the 'real' leaders of the Senate are, for the most part, those in positions of formal authority." [20]

[20] The quotation is from Matthews, *U.S. Senators and Their World*, p. 253. Also see Truman, *The Congressional Party*, p. 285 *ff.*

Senate staff

One dimension of power in the Senate which is subtle and complex but largely unexplored is the influence on their principals of members of professional staffs. There can be no doubt that this provision of the Legislative Reorganization Act of 1946 has profoundly changed and vastly improved the performance of the Senate. Like the President of the United States on an appropriately smaller scale, a senator is an institution. He is what he is plus what he can add to himself by the considerable array of brains and skills the law allows him to buy. The work load now carried by the typical Senate office would be unthinkable without the division of labor among roughly a score of people. Similarly, committees would lose their cutting edge if they lost their staffs. But first-rate professionals do more than carry out assignments. In the offices of individual senators they learn to think like the boss; they determine to some degree who sees him and what importunities reach him. In the committee rooms they identify the problems and provide the facts and questions. The product of the Senate is to some unmeasured and perhaps immeasurable degree their product. Their influence probably would be very easy to overstate, but it does exist.

It is unlikely that staff power has a structure apart from the relationships among senators themselves. A case in point is the loose grouping of the principal assistants of about a score of liberal senators who held regular meetings for a while during the Eighty-second Congress. The membership shifted somewhat in accordance with the issue under discussion. Needless to say, these caucuses had the approval of the participants' principals, and indeed were no more than an extension of senatorial activity.

The most important staff positions in the senatorial office are administrative assistant (the top job) and legislative assistant. Other professionals may be called legal counsel, press secretary, or other titles. These jobs attract some very bright and able people, who sometimes remain with a senator for years, serving him with sacrificial devotion. They are men capable in most cases of achieving successful, perhaps distinguished, individual careers in their own names if they chose to do so. Yet they will submerge their own ambitions and identities in those of a senator, seeing another take credit for their best work, coming in time to think and even talk like him, to exult and suffer with him. Why do they do it?

No one can say with confidence. There is no systematic research into the motivations and satisfactions of these senators' men. Surely the possibility of sharing the power and glory of the supreme office must sustain some of them. Kennedy, Johnson, Nixon, Lodge, and Goldwater all were or had been senators when their parties chose them, and Kennedy and Johnson took their senatorial staffs into the White House with them. But some of the most faithful staff people toil for men who never will be notable beyond state boundaries, and there is a veritable parade of professionals through the offices of some senators with great expectations.

Whatever is revealed by systematic research, one hypothesis may be ventured: the principal staff men share significantly in the exercise of their senators' power or they would not stay. A bankrupt in a millionaire's club is no more contemptible than a man without power in a political system. It is the power over mens' lives and fortunes exercised by the national government that attracts ambitious men to the hazards of elective politics, and the prospect of sharing it which enlists and holds the gifted auxiliaries.

How big should senatorial staffs be? Perhaps much larger than they are, in the case of a few populous states. Perhaps not so large as they are, in the case of the smaller ones. But the indispensability of professional staff should not lead to the easy assumption that there is no limit to the number of staff persons who can be properly employed. Few senators are competent (and some not at all, in fact) to operate a small bureaucracy of their own, and that is not their job anyway. Furthermore, the cushion staff provides between the senator and those who want to see him can become impenetrable, thus destroying the sensitivity to group demands which makes him useful to the system. Finally, any increase in staff beyond what is imperative to keep the work moving probably would be used to court the constituency, making the burden of the non-incumbent opponent—who already must run against the Post Office and the Government Printing Office—quite unbearable.

Are Reforms Needed?

More than any other governmental institution in American life, Congress is under continuous criticism and demand for reform. The Senate shares in the general criticism of Congress and comes in for some directed especially at it. It is not easy to summarize what is said and what has been proposed. *Congressional Quarterly* devoted sixty-two double-columned pages to such a summary in the summer of 1963, with hardly a wasted word. It is possible, however, to suggest some categories of criticism and reform which are relevant to a discussion of power in the Senate.

One is concerned with leadership. Changes are included which would strengthen the hand of elected leaders and encourage them to work more closely with the national leadership, especially the President, and which would weaken the feudal baronies of the committee chairmen. The seniority system is a special target; if it cannot be destroyed, at least chairmen might be required to relinquish their authority at a certain age or the committee majority might be given some choice among the ranking members.

A second category which is more modest includes proposals to bring some coordination to the spending and taxing programs of Congress.

The Legislative Reorganization Act required a joint budget committee composed of the four revenue and appropriations committees of the two houses to meet and set a legislative budget by February 15th of each year, but the provision was unrealistic; it still is law but it has never worked. The two taxing committees have proved that coordination is possible just the same. Their senior members, working through a joint committee and a joint staff, have eliminated duplication and conflict between the committees. Once the House Appropriations Committee successfully produced and passed an omnibus appropriation bill and the redoubtable chairman of the committee, Clarence Cannon, never ceased to think it was an improvement over a dozen different bills. The critics argue that a government which spends $100 billion a year of its citizens' money should attempt, at least, to relate income and outgo and bring a measure of planning to the process.

A third category relates to the effectivness of individual members. Congressional business characteristically lags through the early months of a session and begins to pick up when other people are taking their families on vacation. The hardest work months come in the summer. Congress adjourns, if it ever does, when children are back in school. This result of poor scheduling is typical of a host of small irritations. Only two trips back home each session are paid for by the government; many members go nearly every week. In the case of a senator from the State of Washington, say, this is a major drain which may require steady "moonlighting" if he is not rich. Salaries are raised infrequently because members dread the catcalls from home. Allowances for office help and materials are wholly inadequate for senators from populous states. These are nagging nuisances which reduce a senator's efficiency.

A fourth category of reforms is aimed at the conduct of individual members which brings discredit on the whole body. This is not so much unlawful conduct—senators are punished for that like other citizens— but behavior which falls in a kind of twilight zone where the ethics of the individual must be the regulator. A senator belongs to a law firm, makes well-compensated speeches to interest-group audiences, owns securities in businesses dealing with the government. He makes trips abroad at government expense with no public audit of his accounts. He intercedes with government regulatory agencies on behalf of constituents. No one of these activities is necessarily wrong; indeed many are essential to the discharge of his duty. Most members carry them out with scrupulous regard for what is proper. But some members do not, and there's the rub.

The prognosis for reform varies sharply with the categories. The first two involve a re-structuring of power arrangements, a matter of taking power from those who have it and assigning it to those who do not. Several observations might be made. One is that there does not exist a model of a legislature as it ought to be. Political institutions grow in the soil of national experience. It is unlikely that one can be proven to be abstractly better than another, but even if it could that would not make it a practical alternative; people simply do not choose their institutions that way. Second, altering the power structure is no cure for inability to muster a majority, because more political force is needed to make the alteration than to win on any single issue. A successful reform is a demonstration of effective massing and use of political power, not a prelude to it. National party leadership may dominate Congress one day—when the concern of people with national problems overrides their parochial interests. Third, there may be unanticipated consequences to any change. Reducing the number of committees and clarifying their jurisdictions was regarded generally as one of the unqualified successes of the Legislative Reorganization Act. But the party leader no longer has his choice of several committees for referral of a particular bill; if a chairman is hostile, the leader must try the dubious business of bypassing the committee. Again, when the tyranny of the Speaker was overcome in the session of 1910 and 1911, a strengthened Rules Committee was the chosen instrument. But who is hero, who the villains, in the 1960s? The successful joint operations of the taxing committees provide another illustration: they have resulted in effective domination of federal taxation by the conservative senior members. The liberal members of those committees are not eager to see power over both spending and taxing put in the hands of a single joint committee. They have learned that a coordinating device works for those who control it.

Measures designed to make the congressman's life easier and his work day more efficient ought to be matters better left to the members themselves. This would seem to be true also of standards of ethical conduct, but unfortunately it is not. It is all very well to say Congress should police its own members, but self-regulation is a shibboleth which practically is not within the competence of most groups. What group in American society really disciplines its own members? Doctors? Lawyers? Professors? The public may think so, but the members know better. Perhaps criminal groups do, but adequate documentation is not available. Outside controls are better, and Congress really has none. The electorate obviously should provide them, but just as obviously it does not.

The problem remains and it is a serious one. The effectiveness of a political institution turns in part on the respect in which it is held. Whatever subjects it to ridicule reduces its capacity for winning the unquestioning compliance which is at the heart of civil authority. The Senate should not cease to seek ways to curb excesses, of its committees or individual members, which tarnish the corporate dignity of the body.

Perhaps this has relevance for those two oft-denounced institutions of the Senate, the filibuster and the seniority system. There is weight to the argument that the filibuster has never killed a measure a determined majority really wanted and that the time consumed in its debate of a civil rights measure in 1964 was not disproportionate to that required by the Executive and the courts in their efforts to advance civil rights. Nevertheless epithets like "obscene spectacle" were applied to it without challenge, and it would have been hard to find a defense of the filibuster outside the South. What is almost universally regarded as wrong can be maintained by government only at great cost. Perhaps time will prove that a filibuster like that in 1964 was exactly what was needed to make a more effective limitation possible.

Some modification of the seniority rule seems under a like burden of public disapprobation. Most Americans are required by law or private usage to retire by age seventy at the latest; social security and many private pensions are available earlier than that. Common experience suggests to most people that this is about right. They have observed the diminution of powers which ordinarily occurs at that age. Perhaps congressmen are different; certainly exceptional individuals are. But who is to say who is exceptional? That is why a rule is required. At the minimum, a committee might be permitted to decide for itself in the case of its chairman.

These changes and many others will be suggested, and some will be made. No human institution is above criticism or beyond reform. Nevertheless the history of the republic and the prestige of the modern Senate attest to its basic vitality and to its deep-rooted representativeness, and by inference to the judicious use of power by the men who run it.

Richard E. Neustadt

5

Politicians and Bureaucrats

In the decade of the 1940s an extraordinary element was added to the government of the United States: an executive establishment, a body of officials, which for size, scale, and corporate survival was a new creation, unlike anything our governmental system knew before. This was the institutional deposit of a series of events: New Deal, World War, the Bomb, Cold War, Fair Deal, Korea. The events are irreversible, the deposit is permanent, and for a quarter-century our system has been struggling to assimilate it. This chapter deals with aspects of that struggle.

A few figures help to indicate what happened in the Forties and thereafter. By 1939, before the Nazis marched on Poland, federal civilian personnel, professional and clerical (excluding postal and industrial workers) numbered a half-million, which then appeared a staggering total. Since 1942 their number never has been less than twice that size, not even at the low point of retrenchment between V-J Day and the Korean War. Before the Second World War our military forces had an active officer corps of some 35,000. Since 1945 the number never has been less than 10 times that size, save briefly just before Korea when it fell to a mere 200,000. The change has been both lasting and profound.

CONGRESS AND THE NEW EXECUTIVE ESTABLISHMENT

According to the literary theory of the Constitution, Congress as the "legislative branch" makes policy and a President as head of the "executive branch" administers it. If this theory squared with constitutional practice, or even with the Constitution's plain prescription, our new

RICHARD E. NEUSTADT *is Professor of Government at Columbia University and has been an advisor on the staffs of Presidents Truman and Kennedy. Professor Neustadt is also Special Consultant to the Jackson Subcommittee of the Senate. He is the author of numerous topical and scholarly publications including* **Presidential Power.**

officialdom would be a corporate entity, collectively accountable to Congress through the President and otherwise subordinate to him. But theory is deficient (as it always has been), and bureaucratic structure is a very different thing, the product of a much more complicated context.

Congress, constitutionally, has at least as much to do with executive administration as does an incumbent of the White House. "The executive power" may be vested in his office, but four tangible, indispensable administrative powers rest with Congress: organization, authorization, financing, and investigation. Departments and agencies—the operating arms of the "executive branch"—are created by acts of Congress. They gain operational authority, programmatic jurisdiction, from laws passed by Congress. They gain funds to pay for personnel and programs from congressional appropriations. And their use of both authority and money is subject to "oversight," to inquiry in Congress.

Had Congress been a unit tightly organized and centrally directed, its employment of these powers might have brought us something comparable at the other end of Pennsylvania Avenue: a unified executive establishment. But actually, and naturally, what was produced "downtown" reflects congressional *dis*unity. As preceding chapters show, Congress is not one entity but many, mainly the committees and the subcommittees of each House. "Congress," as Clem Miller once wrote, "is a collection of committees that come together in a Chamber periodically to approve one another's actions." [1] In the administrative sphere, as elsewhere, congressional prerogatives adhere most of the time—and most concretely all the time—to these committees and are exercised by them, piecemeal, on the executive establishment downtown. Its character is shaped accordingly.

Our national bureaucracy expanded in a range of separate agencies, corresponding roughly to traditional departments, each dependent on particular congressional committees for its life-blood: laws and funds. These agencies owed little more to Congress as an entity than chairmen of committees owe, which is not much. And they owed almost nothing to each other. Operational authority ran to the heads of agencies, or to subordinates, not to a collectivity. Personnel systems were built up inside agencies, not among them. Even the general career system, "the" civil service—to say nothing of uniformed or diplomatic services—is "general" in name only. For most intents and purposes it functions as a set of departmental services. Most careerists everywhere live out their lives inside a single agency; their loyalties and perspectives are centered there.

Both organizationally and in terms of personnel the new bureaucracy is a projection of congressional committee jurisdictions—or, more precisely, since 1946, of standing subcommittee jurisdictions. And most committees guard, with jealousy and pride, the separations among agen-

---

[1] Clem Miller, *Member of the House* (New York, 1962) p. 110.

cies downtown. Why, for example, is the Small Business Administration independent of the Department of Commerce? The answer lies in the committee structure of the House. Of course, committee jurisdictions have been influenced, in turn, by organizational developments downtown. Unification of the armed services was matched by unification on the Hill of the committees which had dealt with War and the Navy. Still, the pattern remains one in which particular committees deal with given agencies, and thereby keep the agencies distinct from one another.

Yet in their operations day by day, agencies are much more than "projections" of Congress. They also are competitors with congressmen. Their work defines and embodies public policy, enlisting clients and arousing opposition. They weigh and balance interests while they work. Their regulations have the force of law. Their decisions make news. Their jobs interest partisans. Their expertise helps to get legislation drafted (and committee reports written, speeches prepared, tactics devised). Also, their actions matter at the "grass roots." They carry government into the lives of voters; their "field" officials are in touch with voters. Thirty years ago, aside from postmen and tax collectors (for the well-to-do), the federal presence rested lightly on most citizens. Congressmen could claim to be—and often were—*the* local representatives of "Washington." That time is gone.

Defense contracts and installations underpin the economic growth of many regions. Federal grants-in-aid support the major undertakings of state governments. Federal funds are crucial in the redevelopment of cities. Federal subsidies, direct or indirect, support whole sectors of our industry and commerce—not least commercial agriculture—and become the hope of higher education, private as well as public. And day-to-day decision-making in such spheres as these—on the details of programming and execution which affect constituents concretely—this is done downtown, not on the Hill, and by agency officials, not by congressmen.

This goes hard with the elective politicians who are charged in theory to direct the government and who have won their places through the tests of nomination and election, tests officials do not take. Particularly for new members of the House—among the lowest of the low in Washington's real power-structure—it is frustrating to find that their effectiveness in such decision-making matches neither their own expectations nor the expectations of constituents at home. Oftener than not, the pressures of constituents run to the things that only agencies can do, and congressmen perforce become petitioners downtown, a role which often adds humiliation to frustration.

Frustration is compounded by the fact that men of Congress have not only their entitlement to a great voice in government, legitimated by their popular election, they also have wills of their own, views of their own, ideas of their own. Quite naturally these seem to them at least as worthy of attention in detailed administration as are those of any agency official. There is something to be said for this position; congressional ideas are often apt. But as a practical matter, the officials with immediate authority to act, and the necessity, are bound to make decisions day-by-day which reflect their conceptions and their reading of the issues—and which violate the values of some congressmen. This is understood in Congress but it grates. Repetitive experience of offering advice without material result is likelier to make advisers scornful than humble, especially if they are certain of their right to offer. So it seems to be for many congressmen.

Frustration with an overture of scorn has brought a strong reaction from both houses of Congress, a reaction which amounts to vigorous assertion of administrative powers held by Congress. For twenty years entrenchment of the new bureaucracy has given rise to efforts aimed at tightening congressional control over the details of administrative operations. These efforts have been cumulative for a generation, growing in intensity and ingenuity from year to year. New techniques, almost unknown in prior practice, have been devised to meet the new condition of a vast machine downtown. Congress has not been passive in the face of competition from officialdom. It actively attempts to control its competitors.

The reach for control has taken many forms, but there are three in particular. First is a quite traditional device, the patronage, with special reference nowadays to top appointive posts and to those sensitive subordinate positions—so-called Schedule C positions—which are in the civil service but not subject to its tenure rules. Congressional pressure on the President and on department heads is nothing new, but where postmasterships were once the aim, assistants to assistant secretaries and the like are now a natural target, with good reason. And where "senatorial courtesy" was once the means of putting teeth into congressional desires, hints of trouble in the legislative and appropriation processes now take their place alongside that time-honored technique.

A second such device is untraditional, a novelty, a postwar innovation, rapidly expanding in the last decade. This is the device of annual authorization for agencies themselves and for their programs. More than a quarter of the federal budget now is subject every year not only to appropriations but to prior legislation authorizing a continuation of existing agencies and programs. Among these are the Agency for International Development with foreign aid, the National Aeronautics and Space Administration with space exploration, and the new Office of Economic Opportunity with its poverty program.

A third device for control also is a postwar innovation: the "committee clearance." In recent years we find numerous statutory provisions— some enacted, some rejected, some enforced without enactment—which require that an agency report particular administrative actions in advance to a committee, or, stronger still, which require that an agency "come into agreement" with committee personnel before action is taken or, strongest of all, which require that an agency respect committee veto in a fixed time-period after the fact. These clearances, whatever their strength, have been asserted in the main by Agriculture, Armed Services, Interior, and Public Works Committees, and by the Joint Committee on Atomic Energy, which has a special statutory right of supervision over the Atomic Energy Commission. Taken together, these assertions seem to aim at giving legislative committees (and their members) a hold on bread-and-butter for home districts: site locations, purchase contracts, surplus sales. The impulse is entirely understandable.

Such devices for congressional control have often made an impact on the details of particular administrative operations, and also on the de-tailed distribution of administrative powers in Congress. Indeed the lat-ter impact may, in sum, be greater than the former. Annual authorization and committee clearance are, among other things, devices whereby legis-lative committees gain a share in the surveillance always open to ap-propriations committees. This frequently redounds to the advantage of the agencies concerned, and probably has often been encouraged by them. For legislative committees often champion "their" agencies against economizers in appropriations committees.

From the standpoint of good management as understood in private corporations or as preached by the apostles of administrative rationality, devices of this sort create a host of troubles for an agency official and for his executive superiors. Annual authorization causes turmoil every year, especially in personnel administration. "Agreement" and "veto" mean delay, uncertainty. (Moreover these requirements are constitution-ally dubious.) And "reporting" is a nuisance at the very least. Yet in administrative practice it is far from clear that agency officials are net losers.

On balance, these assertions of control have compensations for official-dom. They sometimes produce good ideas and sensible improvements: congressmen are capable of being very helpful. They may produce a measure of political protection, which is never to be slighted by an agency official. Moreover, they permit an able operator to play his com-mittee "masters" off against each other. Control by two committees of each House can mean control by none, while serving at the same time to dilute direction from above, from the administration.

It is significant that the most heartfelt arguments against these new devices come from central, presidential agencies, especially the Bureau of the Budget. Congressional assertions of control are bound to compli-cate attempts at central management in presidential terms. It does not follow that they have made Congress an effective manager. "Congress" is not involved. Nor are most congressmen.

The competition agency officials offer congressmen is not dispelled by control through congressional committee. Net gainers from this sort of enterprise are likely to be limited in number and are never found exclusively on Capitol Hill. The gainers, ordinarily, are of two sorts: on the one hand, effective agency careerists; on the other hand, well-placed committee members, especially seniority leaders (or their staffs). Control devices can produce a merger, in effect, between particular committees and "their" agencies. Some segments of officialdom are held under the thumb of a strong chairman; others suffer close surveillance by committee staff. Conversely, some staffs are accustomed to take cues from key officials; some chairmen have been known to act as agents of "their" agencies. Either way, there may result a tight relationship between affected agencies and congressmen, restraining competition in the interest of stability for policy and personnel alike. If clients and constituents are brought into the combine to the satisfaction of all sides, so much the better. The outcome then is a monopoly, a true "subgovernment," to adapt Douglass Cater's term, as in the sphere of sugar. Cater writes:

> . . . consider the tight little subgovernment which rules the nation's sugar economy. Since the early 1930s, this agricultural commodity has been subjected to a cartel arrangement sponsored by the government. By specific prescription, the sugar market is divided into the last spoonful. . . .
> Political power within the sugar subgovernment is largely vested in the chairman of the House Agricultural Committee who works out the schedule of quotas. It is shared by a veteran civil servant, the Director of the Sugar Division in the U.S. Department of Agriculture, who provides the necessary "expert" advice for such a complex marketing arrangement. Further advice is provided by Washington representatives of the . . . producers.[2]

But congressmen in general gain no measurable benefit from mergers on these terms, no special hold of policy or personnel, no special claims with clientele. The benefits accrue to members of particular committees and their friends (both on and off the Hill). For all the rest, officialdom becomes more powerfully competitive than ever, buttressed by its links to "Congress" *in committee.*

Moreover, the executive establishment is only ripe for "merger" at the margins of its policy concerns. In central spheres of policy, committees rarely serve the needs of agencies sufficiently to nurture true subgovernments. Bureaucratic organizations may be molded in the image of committee jurisdictions. But agency operations are not. For the very causal factors which brought forth the new officialdom, the same events both foreign and domestic, mix and mingle operations among agencies. Neither in military spheres, nor in diplomacy, nor in domestic welfare, nor in economic management can one agency pursue its statutory mandates independently of aid or acquiescence from others, usually many others. Programmatic purposes and operating problems spill across di-

[2] Douglass Cater, *Power in Washington* (New York, 1964), pp. 17-18.

viding lines on organization charts, entangling jurisdictions in the process. This always was the case to a degree; it now is markedly more so.
Thirty years ago the Departments of State and Agriculture worked in
separate worlds. So did the Department of Justice and the Office of Education. Now even these cross wires rather often, while the operations of
the Departments of Defense and State are always intertwined, to say
nothing of the poverty program, which involves half the government.

Committee "domination" of an agency is constantly imperiled by these
jurisdictional entanglements. "Mergers" do not flourish in the midst of
mingled programs. Overlapping operations force entangled agencies to
deal with one another day by day, and to appeal over each other's heads
when bargaining breaks down. The need for bargaining arenas is en-
demic; so is the need for arbitrators. But in central spheres of policy,
the spheres of greatest overlap, congressional committees rarely offer
either adequate arenas or authoritative arbitrators. Committee jurisdictions usually are too confined for that. And bargaining *between* committees rarely meets the needs of daily work downtown. As a forum for
administrative bargaining, our legislative process has its uses in securing
and defending fixed positions, not in reaching or applying operational
accommodations suited to a job in hand.

Thus even for the privileged few, controls exerted through committee may break down just when and where their use becomes most interesting. For operators with a job to do will sidle out from under the committees and will deal with one another or appeal against each other in
executive arenas at the other end of Pennsylvania Avenue—the White
House end—where congressional seniors, however potent in their own
committee bailiwicks, have limited access and a (relatively) weak voice.

In general then, the politicians on the Hill reach for control of their
competitors downtown without securing a surcease from competition.
On the contrary, these efforts at control have rather helped than hindered
agency officials—and indeed have spurred them on—to play committees
off against each other. For most intents and purposes, much of the time,
detailed decision-making with direct impact on voters still eludes the
politicians, while their agency competitors still flourish as before. Who
controls whom is a nice question. Perhaps officials are as often the
manipulators of committees as congressional seniors are the managers of
agencies.

Congressmen continue to have reason for frustration. When they com-
pare their nominal administrative powers with the actualities of who-
does-what in Washington, the fact that their committees can assert control of relatively marginal affairs is little comfort. When they look down
the Avenue toward the White House and perceive the Presidency, with
its own officialdom, asserting the prerogatives of central management—
as Presidents have done for nearly thirty years—their comfort grows the
less. And when they add what they are bound to see, and so to feel, that

policy initiatives are centered in the White House too, the pain in their position grows severe. Constituents rub salt into the wound. So does a proper pride in the traditions of a parliamentary body.

When the elective politicians on the Hill voice their frustration they are likelier than not to pass over its source, competitive officialdom, in favor of a target more traditional and easier to watch: their constitutional competitor, that Man in the White House. Yet he, an elective politician in his own right, struggles with officialdom no less than they. He too is in a competition with their new competitor.

The President and the Executive Agencies

The Presidency's character shapes what there is of unity in the executive establishment. Every agency is headed by a presidential appointee. (Senate consenting). These appointees are not immune to the old charge of Charles G. Dawes that "members of the Cabinet are a President's natural enemies." But they and their immediate associates do have some things in common with each other and the President which their career subordinates do not: temporary tenure and a stake in his success. Our terminology acknowledges their semblance of community; we speak of them collectively as "the administration," something wider than "the White House," looser than "the Presidency," but different from "officialdom," an intermediate layer neither truly presidential nor wholly bureaucratic.

Within limits, these distinctions have reality behind them: presidential appointees are men-in-the-middle, owing loyalty at once to the man who put them there, to the laws they administer, and to the body of careerists, backed by clientele, whose purposes they both direct and serve. They also owe some loyalty to their own careers, which may make for dependence on each other. And being similarly placed they may have fellow-feeling for each other. All these are two-edged swords. In many circumstances these induce a "scatteration" rather than community-of-interest. But in so far as this exists, the Presidency lies back of it.

The Presidency is a binding force in other ways as well. In many spheres of action the executive establishment can scarcely move except as it invokes the President. One such sphere is a traditional "royal prerogative" where Presidents are heirs to English kings: command of the armed forces and the conduct of foreign relations. A second sphere is of more recent origin, a modern prerogative: the initiative in legislation, authority and funds alike. A third sphere, rooted in our politics, has been transformed by our technology: the appeal to the people, the defense of new departures. In each sphere presidential acts, or delegations, or approvals (as a matter of form at least) are vital for official action, legitimating it as nothing else can. Thus each sphere weaves a bond around all those concerned in action—the bond of common need.

The President's place in defense and diplomacy turns on his role as commander-in-chief, a role created by the Constitution, deepened by history, confirmed by modern statutes, unquestioned today. The essence is that no one else can make him use the nation's troops (or its nuclear weapons for that matter), and no one else can stop him. His place in foreign policy has other sources also, but they pale by comparison with this. The same thing can be said of his authority, long since acknowledged by the Supreme Court, to guard the "peace of the United States" *internally*. Again, the fact that *he* commands the troops is paramount. So, when the use or threat or possibility of force comes into play, officials of all sorts in every agency concerned will keep the President in mind because they must, and each will seek his sanction for the course of action each prefers. The past decade alone is marked by Dien Bien Phu, Suez, Quemoy, Berlin, Cuba, Congo, Lebanon, Laos, Viet-Nam, where troops were either sent or quite deliberately withheld—to say nothing of Little Rock, or Oxford, Mississippi. There is no need to labor the point.

The President's initiative in legislation is a rather different matter, more a product of convenience, of pragmatic adaptation, than a constitutional imperative. Presidents have always had a role in legislation: the veto power and the right to recommend stem from the Constitution. But the process of enlarging these foundations to support initiative across-the-board began only some forty years ago, with the Budget and Accounting Act of 1921. Congress then imposed upon the White House— having nowhere else to put it—the duty to propose an executive budget, a statement of financial need for every agency, in the President's judgment, not theirs. This was conceived by its sponsors as a way to cut expenditures. It also proved a way to make the White House matter more to agencies than it had done before. No other single innovation has so markedly enlarged the practical importance of the Presidency to the whole executive establishment; those sponsors got more than they bargained for. Nevertheless, once done the thing was irreversible. Congressional committees remained ultimately "in control": witness the successes of an Otto Passman, terror of the foreign aid program. But the Presidency held an intermediate control; oftener than not this proved conclusive for the agencies, always, at the least, a problem to them: the starting-line for Congress was the *President's* proposal. So it has remained.

In the years of FDR and Truman, the initial years of our contemporary "big government," White House initiative spread from the spherre of money to the sphere of substance.[3] Ultimately it encompassed the full range of measures coming before Congress. By 1939 the central clearance of all agency proposals and reports on pending measures—whether money bills or not—had been established in the Bureau of the Budget.

[3] For details on this development see my "Presidency and Legislation," *American Political Science Review* (September 1954 and December 1955).

By 1949 the legislative "program of the President" had come to be a fixed, defined, and comprehensive entity, laid down by annual messages and spelled out in a set of special messages in each session. Continuation of both practices through subsequent administrations has accorded to both the sanction of long usage, "ancient custom." There are not many civil servants left who can recall when things were different. Twenty years ago some agencies habitually evaded central clearance. This is rare today. Ten years ago the White House still stopped short of sending bill-drafts with its messages; these went instead from a department head to a committee chairman for introduction "by request"; the fiction was preserved that Presidents themselves did not send bills to Congress. By 1961, however, "John Kennedy" became the signature on draft bills sent with messages directly to the Speaker and the President of the Senate, very much as though the White House were Whitehall. While this has not been the invariable practice since, the fiction disappeared— and no one noticed.

The fact that "no one noticed" is suggestive of the character of this entire forty-year development. It has been among the quietest pragmatic innovations in our constitutional history. The reason for the quiet is that it has proved at every stage to have advantages for all concerned, not least for Congress. What Congress gains is a prestigeful "laundry-list," a starting order-of-priority to guide the work of each committee in both houses in every session. Since it comes from downtown, committee and house leaders—and all members—can respond to or react against it at *their* option. But coming from downtown it does for them what they, in their disunity, cannot do for themselves: it gives them an agenda to get on with, or depart from.

The President's initiative in legislation is accepted on the Hill because it serves a purpose there. And since it serves a purpose there it is respected by officialdom downtown. Inclusion of their own aims in "the program of the President" matters to most agencies—and to their clientele—for reasons both of prestige and of practical advantage. Exclusion is distasteful, at the least, sometimes disastrous. In consequence, both budgeting and program-making are among the binding forces fostered by the Presidency.

So in recent years is "legislative liaison," a matter not of setting the congressional agenda but of keeping up relations between Houses and with agencies in the pursuit of presidential programs on the Hill. The White House has become, long since, a place—almost the only place— where Senate and House party leaders meet with one another on the tactics and prospects of congressional action. The White House telephone has been for many years a major weapon in the hunt for votes, especially when it conveys the President's own voice. But more than this, since Eisenhower's time a special staff for legislative liaison has been established in the White House to monitor the progress of all presidential bills and to assist in rounding up the votes. This staff makes claims on congressmen, and they in turn assert their claims on operating programs in the agencies. The staff attempts to harness agency resources, and the agencies respond by claiming White House help for *their* congressional concerns. Agencies will often have the better of that bargain: a President's connections with the leadership will often serve their purposes more nearly than their help serves his. Because they stand to gain from White House liaison—and liaisoners—this is still another binding tie.

A President's preeminence as spokesman *for* the government and *to* the country is again a different matter, a compound of many things: Madison's Constitution, Washington's propriety, Jackson's politics, Lincoln's martyrdom, TR's energy, Wilson's earnestness, FDR's voice—all mingled with the human need to personalize "government," a need which grows the greater as the government enlarges and its work becomes arcane. In the past thirty years, first radio then television fed that need by offering the *President* at work and play for everyone to hear or see directly, through a form of personal encounter which by now becomes a settled expectation, a matter of course.

After FDR, all Presidents have felt impelled to go before the country, into people's homes (and bars), at every time of gravity in national affairs and at each major turn in governmental policy, to soothe, explain, defend, or urge, as circumstances required. The public expectation is so clear—or seems so—that a Kennedy, who had no native taste for "fireside chatting," nevertheless put himself through these encounters gamely, while elaborating televised press conferences as a congenial form (for him) or partial substitute. No doubt his successors will feel bound to follow suit in their own fashion.

For agency officials who have new departures to espouse, or risky courses to pursue, or clients in deep trouble, it seems natural and proper, often indispensable, to make the President their television spokesman. Presidents may demur, and often do, but their presumed utility is none the less for that. Accordingly, officials never cease to urge. The net effect is still another force for unity originating in the White House—again a force of need.

The President and the "Institutionalized Presidency"

These spheres of presidential primacy give every part of the executive establishment the shared experience, the mutuality of interest (such as it may be), which stems from common claims upon the President. The claims have grown the stronger as officialdom has grown. The same events fed both. But if, while this was happening, the White House had proved institutionally incapable of dealing with these claims, then shared experience would have been sheer frustration, and those spheres would have become bone-yards for agency contention, dog-eat-dog. Actually, White

House capabilities have kept pace just enough to counter separations of that aggravated sort.

It is the "Institutionalized Presidency," another constitutional innovation of our time, which gives concreteness to the elements of unity in our "Executive." The Presidency began to change from man to institution while our bureaucratic apparatus still was relatively small and still in flux, during the New Deal years. The change was guided by a President whose grasp of office and whose continuity in office were extraordinary: FDR. Both timing and guidance appear providential in the light of what came after: stabilized, entrenched officialdom. The Brownlow Report of 1937 and its sequel "The Executive Office of the President" established not alone an organization, but a doctrine: the rightness of a "President's Department," the need for staff resources of his own. These were established in the nick of time. The organization changes, but the doctrine remains. Otherwise, the Presidency as we know it scarcely could have weathered the past twenty years. By now it would have been a hollow shell.

Yet having said this much, it remains to be said that the institutionalized Presidency has not proved an unmixed blessing for the President. In its evolution since the second Roosevelt's years, this institution vividly suggests a basic conflict, probably irreconcilable, between bureaucratic claims upon the White House and a President's own claims upon officialdom. Agencies need decisions, delegations, and support, along with bargaining arenas and a court of last resort, so organized as to assure that their advice is always heard and often taken. A President needs timely information, early warning, close surveillance, organized to yield him the controlling judgment, with his options open, his intent enforced. In practice these two sets of needs have proved quite incompatible; presidential organizations rarely serve one well without disservice to the other.

The National Security Council is a case in point. This Cabinet committee got its statutory start in 1947, as a product of reaction against FDR's secretiveness and "sloppiness" and "meddling" with the conduct of the war and its diplomacy. Yet barring some extraordinary lapses—the German zonal agreements above all—he had managed by his methods to maintain a high degree of personal control during the war, which is what *he* was after. That heightened the reaction. Its ultimate results were seen in Eisenhower's NSC, which came to have a formalized and "paperized" procedure, buttressed by an elaborate interagency substructure. This produced a counter-reaction. In 1961 Kennedy abolished both procedure and substructure to escape bureaucratization of his business. He replaced them, in effect, with a handful of personal aides enjoined to do no business but his own. In the main they gave him what he wanted, and the Cuban missile crisis served to vindicate his whole approach, at least in White House eyes. But outside White House precincts in the great departments, especially at levels twice removed from Cabinet rank, memories of those Eisenhower regularities—and of the access they provided—grow fonder every year. We may yet come full circle to react against Rooseveltian appearances in Kennedy-type performance.[4]

What this instance suggests has pertinence beyond the realm of staffing: not only is officialdom competitive with Congress; it also is in competition with the President. Granted that officials need his sanction, he needs their resources; the dependence being mutual is no bar to competition.

Agency officials, seized by a given problem, rarely seem unequal to the task of making judgments for the government. Nor do they seem inclined to seek a presidential judgment, their's aside, for any other reason than because they cannot help it. The White House would be treated to a novelty if bureaucrats began to ask the President's opinion out of nothing but respect for his good sense. Most careerists see authority as hierarchical —such is the world they live in—and consider that the President is nominally at the top. Because he is on top they can accept his *right* to judge, at least when he asserts it with a show of real authority or when they find it a useful thing to assert against their colleagues. But this is not because they think his judgment better than their own. That thought seems a stranger in officialdom. The usual official view of Presidents is rather like the academic view of businessmen: respect for power, a degree of resignation, a tinge of contempt. Given any chance to work the government without the President, officials will proceed to do so in good conscience, except as they may want his voice or acquiescence for their purposes.

If this does not seem quite the disciplined official style respectful of authority *à la* Max Weber, ours is not a European civil service. In certain other well-established governments, relationships are rigged to minimize, as far as possible, the personal and institutional insecurities of everyone in public life. This seems to be the situation in Great Britain, for example. Not so with us. With us it is almost the opposite: we maximize the insecurities of men and agencies alike. Careerists jostle in-and-outers (from the law firms, business, academic life) for the positions of effective influence; their agencies contend with the committees on the Hill, the Budget Bureau, other agencies for the prerequisites of institutional survival, *year by year*. Pursuit of programs authorized in law can be a constant struggle to maintain and hold support of influential clients, or the press. And seeking new authority to innovate a program can be very much like coalition warfare. Accordingly, most agencies have need for men of passion and conviction—or at least enormous powers of resistance —near the top. American officialdom may generate no more of these than

---

[4] For a statement of the issues see my testimony of March 25, 1963 to the Jackson Subcommittee, U.S. Senate Committee on Government Operations, Subcommittee on National Security Staffing and Operations, *Hearings*, Part 1, Eighty-eighth Congress, First Session (1963).

other systems do, but it rewards them well: they rise toward the top. And there they tend to set the tone of bureaucratic views about all comers from "outside," not least the President.

Yet any modern President will see things very differently. It is routine for White House aides to seethe with irritation at the unresponsiveness of "them," the almost-enemy, officialdom. And aides are but more royalist than the King. Their principals tend to become resigned, but not less irritated. For a President combines in his own person a unique perspective with unique responsibility. Naturally he will consider that the one is relevant to the other, that his own outlook has bearing on the issues which invoke his own official obligations. Moreover, he is not himself an "office" but a human being, eager to make marks upon events, conscious of *his* place in the republic's history, and mindful—now that nuclear weapons are held in Moscow too—of a shared capability to terminate that history. Besides, the human being sees himself in office as the outcome of his own career, topped off by national nomination and election. Ordinarily this is the hardest course to run in our political system. He has run it; in his first term he faces it again; in his second term he faces it at one remove, for a successor (he will hope) of his own choosing. So at least have our Presidents seen things up to now.

To an observer from outside, this seems a reasonable vision of the President's own place. Indeed, our governmental system sanctions it, what we have called "democracy" requires it, the system is legitimated by it, and our history confirms its practical utility—which is with us no small consideration. Too many of our Presidents have done too well in exercising judgment for observers to discount their claims upon the role.

They have done well in part because they often have contributed themselves what none of their executive associates could offer with an equal skill: a first-hand feel for feasibilities across the board of politics, from publics, interests, partisans, to Congress, and officialdom, and governments abroad—a feel for current prospects of support, indifference, toleration, opposition, with respect to lines of action wherever they lead.

This contribution is the province of elective politicians, those who bear the burdens, take the heat, and face the risks of sudden death by ballot box, especially when they share in administrative power and have learned the risks peculiar to that line of work as well. But in the whole executive establishment there are no such risk-takers, short of the White House. Aside from the Vice-President, whose role is bound to be ambiguous at best, the President stands quite alone. Officials cannot make his contribution for him. Few can help him very much to make it. For no one stands on a spot like his, with comparable duties, facing comparable risks. A Lincoln in the months before emancipation, a Franklin Roosevelt in the years after his "quarantine" address, a Kennedy in the weeks after Birmingham, or in the days of his climactic confrontation with Khrushchev —all these were men engaged in calculating feasibilities, and it is not of record that associates could have been counted on to come up with their answers for them. In this trade there is no reliable apprentice-system.

A President does have some fellow journeymen, of course, but they are far away, a long mile down the Avenue on Capitol Hill.

The Common Stakes of Elective Politicians

The separations between President and congressmen are partly constitutional, partly political, partly attitudinal, and in no small degree a matter of semantics. The Constitution's barriers look higher than they are. The barriers of politics may soon start to decline. But differences in attitude may still be on the rise, fed by the connotations of our words.

Constitutionally the President and Congress share each other's powers, from the veto, to appointments, to administrative "oversight," and so down the list. Practically this is a sharing between one man at the White House and a scattering of others who hold key positions in the two congressional "bodies"; they share powers with each other even as they share with him. Politically, these sharers are kept separate by their differing dependence upon different electorates. These differences are sharpest at the stage of nomination: Senators and congressmen will owe their seats to separate sets of nominators; chairmen owe their powers to seniority acquired by repeated nomination. The President, by contrast, owes his place and powers to a nominating contest of another order, as far removed from theirs, in timing and geography and personnel alike, as theirs are separated from each other. The fact that nominators everywhere would like to win elections has not served to produce like-minded party candidates—far from it. Terms of party competition and conditions of survival and electoral arithmetic have differed far too much. Realignment of congressional districts, reapportionment of legislatures, and Republican attempts to break the "solid South" *may* now combine to change this situation, to reduce those differences, to force more uniformity on nominators, and hence on candidates. If so, then there will be a narrowing of separations among senators and congressmen and Presidents—a narrowing, at least, of gaps induced by politics. But that time is not yet.

Even if it comes, there will remain the gaps induced by attitudes of mind, by habit, custom, way of life, and ways of doing work. In some respects our Constitution and our politics tell less about what separates the Presidency from Congress than our architecture does. For the White House and the Capitol as structures almost perfectly express these underlying differences of attitude: the former has an exterior which at first glance looks simpler than it is, and inside all seems orderly: rectangular rooms mostly, connected by straight corridors, as neat-appearing as an organization chart. The latter is almost rococo in externals, appearing more complex at first than on long knowledge, and within it seems all twists and turns: passages which lead in circles, little-known connections, sudden detours, hidden treasures, obscure sanctuaries, walls in curves.

The men who work inside these buildings literally work in different worlds. Their attitudes are shaped accordingly.

The Senate and the House, of course, are not identical workplaces. For most of its inhabitants the Senate is a pleasant place, possessed of quite enough prestige and power (or its semblance), and amenities of staff and space, and time to enjoy them (six years at a crack), so that it alone remains what much of government once was, a refuge for the spirit of political free-enterprise, unfettered either by undue responsibility or the restraints of size. The House, however, offers comparable enjoyments only to a few, the men of great seniority or great good luck. The rest either content themselves with marginal existences or scramble for political and personal identity amidst the ruck and ruckus of large numbers, rigid rules, demanding lobbyists, disdainful agencies, unheeding press, importunate constituents, and pitifully short tenure. No wonder that the House is seen by many of its members as a stepping stone, a place to be endured on the way up and out. It may well be the most frustrating place to work in Washington. It certainly ranks high among such places.

Even so, the contrasts between houses pale compared to those between the work of either and of men downtown. Tiber Creek is gone, but there remains a great dividing line across the Avenue.

This is the product not alone of work-ways but of substance, not merely who-works-how but who-does-what. So much of the decision-making critical for all of us is centered nowadays in the executive establishment that congressmen and senators feel cheated of a birthright. They are, for the most part, men of seriousness, intelligence, and patriotism, to say nothing of experience. They also are men of elections, voted into office by a portion of the citizens and sharing with the President the risk of death by ballot box. Yet others have a greater voice than they in numbers of decisions, day by day, which touch the lives of citizens. They may accept this, but they cannot like it.

For instance, the most critical of government decisions, the war-or-peace decisions, have been snatched away from Congress by technology, despite the plain words of the Constitution. No congressman disputes the *fact* and few have any eagerness to take upon themselves the heat of presidential choices. But many, perhaps most, dislike to draw the corollary, that they have no choice at all and not even a voice, except by presidential courtesy, in presidential prudence. When it comes to lesser instances, where courtesy and prudence are prerogatives of a mere appointee or even of a careerist, then their sense of deprivation will be stronger still, and for good reason.

Hurts like these are rendered the more painful by the press, which centers its attention on the President. Publicity is far too great a prize for politicians to make this a happy outcome for most members of Congress. Only elders can remember when the Hill was the best-covered part of town. Franklin Roosevelt's Presidency put an end to that. But even juniors are impelled by sheer professional concern to nurse their disadvantage as a grievance.

Such feelings are returned with interest from downtown. In executive eyes, Congress is at best a necessary nuisance and at worst a great conspiracy against efficient government. All Presidents will wish they could make Congress serve them as a rubber-stamp, converting their agendas into prompt enactments, and most Presidents will try to bring that miracle about, whenever and as best they can. Most presidential appointees will grow despairing about drains upon their time, skill, energy, and ingenuity —to say nothing of reputation—occasioned by the legislative (and investigative) process with its "endless" repetitions in committee hearings, correspondence, phone calls. Most careerists, even if their agencies show profit, will grow sick, or cynical, at seeing "rational" solutions twisted out of recognition by committee compromise. And most of them, reacting in anticipation, become do-it-yourself types, compromisers-in-advance, despite the risks of amateurish outcomes. (Amateur careerists, in turn, sicken the politicians; some, however, do acquire near-professional standing.) Underlying all of this is a persistent puzzle: why should "they" be so blind to imperatives of good administration? It is the obverse of a question constantly occurring on the Hill: what makes "them" so obtuse about the necessities of the legislative process and of political survival?

"They" and "them" are optical illusions, but these make the sense of separation all the sharper. Administrators may know well, from personal experience and frequent exploitation, how disjointed is the power-structure on the Hill. Yet most of them would say and feel with Kennedy:

> ". . . the Congress looks more powerful sitting here than it did when I was there in Congress. But that is because when you are in Congress you are one of a hundred in the Senate or 435 in the House, so that power is so divided. But from here I look at a Congress, and I look at the collective power of the Congress, particularly the bloc action, and it is a substantial power." [5]

And most members of Congress may be quite aware that any one of them, with influence enough, can penetrate or even dominate the programs of some agency or other. Yet looking down the Avenue at the array of agencies—the rows of office buildings, the outpouring of officials, the interminable corridors, the bustle of department heads departing for the White House from their grandiose office-suites—these legislators see an entity of monolithic aspect, the executive Branch, apparently commanded by one man, the President: that other and more grandly placed elective politician whose hold upon the agencies seems mighty in comparison with theirs.

These visual impressions are confirmed by our semantics, reinforced by words in common use: *the* Congress, *the* Executive, "legislation," "admin-

[5] Television and radio interview, December 17, 1962, *Public Papers of the President: John F. Kennedy* (1962), p. 893.

istration." A quarter-century ago the coming of the "Institutionalized Presidency" was justified by experts outside government (and by officials near the White House) as essential to the role of "Chief Administrator," a presidential role read into constitutional provisions by analogy with private corporations. The analogy has stuck, and with it the suspicion that all efforts to enlarge a President's resources threaten the prerogatives of *Congress,* striking at committee rights to authorize, finance, investigate, and "oversee." Presidents in fact are merely fighting for their rights as independent operators, threatened with engulfment by official claims upon them. This is a fight which should enlist the sympathy of fellow-politicians on the Hill. But phrases twist the fact into a contest between President and Congress.

This is symptomatic of a great confusion about who is fighting whom and who is winning in our government. Bureaucracy has brought a new contestant into play: the great prospective struggle is between entrenched officialdom and politicians everywhere, White House and Hill alike. Officialdom already is competitive with both. Its strength is sapped by institutional disunity, the gift of Congress. Temporarily, at least, this shields the politicians from the consequences of their own disunity. But it seems far from certain that the bureaucrats will not learn how to close their ranks in better order, faster, than their showing up to now. What then would happen to the politicians separated as they are by all the factors just described?

We now are ending our first generation of experience with an executive establishment in modern dress. Even now, experienced officials tend to work across their lines of jurisdiction with an ease and understanding little known some twenty years ago. Relations between Pentagon and the Department of State exemplify the trend. Their disputation still remains incessant, as before, but temperature and tempo are decidedly below the levels of, say, 1949. If this trend should continue and accelerate, encompassing domestic agencies as well, a President and congressmen might confront competition too intense for them to meet in isolation from each other. If so, they either must array their own ranks or our government will risk losing what they uniquely bring to public policy: the feel for feasibility of men who take the heat from an electorate. It is a risk not only to their power but also to our polity.

Fortunately for the politicians, there is little likelihood that bureaucrats will soon be tightly united. The separations among agencies, induced by separations on the Hill, run far too deep. The risk lies not in an official unity but simply and more subtly in a heightened sense of official community. And nowadays not only are there signs of fellow-feeling among "second-generation" bureaucrats, there also are great efforts being made by private sources to induce communiy spirit through enhanced professionalization. Our schools, foundations, and study groups make no such efforts for our politicians.

The moral is plain. To paraphrase Karl Marx: Politicians at the two ends of the Avenue unite! You have nothing to lose but your pieces of power—and even now these may be slipping out of reach. To call for unity in form would be absurd. To call for sheer subservience of Congress to the President, or *vice versa,* would be futile. But to urge some change of attitudes at both ends of the Avenue, to urge awareness of joint stakes and common risks is not perhaps to ask too much of our established system. This might induce a unity sufficient for the purpose. Moreover, politicians might enjoy it when they thought about it. Opportunities to think, however, will come hard unless outside observers—academic and other—set about repairing our semantics. We might begin now.

Harvey C. Mansfield

6

The Congress
and Economic Policy

Any observer can assert, and none can prove, that the country is lucky the Congress does what it does; or to the contrary, that we would be better off if it stayed home, or if some other body, somehow differently organized, replaced it. The present essay has a more modest, expository aim: to illuminate the ways in which the Congress and its component parts go about their varied activities in the field of economic policy, and to account for some of the whats and hows and whys of their actions. A general theme is the continuing tension between the needs and forces calling for an over-all view of national policy—usually a distasteful discipline for congressmen—and the more congenial course of responding to special claims. Not all special interests, luckily for everyone, are inconsistent with a general interest, however defined. But the notion will not down, vague as it is, that there is a general interest to be advanced; and its identification and fostering require analysis and policies addressed to the aggregate performance of the national economy. This the institutions of Congress are ill-adapted to supply. For the Congress is itself a part of a larger political system, and so only partly a master of its own destiny. It is seldom the source of major initiatives or innovations; its characteristic outputs are the products of interaction with outside forces and display

HARVEY C. MANSFIELD, *Professor and former Chairman of the Department of Political Science at Ohio State University, has been on numerous occasions a consultant to various government commissions and committees. In 1953 he was a member of the faculty of the National War College. Since 1956 he has been Managing Editor of* The American Political Science Review. *Professor Mansfield is the author of numerous books and professional articles, including two in earlier American Assembly publications.*

patterns characteristic of the ways those forces combine and collide in the congressional setting.

CONGRESSIONAL POWER IN THE PREMISES

In the field of domestic economic policy, Congress deals from constitutional strength. It can have a large say if it wants one—if it is moved and organized, that is, to exert its full potential. Its enumerated and implied powers (Article I, section 8) are sweeping if not plenary: to tax, borrow and spend; to regulate interstate and foreign commerce, currency and credit (and the lack thereof, bankruptcy); to grant patents and copyrights and establish post roads; and to order the organization and procedures of the judicial and administrative establishments. These powers have been broadly construed in their exercise and in the realm of economic policy they are not seriously hemmed in by the constitutional powers lodged with the President or with the courts.

The President, to be sure, is vested with the power to make appointments to the offices that Congress creates or authorizes. This is a source of influence over policy; and he has other means of influence. But his overriding constitutional power as Commander-in-Chief, which bulwarks his position in foreign and military affairs and also enables him ultimately to intervene decisively when domestic federal authority is forcibly defied —as in the school segregation cases—is of little avail in economic controversies in peacetime. This much, at least, is the teaching of President Truman's experience when he ordered the seizure of the steel mills in 1952. The President's "executive power" and his responsibility to "take care that the laws be faithfully executed" have not, for present purposes, proved to be significant sources of independent power either.

The federal courts have done much to vindicate congressional power in economic affairs and little to curb it except by insistence on procedural requirements—at least since 1937, when the Wagner Act and the Social Security Act were sustained. With constitutional controversies transferred in the main to the civil liberties field since then, the function of the courts in economic disputes has been confined chiefly to statutory construction. Where the statute involved is broad and vague, like the Sherman Act, this still leaves a good deal of scope for judicial discretion. But when the Congress does not like the result—for instance in the *Southeastern Underwriters* case in which the Supreme Court held insurance to be interstate commerce subject to the Antitrust law—it has been possible to undo the effects of the decision by changing the law, as was done in that case. During the five sessions, from 1957 to 1961, at least eight acts or amendments were passed to reverse the results of some thirteen Supreme Court decisions. Most of these were tax cases; the best known of them cushioned the duPont divestiture of General Motors stock, but two dealt with transportation rates and one, the Landrum-Griffin Act, with labor relations.

Occasionally the Congress pushes an economic regulation to the limit of its power, approaching absurdity. There is the law, for example (U.S. Code, Title 21, section 347c), which says that every restaurant in the United States must, if it serves oleomargarine to its patrons, serve it in triangular pats—lest they mistake it for the high-priced spread. But ordinarily the politics of legislative processes keep the final exertions of congressional power well within the borders of constitutionality.

As nearly any enactment has some economic aspect, there is no precise answer to the question, what proportion of congressional time and attention is devoted to those regulations of "interfering interests," deriving from the unequal distribution of property, that Madison saw as the "principal task of modern legislation." Some crude notion of the distribution of activity by subject can be gained from Table I, which classifies—but does not weigh—the bills acted on in the 1962 session. Lumping together the items tabulated there under the headings of Agriculture, Appropriations, Welfare, Housing, Public Works and Resources, and Taxes and Economic Policy, it appears that 384, or 44 per cent, of the 872 public bills that reached at least the stage of a committee report, and 272, or 45 per cent, of the 599 bills that ultimately passed in that session, can be counted in the realm of economic affairs primarily. This only sets the stage for the question, what kinds of policies and interests are at stake in these bills? For Madison the answer to this question was plain: interests are particular, and interfering interests must be moderated by public authority, lest the society fly apart. Today this answer is only a partial truth, because its premise—that economic activity is private—is no longer wholly descriptive. Today the government is a direct and large-scale participant.

MACRO- AND MICRO-ECONOMIC POLICIES

Economic thinking about the economy, and in its train political thinking about what the government could and should be doing, have undergone a revolutionary transformation since the impact of John Maynard Keynes became felt in this country during the 1930s. Prior to the depression, economists—following in the steps of Alfred Marshall and the classics—concentrated on price analysis, since every transaction has a price, and setting that price seemed to be the key decision for the participants. On the limited range of economic questions the government could decide, economists lined up for or against free trade or protection, the gold standard, and free competition as against the regulation of monopolies or public ownership of utilities. A stray Veblen scoffed at them from the sidelines without deflecting their concerns. After World War I, specialties in agricultural and labor economics began to develop, and Wesley Mitchell launched his pioneering studies of business cycles. Orthodox public finance economists preached the virtues of an annually balanced budget, on the tacit assumption that the government should be a neutral factor

Table I

DISTRIBUTION OF BILLS ACTED ON (COMMITTEE REPORT OR BEYOND),
BY SUBJECT CATEGORY, EIGHTY-SEVENTH CONGRESS, SECOND SESSION (1962)

Subject of bill	Completed	Unfinished
Agriculture	41	9
Appropriations	19	3
Education and welfare		
Education	3	12
Health	3	2
Welfare	17	8
Housing	3	0
Veterans	26	12
Foreign policy		
International affairs	22	7
Immigration	4	1
General government		
Congress	18	5
Constitution and civil liberties	1	5
Government operations	17	6
Post Office and civil service	14	17
District of Columbia	52	30
Indians, territories	37	15
Judiciary	34	17
Commemorative	38	20
National security		
Armed services and defense	48	10
Atomic energy and space	10	2
Public works and resources		
Lands	29	12
Resources and public works	51	28
Taxes and economic policy		
Economic policy and regulations	31	6
Commerce	21	9
Labor	4	5
Transportation	27	16
Taxes	14	11
Tariffs	15	5
Totals	*599*	*273*

Source: Congressional Quarterly Almanac 1962 (Washington, D.C., 1962), pp. 770-795.
The tabulation includes one Senate Resolution and eleven House Resolutions deemed
substantively significant by the *Congressional Quarterly* compilers; these are neither
"laws" nor "bills."

in the economy, taking out as much as it put in—and the less of either, the
better. Texts on money and banking taught the need for a system of
currency and credit firmly anchored to hard money reserves and automatically regulated in volume by the level of business demands.

Keynes' doctrine, that the national government should use its fiscal and credit powers to play a deliberately compensatory role in the economy —buoying it with deficit spending in times of slack demand and running a budget surplus in inflationary periods—found a cordial reception (where and when it did) partly, no doubt, because it provided a theoretical rationale for what the government was, after a fashion, already doing—and being criticized for doing. But the impact was more than political. It directed attention away from preoccupation with the behavior of prices to focus instead on aggregate income and savings in relation to demand for consumption and investment, and on output, actual and potential. Looking at aggregates meant taking a national view of the behavior of the economy as a whole.

In the state of the art at the time this was not easy to do. For some sectors of the economy statistical series were highly developed; for others they were inadequate or nonexistent; nowhere were the parts put together regularly and comprehensively. In the late 1930s Simon Kuznets and some co-workers set about developing a statistical basis for expressing the then novel concept of the Gross National Product. This might have occupied a quiet academic generation, but for the advent of World War II. The imperative need of the War Production Board to know the GNP and its components, as a prerequisite to refashioning that product to serve the purposes of war mobilization, put the full resources of government into the statistical task. Starting in 1940 the Budget Bureau circulated confidentially to the upper ranks of officialdom in Washington, particularly among those connected with the war agencies, a monthly statistical compilation under the title of *Defense Progress* (August 1940-December 1941) and *War Progress* (January 1942-October 1945). This was the precursor of *Economic Indicators,* prepared by the Council of Economic Advisers since 1947 and published monthly by the Joint Economic Committee. All the main federal agencies concerned with financial and economic affairs—Treasury, Federal Reserve, Budget, Commerce, Labor, SEC, and so on—contribute their figures to this compilation. Since the war, analysis of the national income and of the GNP has been the starting point for official as well as private professional studies of economic policy.

Statistics, of course, are the instruments, not the authors of policy. Two complementary developments in the institutions and financial practices of the government have had more weight in bringing about the transformation in economic thinking. On the institutional side the passage of the Budget and Accounting Act in 1921, which created the Budget Bureau, was the first long step—since the days of Hamilton and Gallatin—toward focussing on the President a government-wide responsibility for a government-wide view of fiscal policy. In practice, the Bureau's effectiveness was enhanced after 1935 by the renovation in Treasury accounting procedures and organization—introduced in order to keep current and accurate track of federal relief expenditures—that for the first time provided reliable monthly data on governmental cash outlays. The Bureau's position was strengthened further in 1939 when it was moved from the Treasury to become the key unit in the newly formed Executive Office of the President, following the passage of the Reorganization Act of that year. The Bureau introduced another tool of over-all analysis after the war when it began reporting the consolidated cash budget—reflecting social security and other trust fund receipts and payments—alongside the traditional administrative budget, which was limited to new obligational authority. The Bureau's jurisdiction, however, was still confined to fiscal policy and, as a practical matter, chiefly to appropriation requests.

The passage of the Employment Act of 1946, therefore, marked a second long institutional step toward the development of national economic programs. For although it endowed the government with no new powers beyond the vehicle of an annual economic message and report, it announced a set of goals for the economy as a whole—not just the government sector—and committed the government to a new degree of political responsibility for pursuing them. To provide organs of planning and deliberation it created the Council of Economic Advisers in the Executive Office and a congressional Joint Committee on the Economic Report (later renamed the Joint Economic Committee).

Two other institutional developments fit in with the trend. By the Reciprocal Trade Agreements Act of 1934 the Congress gave over its nineteenth century practice of piecemeal enactment of individual tariff rates, in favor of a process of collective bargaining with other nations. The Trade Expansion Act of 1962 reaffirmed and extended this approach. Finally, in the 1960s and without any new statute, the Federal Reserve and the Treasury entered a new era of close and informal cooperation—in sharp contrast to the tensions that had often marked their previous relations—in the exercise of their powers over money and credit; this because of their converging concern over the balance of payments deficit.

Underlying these institutional changes and providing the basic drive toward an over-all perspective were a series of developments in federal finances too familiar to need elaboration: the income tax, which established a revenue base sufficient to sustain federal borrowing on an unprecedented scale without bringing the government's credit into question; Supreme Court decisions that quieted any doubts about the constitutionality of federal spending; the power of the Federal Reserve to create money (in the form of bank reserves) and so to sustain a market for government securities in virtually unlimited volume; the technological innovations in machine checkwriting on IBM punch-cards that made it physically and administratively possible to issue checks by the millions, quickly; and demands for federal expenditures on a scale that in 1944-45 approached 45 per cent of the annual GNP. Governmental instruments of such capabilities called for conscious management and direction with an eye to their aggregate impact. They were too potent to be left to the chance play of private influences.

The deliberate marshalling of economic processes in wartime was one thing; to talk of economic planning after the cessation of hostilities, unless in the most general terms, was something else again, as the debate on the Employment Act showed. An appreciation of Keynesian teachings spread slowly from professional to political quarters During the Truman and Eisenhower Administrations the virtue of balancing the budget—i.e., ignoring the social security fund surplus and neutralizing the aggregate effects of government budget spending—and of reducing the public debt, an anti-inflationary move, were still official doctrine. But practical responses to practical conditions belied the doctrine on decisive occasions. In 1948, with price inflation waning and the Treasury running a heavy surplus, a Republican Congress preferred tax reduction to debt reduction in an election year—to the extent of overriding a Democratic President's veto. In the 1958-59 recession a Republican administration, with the acquiescence of a Democratic Congress, ran a deficit of unprecedented peacetime proportions (over $12 billion) by sustaining expenditures while revenues fell off sharply. Finally, in the early 1960s, bipartisan political judgments and Keynesian doctrine converged overtly. At a time when the balance-of-payments deficit dictated a rise in short-term interest rates, while a lagging growth rate forbade higher long-term rates and an unemployment rate near 6 per cent called for an expansion of aggregate demand, the administration in 1963 proposed a major tax reduction even though a budgetary deficit was already in prospect. The Revenue Act of 1964 was the result, after more than a year of congressional debate. Reviewing the experience, Secretary of the Treasury Douglas Dillon said:

> . . . the past three and one-half years constitute a significant water shed in the development of American economic policy. For they have borne witness to the emergence, first of all, of a new national determination to use fiscal policy as a dynamic and affirmative agent in fostering economic growth. Those years have also demonstrated, not in theory, but in actual practice, how our different instruments of economic policy—expenditure, tax, debt management and monetary policies—can be tuned in concert toward achieving different, even disparate, economic goals. In short, those years have encompassed perhaps our most significant advance in decades in the task of forging flexible economic policy techniques capable of meeting the needs of our rapidly changing economic scene.[1]

The Secretary nevertheless included one caveat in his otherwise optimistic survey:

> There remain, in my opinion, great obstacles to the use of tax policy for purely counter-cyclical purposes. The chief of these obstacles is the fact that, within our constitutional system, a long lag typically intervenes between a

[1] Speech at the Harvard Business School, June 6, 1964.

request for a change in tax rates and legislative approval. Unless and until some method is worked out—acceptable to the Congress and consistent with its prerogatives—whereby tax rates can be varied without undue delay, the purely counter-cyclical function of tax policy will remain outside our arsenal of economic tools.[2]

In the upshot it seems fair to conclude that the transformation in economic thinking over the past quarter-century has been translated into official policy to a considerable degree. At least until the Goldwater campaign in 1964 reopened the issue in a frontal assault, the transformation appeared to have reached the point where the great, and greatly expanded objects of national policy—the political commitments of the Employment Act, or, in economists' terms, an adequate and sustainable growth rate, near-full employment, price stability, a tolerable balance of international payments, and a satisfactory minimum standard of living (health, education, and welfare) for the underprivileged—were widely accepted in general terms as the legitimate agenda of the federal government. Where these can be forwarded under existing statutes, as by Federal Reserve operations in the money market, little objection is heard. But where they depend on new and timely legislation that runs counter to still-cherished doctrines of an earlier generation, a major political battle in Congress ensues. All the resources of the administration become engaged in such a battle and these may not suffice to carry the day, the distribution of power and prejudice in Congress being what it is. So, although the tax reduction was ultimately enacted, it was beyond the reach of the Kennedy Administration in 1963. And a considerable list of other measures on the agenda, long agitated, are indefinitely stalled: tax reforms to close loopholes; the removal of the debt ceiling; the repeal of the domestic gold reserve requirement so that all gold stocks can be used to support the international position of the dollar; medicare; block grants-in-aid to the states; and variable tax rates and contingent public works appropriations linked to counter-cyclical indicators, among others.

Measures such as these affect the long-run balance of power between the Executive and Congress, by making permanent delegations of discretionary authority to act; or else they effect a significant redistribution of income, taking from some in order to pay others, in the name of social justice. Either way, such measures array the administration against major pressure groups as well as instinctive congressional reluctance. Victories in any one year can usually be counted on the fingers of one hand.

Meanwhile, and alongside these major grapplings, the Congress continues to be preoccupied with the perennial and far more numerous contests for advantage among interfering interests that make up the ordinary stuff of politics: who gets what. Several categories under this general heading can usefully be distinguished, marking different types of advan-

[2] *Ibid.*

tages to be had and perhaps suggesting characteristic patterns of conflict and accommodation.

One such category is the disposal of the public domain—literally and figuratively the parcelling out of the tangible and intangible resources and benefits that are inherently within the power of the government to bestow on claimants thought to be deserving. Historically, titles and rights to public lands and protective tariffs exemplify this category; it includes also a good many kinds of appropriations, for public works and grants-in-aid, for instance. Latterly, access to the virtually unlimited store of government credit (or credit guarantees or insurance) and commodity price supports have become favorite forms: more federal money is invested in the stockpiles of strategic materials than in holdings of farm surpluses. Whatever their intrinsic merits, all these function also as types of patronage. Various general principles may be mustered against them, but seldom any major organized interests outside of the government; for it is a thankless task to argue that the government should keep what it can give away if someone really wants it. So congressional committees listen to the claimants and preside over the process of disposal, in ways that tend, like patronage generally, to fortify the *status quo* in the political system. If the supply is ample the process is painless. If giving to one means denying another, a test of access and power ensues. If the claimants are individually weak, a logrolling omnibus bill is the typical result.

A second category consists of regulations that the Congress may impose, directly or by delegation to administrative agencies. Here the benefits conferred come not from some government store but from restraints laid upon those who are regulated. In the long run it may well turn out that the regulations benefit the regulated too, as by increasing the confidence of their customers or by eliminating some forms of competition; but they don't usually see it that way at first. So a regulatory proposal—for example, the Bank Holding Company Act of 1956, or the Motor Vehicle Act of 1935 that brought the trucking industry under ICC control—typically arrays well-organized interests (and stimulates their formation or strengthening) pro and con, in a parallelogram of forces operating in a congressional matrix. A common variant of this category occurs when it is proposed to upset the *status quo* by repealing or relaxing an existing regulation around which settled expectations have grown up—for example, by permitting commercial banks to open branches outside their home-office territories, or by lifting FPC controls over the field prices of natural gas. Parties with a stake in the continuance of the regulation react as though they were themselves about to be regulated.

A third category is made up of exemptions and dispensations, partial or complete, from burdens otherwise generally applied. Any broad regulation brings applications for exceptions or special treatment, on grounds of hardship or inequity; much of the language in the revenue code is devoted to spelling out congressional responses to such applications. In considering a plea of this sort a congressional committee confronts a highly concentrated and sharply focussed pressure from a limited source, working often through a single, friendly, well-placed congressman. The Treasury or another government agency may take a stand in opposition, on behalf of a more general interest, but countervailing pressures from other organized interests are ordinarily not in evidence unless the exemption sought will confer a marked competitive advantage. If that is the case, the easiest course is to broaden the exemption proposed, to cover the competitors as well. On the other hand, if the exemption has no merit but the influence of the member sponsoring it, the committee may write the exemption so narrowly that only a single person or firm will qualify under its terms. A classic instance of this was the "Louis B. Mayer amendment" of 1951, estimated to have saved the movie executive $2 million in taxes on the settlement of his contract with MGM after his retirement. A more recent case, involving a Wisconsin mortgage guaranty company, gained some temporary notoriety from its connection with the Senate's Bobby Baker investigation; it was settled when the prospect of a special amendment led the Treasury to reverse its initially adverse position. A knowledgeable reporter observed:

> No one denies that there are a dozen or so cases in an average year in which one-company legislation is passed by Congress because of the intense interest of a single member who is accommodated by his fellow legislators. These cases are not secret, however. It is just that no one other than those concerned generally pays any attention.[3]

The same forces and methods that secure legislative dispensations commonly operate also, by logrolling, to defeat most efforts to close tax loopholes—a lesson that caused President Kennedy at an early stage to abandon his attempt to combine tax reform with tax reduction in 1963. The one major loophole-closing salvaged in the 1964 tax act, the repeal of the 4 per cent dividend credit, is reported to have cost the administration a federal judgeship in Kentucky.[4] And this repeal illustrates a further lesson: in the absence of a consensus on where the burdens of taxation—or of any economic regulation, for that matter—should be laid, one man's justice is another man's loophole. The dividend credit was advocated by the Eisenhower Administration as a measure of equity; it was repealed by the Kennedy Administration in the name of reform.

The fate of particular measures in any of these categories is affected

---

[3] *New York Times,* November 11 and 18, 1963. Private laws are common in other fields; the judiciary committees, for instance, handle a great many that give relief from the stringent provisions of the immigration and naturalization laws. When they are passed as individual acts they are subject to a presidential veto; special tax relief measures, however, are usually incorporated as amendments to major tax bills that are veto-proof.

[4] *New York Times,* February 27, 1964, p. 19.

by a great many factors, of course; it is especially influenced by the structure of organized economic interests and by the nature of the relevant congressional committees.

SOURCES AND CHANNELS OF INFLUENCE

Economic interests seeking to influence congressional action may follow any of several paths, all leading sooner or later to the various committees having jurisdiction in the two houses. Giant firms, major labor unions, and farm co-ops can take up their specific legislative concerns directly or by way of top officials in whatever departments or agencies are also involved. GM, Kodak, Chase Manhattan, the telephone company, the railroad brotherhoods, the teamsters, the Farmers Union, and the like, have permanent offices and informal contacts in the capital; they know their way around and do not need intermediaries; they have connections with both parties. New firms and small firms without permanent Washington representation can start with their congressmen, or go to the Small Business Committee in either house if they can interest a member in their desires, or they can employ *ad hoc* brokers or lobbyists. But for problems that are generic rather than specific, associations are the main channels for aggregating and applying pressures, direct and indirect. And because the attitudes of the administration and the agencies affected by a particular proposal are apt to be critically important—especially if these are negative—the associations cultivate executive as well as legislative ties.

We can put aside here the ideological pressure groups that seek a better world for no mercenary reason and the status groups—veterans, AMA, NAACP—that seek a better standing for their own order, though their demands may have economic overtones. Our present concern is the organization of frankly economic interests.

Characteristically, in each of the broad areas of business, agriculture, and labor there is room for one or two nationwide, all-embracing general-purpose organizations—the U.S. Chamber of Commerce, the American Farm Bureau Federation, the AFL-CIO. These speak with a mighty voice before Congress on issues that command a fair degree of consensus among their members—taxes, price supports, labor relations. But, like the national parties, their members are divided or indifferent on most specific matters: the corn grower's price is the poultryman's cost; sectional producers compete in metropolitan markets; fruit growers don't care what wheat growers get, etc. So except on a handful of major issues the voices of the major organizations are muted or ambivalent, their wills paralyzed by internal divisions. This leaves room for a host of more specialized associations, organized around a commodity, a product or service, a craft, a distinctive method of doing business, a limited geographical area, or a combination of these. Specialization is carried as far as is needed to express an undiluted interest with a stake sufficient to warrant the costs of maintaining an organization. Most legislative proposals are specific fragments, and most of the arguments over them are urged before Congress by these specialized and inherently parochial associations. If no one else is paying attention, they may get their individual desires piecemeal. More commonly they jostle each other and must work out their cross-purposes by the tactics of coalition.

POLICY SECTORS AND COMMITTEE CONTROLS

Congressional action depends so much on committee action and the committees differ so in their attitudes and modes of operation, that economic policy-making tends to be a function of committee jurisdiction. Two pairs of committees—Appropriations and Government Operations, the House Rules Committee and the Joint Economic Committee—all have, in varying ways, nearly universal jurisdictions. The Small Business Committees likewise can roam at large wherever their clients' interests reach. By contrast the taxing and other legislative committees—Banking and Currency, Commerce, and so on—have sectors defined by rule and precedent, designed to effect a division of labor and responsibility. As between the two houses, committee names and jurisdictions match each other roughly but not exactly. The Senate standing committees have, in addition to legislation, the confirmation of appointments to the agencies within their jurisdictions. Left to themselves, committees tend to go their separate ways, but inevitably they impinge on each other. Jurisdictional rivalries are consequently inherent, and, with them, contests for power and its policy stakes.

THE SPENDING POWER

By rules of the two houses adopted in conjunction with the passage of the Budget and Accounting Act of 1921, jurisdiction over all appropriations was vested in a single committee in each house; and corollary rules, imperfectly observed, forbid legislation in appropriation bills. In this way the Congress braced itself to deal with the unified budget it directed the President to submit. Since nothing moves without money, it might be supposed that the appropriations committees, thus endowed, if they were so inclined and adequately informed, might control the fiscal policy of the government—allowing a discretion to the taxing committees in raising the sums appropriated. In fact, the appropriations committees wield formidable concentrations of power, but not to that extent and not in ways designed to effectuate a general economic program. They have to reckon with some practical limitations, and they also have objects in view that are inconsistent with an over-all concern for fiscal policy.

The limits are of several sorts. One is the sheer labor of reviewing the details of budget estimates, a labor so burdensome as to force reliance on subcommittees which ratify each other's work when the full committee assembles. For 99 per cent of the items, subcommittee action is committee action and House action as well. No subcommittee can get its own work done and also take an over-all view. Another limit is the independence of the taxing committees and the shifting yields of the tax laws, depending on the state of the economy. The appropriations committees must take the revenue estimates as given. A third limit consists of legislation handled by other committees that makes certain appropriations mandatory. The appropriations committees may themselves mitigate the rigors of an annual review by making permanent appropriations (as for the interest on the public debt) or lump-sum appropriations (as for military pay) or "no-year" appropriations (as for construction projects); but their hands are forced by laws that stipulate payments (pensions to veterans, for instance, or grants-in-aid to states, or farm price supports) at specified rates to all applicants who qualify. Their discretion is altogether foreclosed by laws that earmark the proceeds of specified taxes as trust funds or automatic appropriations for designated uses, such as the Highway Trust Fund, social security taxes, and the 30 per cent of customs receipts allocated to the enlargement of outlets for farm products. And not only discretion but also jurisdiction is foreclosed by laws that authorize various agencies to operate with funds borrowed from the Treasury (e.g., the REA) or from the public (the TVA), or generated by their own operations (Federal Reserve Banks, Export-Import Bank), or assessed against their clienteles (Board of Governors of the Federal Reserve System, Farm Credit Administration, FDIC). The Government Corporation Control Act requires some, but not all, of these agencies to get appropriations for their administrative expenses and approval of their planned scale of operations.

Within these limits the appropriations committees go about their work, toward goals largely of their own making over the past forty years—goals that differ somewhat for the two committees and, in the case of the House group at least, have become embodied in a set of settled doctrines for committee behavior.

The House committee and each of its dozen subcommittees for the bills assigned to them, aim first of all to reduce the President's total budget figure, whatever that may be ("I've never seen a budget that couldn't be cut"); and in this they succeed, with occasional exceptions, at least until the conference stage is reached. They aim next to revise the judgments expressed, and reduce their grants below the authorizations established, by the legislative committees for programs the appropriations group is not enthusiastic about. The legislative committees are thought to be "soft" on the agencies, and in need of disinterested discipline. But this is a delicate operation, involving the confidence of the whole House in the committee: the committee must listen to the importunities of other members and distribute or withhold its cuts in ways that consolidate support —it cannot rely altogether on moral exhortation and rhetoric. Next, the committee has its own sparing enthusiasms and must make room for additions to the budget estimates under these headings without pushing the total back up to the President's figure. Further, the committee aims to make it unmistakably clear to agency spokesmen that, in any conflict of purposes, they are to take their marching orders from the committee. A variety of sanctions, mild and harsh, are available to enforce this intent. Finally the committee, extrapolating the revenue-originating prerogatives of the House, aims to oblige the Senate to accept its judgments; in this it is only partly successful.

In aid of these objectives the committee meets only in executive session and ordinarily hears only agency spokesmen and other members of Congress; it releases the printed testimony when a bill is reported and floor action scheduled—too late and too voluminous (and unindexed) for general use in debate. The committee maintains a small permanent staff, supplemented by investigators detailed for limited periods by the FBI, GAO, or other agencies—these for field studies to go behind the justification sheets that accompany the budget. It gives no apparent attention to the "cash budget" (the net results of federal receipts and expenditures, including trust fund operations) or the national income accounts, which also appear in the President's budget.

The Senate Appropriations Committee, unlike its House counterpart, makes no effort to canvass all the items in the estimates. Instead, it waits until the House has acted, listens to appeals from cuts the House has made —granting some and denying others—and then makes some additions of its own. When it listens, it hears the same general kind of evidence the House has heard. Its members are fewer (twenty-seven as against fifty in 1963), also senior and frequently ex-members of the House; they choose their subcommittee assignments, according to seniority and interest, instead of being appointed by the chairman or ranking minority member; and certain legislative committee members may sit *ex officio* when their committee interests are involved. Because of the freedom of floor debate, legislative riders inserted in the House, and protected there by the Rules Committee from points of order or separate votes, can be more easily removed in the Senate. And because appropriations usually reach the Senate floor late in the session, the floor leader's help in scheduling means a good deal to the subcommittee chairman managing a bill.

The final shape of appropriations is fixed in conference, where the senior subcommittee members from both houses meet and bargain. Occasionally the House managers are adamant, as they are apt to be about money for the District of Columbia. Concessions come from both sides, especially at the expense of insertions sponsored by junior members or added by floor action; some items are taken to conference only for trading purposes. But the Senate managers usually succeed in making most of their changes stick, wholly or in part. As likely as not, the final bill is higher than the President's budget, except in election years. Since the

Senate considers only a few of the items, however, and is more apt to raise than reduce what it looks at, the House subcommittees have the more pervasive influence. This fact, coupled with the stability of membership on the House committee, makes it, in the eyes of many bureaucrats, the nearest thing to tyranny in our legislative institutions.

One device for frustrating the appropriations committees, as already noted, is the "back-door financing" method of authorizing the use of funds borrowed from the Treasury for designated agencies or programs. It came into wide use during the depression and again during World War II. The Government Corporation Control Act of 1945 was a compromise attempt to curb its employment or extension, but it has survived for at least a score of agencies. Senior members of the House Appropriations Committee and Chairman Smith of the Rules Committee—"economizers" —see it as an evasion of constitutional controls; certain legislative committees—notably Banking and Currency, Veterans, Foreign Relations, and Agriculture—and powerful agencies in these areas, as well as many senators, and "spenders" generally, have a stake in preserving it. During the 1960s it has been a recurring subject of controversy. In 1963 the issue flared in connection with the renewal of the Export-Import Bank's charter, and was settled inconclusively. Chairman Wright Patman got nowhere with his proposal in 1964 to subject the Federal Reserve to appropriations control. *Ad hoc* balances of power, rather than triumphs of principle, govern the outcome each time the issue is raised.

Another and more unwieldy device has been introduced in the past decade. This is the requirement of an annual authorization act, emanating from the legislative committee, prior to consideration of an appropriation. First employed by the Foreign Affairs Committees in connection with foreign aid, it has been picked up by the Armed Services Committees and applied to major military procurement areas, amounting to about a third of the defense budget. Against it are the delays and duplications of testimony involved; in its behalf, Foreign Affairs Committee members argue that, since appropriations are considered in executive session, the open hearings of the legislative committees give the foreign-aid agency its only chance to get its case before the public. Plainly, annual authorizations give increased leverage to the legislative committees.

For present purposes, two related conclusions can be drawn from this sketch of familiar matters. First, the appropriations process has only an inadvertent bearing on the fiscal policy of the government. And second, the appropriations committees are mainly concerned with the oversight and control of executive agencies and their programs, as against other contenders for that prerogative. They are not oblivious of the economic effects of individual appropriations on particular industries and areas —far from it—but they do not employ their powers as instruments for achieving a calculated impact, in the public sector, on the national economy.

INVESTIGATING COMMITTEES

The two Government Operations Committees (successors since 1946 to the old and ineffective Committees on Expenditures in the Executive Departments) typify but by no means monopolize investigative activities in Congress. Like the appropriations committees, they have government-wide jurisdictions and the authority as standing committees to report bills. Conceivably, their investigations might sometimes take them into the realm of economic policy and lead them to make broad analyses and recommendations. In practice, however, this function has been assumed by the Joint Economic Committee, as will be noted later. The Government Operations Committees deploy their energies almost entirely through subcommittees that enable their members to ride individual hobbies—which may be broad themes or particular cases. The jurisdictional base that once launched Senator McCarthy now serves Senator McClellan in his crusade against racketeering and, on the House side, Congressman Moss in his campaign against secrecy in government. During the Eisenhower Administration it was Senator Jackson's base for comprehensive studies of national security organization.

The subcommittees touch economic questions sporadically, and when they do, members encounter the fact that one or another of the other legislative committees also has jurisdiction and may be jealous of intrusion. When a California congressman, for instance, used his Government Operations subcommittee to go after the Home Loan Bank Board for its summary action against an ailing savings and loan association in Long Beach, the Senate Banking and Currency Committee, sympathetic to the Board, monitored the lengthy and acrimonious hearings, to be prepared for intervention if needed. On the other hand, when Congressman Reuss of Wisconsin, during the second Eisenhower Administration, found himself lacking support in the House Banking and Currency Committee, he was able to use a Government Operations subcommittee base for his campaign to put more teeth into the Employment Act.

If congressmen with prime interests in economic policy are put on the Government Operations Committee, it is an accident of the processes of committee assignment. The committees rank low on the ladder of prestige. For both reasons, these committees are unlikely locations for sustained attention to broad economic policy or influence upon it.

TAXATION

Congressional control over the revenue and borrowing side of fiscal policy is centralized in the Ways and Means Committee of the House and the Finance Committee of the Senate; and in practice, concentrated in the hands of the ten senior members—five from each body, three from the majority and two from the minority—who comprise the Joint Committee on Internal Revenue Taxation. The full committees have an older tradition and rank at least equal to the Appropriations Committees in power and prestige. The leverage of Appropriations members is matched by the opportunities of taxing committee members to be helpful to others with tax amendments. In the House, the Democratic members of Ways and Means, each with a geographical zone of several states as his province, also constitute the party's committee on committees. By cooptation, Ways and Means itself, on the Democratic side, is a self-perpetuating body. Other House Democrats who want to improve their committee assignments are well aware of the bargaining situation this entails. This explains why, at a critical stage in floor consideration of the 1963 tax-cut bill, Chairman Mills preferred to use his Democratic colleagues for a canvass of the close prospective vote on the recommittal motion coming up, rather than depend on the parallel organization of the party whips, who also have zone captains assigned to keep track of Democratic voting.

Two differences in the work of the spending and revenue committees are inherent. Most appropriations are annual, so that the round of bills must be done over each year. Tax legislation, except for some excises with expiration dates needing periodic renewal, is "permanent"—i.e., fixed until changed. So the Appropriations Committee always has a dozen balls in the air at once, while Ways and Means can concentrate on one major bill at a time. The public debt ceiling is the only item the revenue committees have kept on an annual—or even shorter—basis. Another difference is that the Appropriations Committees are acutely sensitive to the geographical distribution of federal outlays, while the revenue committees deal with classes of taxpayers, wherever located. The whole domestic wine industry is regulated by the Alcohol Tax Act; extractive industries have their own depletion allowance; manufacturers have one set of rules for valuing inventories, department stores another; savings banks, commercial banks, and insurance companies have different allowances for tax-free reserves, and so on.

Two other contrasts between Appropriations and Ways and Means are sharply marked. Appropriations gets nearly all its work done through subcommittees; ratification of their decisions is nearly automatic. Ways and Means, on the contrary, has no standing subcommittees, and when *ad hoc* subcommittees are occasionally employed they are not empowered to draft or recommend bills. Further, the House Appropriations Committee has a tradition of fierce independence, not only of other House committees (except Rules) but more especially of the Senate; it is forever insisting on its prerogatives as against Senate revisions. The senior members of Ways and Means, on the other hand, while they will not delegate power to their junior committee colleagues, work hand-in-glove with their Senate counterparts—this despite the fact that their prerogative of originating revenue bills is clearly spelled out in the Constitution, while the corresponding assertion by the Appropriations Committee is plain usurpation.

The mark of these differences is the Joint Committee, established in 1926 to police large tax refunds after an investigation of dubious cases during the regime of President Harding's Commissioner of Internal Revenue. It still performs that statutory function. But like so many institutions, it has since acquired others not mentioned in the statute and not anticipated by its founders or that dwarf its formal duty and give its members a generally firm control of tax policy. Limited to seniors, it is conservative, it is bipartisan, its membership is fairly stable, it employs the principal staff that works for Congress on tax bills, and its members are usually the conferees who settle differences between the two houses in the concluding stage of tax legislation.

The staff, headed since 1938 by Colin Stam (who had spent the previous decade codifying the tax laws for the committee), was the first genuinely professional staff maintained by a congressional committee, antedating the Legislative Reorganization Act of 1946. It does not change with shifts in party control. It is a team of tax experts—lawyers, statisticians and economists—who work closely with Treasury staff but keep their loyalties exclusively for the senior committee members. Since the accession of Chairman Mills the Ways and Means Committee has begun to build some staff also, on whom he draws increasingly; Chairman Byrd has a single professional, besides the chief clerk and assistant chief clerk, for the Senate Finance Committee. Junior committee members, not on the Joint Committee, must accordingly depend on their own resources, or look outside, for technical help. And the tax laws are too complicated, and the consequences of changes too uncertain and potentially far-reaching, for anyone to intervene effectively without skilled help.

In this general setting, tax revisions since the Korean War have come about slowly, with the attention of nearly all participants preoccupied with the details of particular provisions. The Joint Committee staff are technicians, not policy analysts or planners. They stay with the process from the beginning stage of months of homework through House, Senate, and conference action. They are concerned with the complexities of drafting and calculations of the revenue consequences of alternative phrasings. The senior committee members are political conservatives who utilize their positions and skills to distribute the burdens and benefits of tax provisions as they think best, and to keep others from imposing different views. To do this they must win votes or forestall them from being taken. Much of their time therefore must be occupied in assessing the opposition to particular provisions, finding acceptable alternatives, and assembling and mustering the shifting coalitions that produce majorities at the successive stages when votes are needed. This does not leave much time, if they had the inclination, for escape from the narrow concerns of technicians and organized interests in order to entertain questions about the use of the taxing power to attain broad social goals.

This review teaches that in the current political context it is possible to concentrate power in Congress, in the tax field; though it is not the kind of concentration that champions of party responsibility advocate. As Professor Huitt observed in an incisive study for the Commission on Money and Credit:

> There is almost no way that the nation's voters could register 'no confidence' in the tax policies of a handful of senior congressmen of both parties and absolutely no way they could turn them out so long as Congress continues to work as it has in this century.[5]

It does not follow that a similar concentration could be put together and maintained over other fields, as has often been suggested—say, over appropriations, let alone over expenditures and revenues combined—or that, if feasible, it would long be politically tolerable. Indeed, the experience of the Revenue Act of 1964 suggests some of the difficulties in keeping it where it already exists. With or without a change in party control there is no apparent successor to the influence once wielded by Senator Byrd, who this time could delay and force concessions but not stop the passage of a tax bill he refused to pilot through floor debate and voted against, precisely because it embodied a novel and unwelcome concept of the relation of tax policy to national economic goals. If some of the junior and more liberal committee members scale the seniority ladder far enough to break into the inner circle, the conservative consensus that holds the Joint Committee together would be strained.

A related difficulty is discernible in the experience with social security legislation, which, because taxes are involved, is in the jurisdiction of the taxing committees, not those that handle other labor and welfare matters. Organized interests, such as the AMA, are at work here too, but they are arrayed in a very different configuration that pits employers and beneficiaries in direct opposition. Ideological controversies are more prominent and more clearly polarized than in the obscure moralities of income and selective sales taxes. Ideological controversies lend themselves to presidential dramatization. During the past decade the taxing committees have been on the defensive against enlargements of Social Security benefits, fighting a holding or rear-guard action. The conservative consensus on the Joint Committee is more secure when it does not need to be explicit.

MANAGEMENT OF THE PUBLIC DEBT

The management of the public debt has been confided to the Treasury by broadly phrased delegations of authority and permanent indefinite appropriations of whatever is needed to pay interest and principal when due. The nuisance value of congressional attachment to orthodoxy in public finance, however, and the political mileage to be got out of it,

---

[5] Ralph K. Huitt, "Congressional Organization and Operations in the Field of Money and Credit," in *Fiscal and Debt Management Policies* (Englewood Cliffs, N.J.: Prentice-Hall, Inc., 1963), p. 456.

are well illustrated in the recurrent controversy over the public-debt ceiling, another item in the jurisdiction of the taxing committees.

A statutory limit on the total of government debt outstanding at any one time was first fixed in the Liberty Loan Acts of World War I. It gave no practical trouble, being revised upward as needed, until after World War II. But during the past decade it has required an amendment nearly every year (three in the fiscal year 1963-64). These amendments are adopted usually on the last day allowed by the previous extension. In form they permit a stipulated "temporary" excess for a limited period over a "permanent" ceiling that was exceeded some time ago—as though the debt total would drop when the extension expires.

No economic warrant exists for a debt ceiling—at least in the present range of magnitude—and economists and study groups like the Commission on Money and Credit have repeatedly recommended the outright repeal of the existing provision: the debt is the automatic result and measure of the accumulated difference between revenues and expenditures, plus some allowance for Treasury cash balances. The practical bearing of the ceiling is on the size of these balances and on the elbow room they leave for Treasury discretion in handling current payments, debt issues and refundings, etc. The amount and placement of cash balances, to be sure, has a direct effect on the supply of bank credit, though it is an effect easily dwarfed by Federal Reserve open-market operations. Substantial Treasury cash balances kept in interest-free tax and loan checking accounts in the New York banks where they accumulate, are a cost-free source of profit to the banks, as Congressman Wright Patman has pointedly observed. But if the management of these balances were the main issue, they could be regulated in separate legislation. Why, then, the ceilings and their short-term expiration dates?

Part of the answer appears to lie in the fond hope, expressed by Congressman Curtis (R., Mo.) of Ways and Means, among others, that the ceiling can somehow be used to make good the failure of the Appropriations Committees to avoid a deficit. Let the Treasury reduce its spending to the level of revenues, lest it default on obligations; or let the leadership, after consulting the Treasury and Budget in periodic appraisals, enforce a further retrenchment in appropriations. But this is an exercise in buck-passing. It invites the retort, even from those who agree to the need for a continuously balanced budget, that it is the business of Ways and Means to find the wherewithal to meet the outlays Congress has authorized. In practice, after last-minute conferences with the Treasury, the ceiling is always raised, or the previous raise is extended.

A more realistic answer appears to be that the expiration date gives the taxing committees what the budget gives the Appropriations Committees, an automatic occasion for summoning Treasury officials to listen to some public badgering and to respond to some informal exertions of leverage. The leverage, therefore, is proportional, among other things, to the strength of the Treasury's commitment to a balanced budget. During the Eisenhower Administration, when that commitment was high, the response was partly sublimated in bookkeeping devices that improved appearances and in uneconomic postponements of expenditures. High or low, the confrontation against a deadline creates a bargaining situation the taxing committees are unlikely to forgo.

LEGISLATIVE COMMITTEES

Apart from the taxing and spending committees, subject-matter jurisdiction is parcelled out among fourteen other standing committees in the Senate and eighteen in the House. All but four or five of these on each side have substantial segments of the economy within their province; none have more than segments. Space forbids any systematic review of their work, but some generalizations more or less applicable to all of them are in order, as are some examples.

First, they tend to go their autonomous ways, and to multiply these ways by setting up subcommittees that, once established, tend to develop their own permanence and autonomy. Jurisdictional disputes are frequent. A good many questions of economic policy consequently have as many partial answers as there are committees and subcommittees participating. If it be asked, for instance, what congressional policy governs the federal sharing of expenses with the states by way of grants-in-aid, or the utilization of private contractors to provide governmental services, or the terms for lending federal funds, across-the-board canvasses of a host of distinct committee actions would have to be compiled before attempting an answer. The House and Senate leadership, moreover, are not program-makers for the committees. They may prod a committee chairman for a bill that can pass and help to see that it does; the content of the bill, within some limits, is up to the committee.

Second, as the saying goes, "everything depends on the chairman," and the caliber of staff he assembles. A change in chairmanship is seldom as dramatic as the one that occurred when Adam Clayton Powell (D., N.Y.) succeeded Graham Barden (D., N. Car.) as the head of the House Education and Labor Committee in 1961, but a substantial reorientation of committee activity is to be expected from any change in leadership. To take a purely hypothetical case, a shift in party control of the Senate after the 1962 elections would have made Senator Goldwater chairman of the Labor and Public Welfare Committee, in place of Lister Hill (D., Ala.); a party shift after the 1964 elections would have given the chairmanship to Senator Jacob Javits (R., N.Y.).

Third, the extent of discretion already conveyed to administrative agencies by past legislation shapes the room left for committee activity. The Federal Reserve Act, for instance, launched an agency that has become self-sufficient in authority and more so in funds; it needs little from Congress but to be let alone; the Banking and Currency Committees are outsiders looking in. The same is true of the Farm Credit Administration's complex of banks, which have repaid their federal grubstakes, vis-à-vis the Agriculture Committees. The Interstate Commerce Commission has a broad statute, a tradition of independence, an unwieldy top structure with 11 commissioners, and an unmanageable case load. It needs annual appropriations for administrative expenses, but the legislative committees leave it alone too, lest they get lost in a thicket of trucking rivalries. On the other hand, where regulation is combined with subsidies, as with public lands, public works, defense installations and contracts, housing, merchant marine, air transport, and many other fields, the legislative committees are active intervenors.

Fourth, the legislative committees tend to attract members with a special interest—usually favoring, but sometimes hostile—in some part of their jurisdiction, though this is not the only consideration in committee assignments. This shows up most strongly on the Agriculture Committees, where farm constituencies are the nearly universal rule—a Democrat from Brooklyn served briefly and unhappily from 1955 to 1959 on the House committee, as a party duty in an experiment, and escaped at his first opportunity. The rules and standards regarding conflicts of interest, applicable in the judicial and executive branches, are matters for the individual consciences of elected legislators, so a wide range of behavior from the near scandalous to the austere, may be found in the same committee.

Banking and currency. These generalizations can all be illustrated in the two Banking and Currency Committees. Their jurisdictions are extensive but not exactly co-extensive. The Senate committee controls securities legislation but not the international lending agencies, which are under Foreign Relations; in the House, the former belongs to Interstate and Foreign Commerce, the latter to Banking and Currency. Both have an active housing subcommittee to handle the omnibus housing bill, which has become a popular annual feature, somewhat after the model of public works. The Senate committee had a period of broad activity on many fronts when Fulbright headed it (he took with him the international lending agencies, which Vandenberg had not wanted, when he moved to Foreign Relations), while Senator Willis Robertson (D., Va.), a successor, has confined himself inconspicuously to his specialty, the banking laws. The House committee had an unaggressive era in the regime of Brent Spence (D., Tenn.); Wright Patman (D., Tex.), an inheritor of the Populist tradition, has made it a gadfly of large eastern financial institutions and especially of Chairman Martin of the Board of Governors of the Federal Reserve System—a case of pursuing an interest in order to reform it, not to profit from it.

Little formal collaboration between the two committees is in evidence, beyond the necessities of conferring on legislation pending between the two houses. For instance, when Chairman Patman secured a set of minutes of meetings of the Federal Reserve's Open Market Committee, under a stipulation that they would be available in his office to both committees, Senate committee members later complained that they had not heard of the arrangement. But the sharp divisions are within the committees rather than between them. Staff relations are cordial but not close; the House committee staff, except for its minority member, turned over almost completely in 1963; its general counsel left to become legislative counsel to the Federal Reserve.

Staff contacts with downtown agencies in the committees' realms are maintained, but much more closely with some than others. In part, staff assistants are alert to cues from committee members, especially senior members, as to agencies and topics they want watched, or are indifferent to. In part, some agencies are more in the limelight or more in need of committee action.

But it does not follow that because a controversial situation develops, the committees will necessarily plunge in to resolve it. For example, in 1963 the Comptroller of the Currency, reversing previous interpretations of the apparently flat prohibition in the Banking Act of 1935, ruled that national banks could underwrite municipal revenue bond offerings. The Federal Reserve protested publicly. Commercial bankers came to the House committee, pressing a bill that would have confirmed the Comptroller's interpretation and extended it to state-chartered banks as well. The investment bankers' association appeared in opposition to this. Facing the unlikely line-up that ranged Chairman Patman alongside Chairman Martin and the investment bankers, against the Comptroller and state banks, the committee looked for an out. More fingers would be burned than chestnuts extracted. The committee took no action on the bill and suggested instead that an official opinion of the Attorney General be requested, interpreting the 1935 law—an opinion it was not altogether clear the Comptroller would accept as binding, though the Federal Reserve, in an even more independent position, promised to do so.

Similarly, the committee took no action on several other bills, implementing recommendations made by the Commission on Money and Credit in 1961 or by the President's interdepartmental Committee on Financial Institutions in 1963. These would have realigned bank supervisory jurisdictions and relaxed restrictions on competitive practices among various types of banks. It took no action either on recommendations of the Comptroller's Advisory Committee on Banking, a clientele group he sponsored as an offset to the ABA, to advance the competitive position of national banks.

The House committee, giving rein to its chairman's interest, is willing to study what it will not act on. On the fiftieth anniversary of the Federal Reserve Act, it commissioned a series of studies and summoned all the

Board members and Reserve Bank presidents *seriatim* to extended hearings. But it did not back Chairman Patman's bills to alter Federal Reserve structure.

The two committees have been deeply embroiled for several years in the running controversy over back-door financing, as already noted, and they are more or less continuously engaged on housing matters. Otherwise, except for Patman's persistent preoccupation with the Federal Reserve, their legislative activities appear to be *ad hoc* responses to external stimuli. Ideological splits prevent the kind of cohesion the Appropriations Committee has developed and the taxing committee's formula for concentrating power is not in evidence.

Special cases. Two House committees with jurisdiction over far-reaching questions of economic policy deserve note not so much for what they do as because, in different ways, their bases of composition depart sharply from the prevailing pattern. These are Education and Labor, and Agriculture.

The Education and Labor Committee for years has been the arena for contesting issues—labor-management relations, school aid and its corollaries, racial segregation and help for parochial schools—animated by many of the most burning emotions in American politics. Consequently, as a student of the subject put it, "this assignment is no place for a neutral when there are so many belligerents around." [6] On this ground South Dakota Democrat (later Senator) George McGovern, a history professor and Ph.D. when he was elected to Congress in 1957, was given a transfer from Education and Labor to Agriculture after it developed that school aid had become a major campaign issue in his farm district. Any position he took in his previous committee only hurt him at home. As a rule, the Democrats have put on this committee some anti-union Southerners and more Northern city Representatives with strong union support. The Republicans name members who can safely survive union opposition. The rival forces battle it out. The result has usually been something of a standoff between antagonists and lengthy periods of stalemate within the committee.

The Agriculture Committee is responsible for programs entailing budget expenditures in the range of $5 to $7 billion annually, in the years from 1959 to 1964, distributed according to the political strength of the claimants as well as according to need. Compromising the claims has become increasingly complex and difficult in recent years, in the face of divided counsels from farm interests. This is no work for outsiders. Committee seats are a monopoly of members from the farm areas. An urban spokesman for consumer interests would be a sitting duck for crossfires from farm lobbies he knew little about, and besides, the farm members need the places to protect their tenure in office.

[6] Nicholas A. Masters, "House Committee Assignments," *American Political Science Review*, 55 (June 1961), 354.

Ten of the committees' eighteen subcommittees handle specific commodities that can be broadly grouped in a half-dozen categories: (1) corn and livestock; (2) cotton and rice; (3) dairy, livestock, small grains; (4) wheat; (5) tobacco; and (6) diversified (non-"basics"). Members cluster on the subcommittees closest to their constituency interests. Commodities have partisan as well as sectional identifications: wheat, corn, livestock, and dairy products are Republican, and cotton, rice, tobacco, and peanuts Democratic. Sugar is a complex story, involving overseas supplies as well as Democratic cane and Republican beets; it has a separate, long-term bill. Among the "basics," some crisis arises for one or another each year, to which producers of other commodities are more or less indifferent.

The general procedure usually operates on logrolling principles—letting each subcommittee write its own ticket in a series of titles in an omnibus bill, in order to get something the full committee can report, and modifying or abandoning the weaker of these on the floor, in order to get something the House will pass. If calculations are upset by a presidential veto, as happened in the Eisenhower Administration, or by an adverse vote of growers, as happened for the first time in the 1963 wheat referendum, the participants start over again.

By a parity of reasoning, assignments to some other legislative committees—e.g., Interior and Insular Affairs, and Merchant Marine and Fisheries—are also closely related to the environments of their districts, but these are of less consequence in the total economy.

Non-Legislative Committees

A formal way for Congress to transcend the jurisdictional boundaries it has set for its standing committees, in order to focus concern on a problem that cuts across them, is to establish a study committee. Without authority to report bills, it avoids the jealousy a claim-jumper would arouse. It can study, hold hearings, issue reports, and agitate. Its members also sit on legislative committees; if they are persuasive they may obtain results there.

Small business committees. Two examples of this approach are the Select Committees to Study the Problems of Small Business, one in each house, created in 1940 and made permanent in 1950. They undertake to help small firms get favorable tax treatment, get credit when it would otherwise be unobtainable, get government contracts or subcontracts, get attention from government agencies, get antitrust relief from large competitors, and so on. They are a convenience to other members, who can refer constituents to them as a complaint bureau. As official lobbyists, so to speak, for a frankly labelled bias and clientele, they give strength and legitimacy to what might otherwise be dismissed impatiently as a nuisance.

The Senate committee owes much to the energy of Senator Sparkman (D., Ala.), its chairman continuously since 1950 except during two years of Republican control. The House committee has an outspoken champion

in its chairman, Wright Patman. Working with the other committees,
they have sponsored a surprising amount of legislation that has been
enacted, including the establishment of the Small Business Administration, chartering of Small Business Investment Corporations, tax concessions, and set-asides of procurement orders. Patman also has gotten out
voluminous studies of chain banking and of the operations of tax-exempt
foundations. It may be no accident that the committees have had their
greatest successes with projects in the legislative province of Banking and
Currency, since Sparkman is the ranking Democrat on that committee in
the Senate and Patman and Congressman Multer (D., N.Y.) are the two
ranking Democrats on both committees in the House.

The small business committees demonstrate an effective method of
institutionalizing a bias, a needed reminder and sponsor of a neglected
interest. It is their virtue that no one mistakes them for more than that.

The Joint Economic Committee. A very different sort of study group
is the Joint Economic Committee, the nearest thing to a central economic
analysis unit that Congress possesses:

> In many ways the Joint Economic Committee is the most exciting contem-
> porary invention of Congress. Established originally to react to the annual
> Economic Report of the President, it roves at will over the economic spectrum,
> studying broadly or intensively any problem which attracts the interest of
> Committee or congressional leadership. The Joint Economic Committee is a
> congressional anomaly. It is a planning and theory group in a culture fiercely
> devoted to the short run and the practical. It is committed to the panoramic
> view in a system which stresses jurisdictional lines. It signifies recognition that
> economic problems are related, by a body which deals with them piecemeal.[7]

The JEC is made up of sixteen members who request the assignment,
divided five and three, majority and minority, from each house. Since
1955 the chairmanship has alternated biennially between Senator Paul
Douglas (D., Ill.) and Congressman Patman. Neither is in the inner
leadership circle of his chamber, but there is muscle in the group as well
as brains: on the House side in 1964, three from Ways and Means, one
from Rules and four from Banking and Currency; on the Senate side, two
from Finance, two from Foreign Relations, four from Banking and Currency, as well as representation from Agriculture, Labor, Public Works,
and Government Operations. Noticeably absent from this array, after an
early nominal trial, is any representation from Appropriations.

The JEC publishes an annual report in the spring, commenting on the
President's Economic Report. It publishes the monthly *Economic Indicators* prepared by the Council of Economic Advisers, a thirty-six-page
compendium of statistics without commentary. And it makes and publishes studies on its own initiative, according to a method resembling a

professional seminar, novel to Congress and designed not only to enlist first-rate professional advice but also to overcome two of the notorious frustrations of congressional hearings—the tendency of senior members to monopolize the time for questions and the tendency of witnesses with axes to grind to contradict each other without ever meeting on the issues. For these studies the JEC commissions the preparation of papers and monographs by outside experts—sometimes also arranging for panel discussions with the authors—and staff analyses. The staff is on easy terms of professional familiarity with experts in the CEA, Treasury, Federal Reserve and other agencies, and with leading academic scholars.

Some monumental tomes have resulted—*Monetary Policy and the Management of the Public Debt* (1952), *Federal Expenditure Policy for Economic Growth and Stability* (1957), *Employment, Growth and Price Levels* (1959), *State of the Economy and Policies for Full Employment* (1962), among others, together with scores of shorter works which have sold in the hundreds of thousands of copies and are frequently required reading in college courses. The committee's work therefore has a double effect, one direct, as the members go about their other business in Congress, and the other indirect, as the outside impact of their publications is reflected back on other members. Unquestionably, the committee has been a notable educational influence outside as well as inside Congress and has contributed to a marked increase in the level of sophistication, since 1947, in public debate on economic policy.

If the JEC has helped change the climate of thinking, it would be something else again to argue that it has been specifically responsible for any identifiable policy change. A study group is not an action group, let alone a policy-making group. Before 1955 its annual reports were unanimous, or nearly so; since then, majority and minority reports, strictly along partisan lines, have been the rule. Some critics have deplored this; Senator Douglas welcomes it, on the ground that unanimity necessarily requires covering over real differences with innocuous generalities. A middle course might seek to state matters of agreement and isolate differences, in order to define issues more sharply; but this would not be easy where differences are ideological and not merely technical, as economic arguments are apt to be. Other critics have urged changes in procedure and format to dramatize the committee's output; experiments in this direction will probably have to wait on changes in leadership that would make them congenial.

It is perhaps significant that the committee's work, like Senator Jackson's studies in the field of national security organization, attracted the greatest attention in a period when Democrats controlled the Congress and Republicans the White House. When the same party controls both, there is less room—and less incentive—for developing, from a congressional committee base, major alternatives in policy to those espoused by the administration in office.

THE QUEST FOR COORDINATION

At this point the problems of Congress and economic policy merge into the larger problems of the place of Congress in the general scheme of things. We confront a number of dilemmas, not apparently soluble without larger readjustments.

Congress acts on economic matters in piecemeal fashion, from limited perspectives. The committee system permits technical expertise and political appraisals to be brought to bear on these actions, the appraisals reflecting the dominant organization of power at the particular time and place. Most of the time this is perhaps as much as can be asked. The economy is huge and complex, and most people want their changes in small doses, with a minimum of disturbance.

Nevertheless, though the economy is huge and complex, it is not beyond the reach of human purpose. Economic understanding has advanced sufficiently so that its larger movements, and forces behind them, can be apprehended, if not always with a desirable degree of clarity or precision. Economic goals are formulated and programs to secure them developed. Potent instruments are available to the government to further them. Once their potentialities begin to be appreciated, it is idle to say that the instruments should be put away; and it is better that they be used consciously than blindly. Even small moves need the guidance of larger perspectives. Yet these perspectives are missing in the conduct of congressional business.

The experience of the Joint Economic Committee testifies that it is possible to organize a unit in Congress that can open up national perspectives on the economy and draw on the most advanced techniques of economic analysis to make prescriptions. But it is not conceivable that the JEC could acquire the power to enact them; it is a teacher, not a governor.

The experience of the Joint Committee on Internal Revenue Taxation testifies that it is possible to organize a unit in Congress sufficiently powerful to control the use of the taxing power. But it is not conceivable that the taxing committees, in doing so, will apply the prescriptions, or even adopt the perspectives of the JEC. Except for atomic energy, it is doubtful that any other subject-matter field lends itself to as much concentration of power across the two houses at the committee level as does taxation.

The experience of the leadership in both chambers testifies that power over procedure will bear no corresponding responsibility for the substantive content of a program. And precedents from by-gone days when the leadership could control the substance of legislation do not encourage efforts to return to them.

Three general conclusions emerge. First, the basic problem is not in the organization of Congress as it acts on economic policy. A going organization can confer power, but a growing power can also create organization. It would be unrealistic to expect that creating new committees on economic policy would bring about material changes unless the forces that control present arrangements were somehow realigned. This could come about imperceptibly through education or through gradual shifts in the electoral base.

Second, those who control the proceedings in any segment of congressional machinery can be expected to use their power to impose their own terms. Power is not neutral.

Third, experience with the Budget and Accounting Act and the Employment Act suggests that the way to influence the Congress to view the economy in a broader perspective is to impose on the President a duty to do so first, and in a public stand that requires a response. A focal point for a coordinated approach is to be found in the White House, or nowhere. If one is articulated there, in connection with action programs that Congress cannot ignore after he has committed himself, wider influences will be released. In a political system as loose of access as ours, Congress is a poor place to assemble sufficient force for a coordinating, i.e., a governing initiative; it cannot avoid being a reactor, or ignore the perspective in which the initiative is publicly presented.

Holbert N. Carroll

7

The Congress
and National Security Policy

To one President, the demand of the House of Representatives for executive correspondence relating to negotiations with another nation, and the threat of the House to refuse funds to implement the commitment, jeopardized the balances of the Constitution. In a major address, he later solemnly warned the nation about the hazards of dissension, partisanship, and prejudice in foreign policy.

To another President, a House action would be the signal for other nations "whether they are to deal with a strong or a weak President." He admonished the representatives that the amendment to deny him discretion "places handcuffs upon the President and leaves the key in the possession of a body of men who cannot possibly act with the speed frequently required in international negotiations." [1]

Both Presidents prevailed. President Washington in 1796 overcame a defiant House on the Senate-approved Jay Treaty. In 1963, President Johnson got the discretion he sought to underwrite Soviet credit for the purchase of American wheat.

These events, separated by 167 years, reveal the persistent tension of the political system between the requirements of a Constitution dividing and limiting the powers of government and addressed primarily to the

---

HOLBERT N. CARROLL *is Professor of Political Science and Chairman of the Department of Political Science at the University of Pittsburgh. Long a student of the formulation of United States foreign policy, Professor Carroll has been a consultant on the subject at The Brookings Institution and a contributor to numerous journals and policy studies. He is the author of* The House of Representatives and Foreign Affairs.

[1] *New York Times,* December 24, 1963.

achievement of "domestic tranquillity" and the exigencies of conducting the external affairs of the nation. Today, the formal allotment of powers between the President and the Congress remains exactly as when the Constitution was adopted. The allotment compels, and tradition supports, congressional participation in defining both the domestic and external purposes of the nation and in achieving the goal of national security, always fervently shared by the President and the Congress. Presidential dominance in conducting the external relations of the nation and congressional preoccupation with the domestic tasks of perfecting the Union represented a rough accommodation through history to the tension of the system. National security was the happy sum of their efforts. It was a general goal like freedom or justice. It rarely demanded concentrated attention.

Radical changes in the requirements of national security, especially since the 1930s, have spurred fresh adjustments to the tension of the political system of divided and shared power, now so inextricably drawn into the fantastically complex affairs of every part of the globe. From the President's perspective, national security policy spans that range of national policies identified in a summary way in the tasks of the National Security Council to advise him on the integration of "domestic, foreign, and military policies relating to the national security. . . ." [2] His perspective is thus the whole of national policy as it bears on relations with foreign nations.

For the Congress the boundaries are more confined. To the Congress national security policy is preeminently military policy and much of foreign policy. In these sectors the Congress generally acquiesces in presidential dominance. Its mode of behavior, by necessity or choice, has become primarily that of monitoring the executive branch. Looking back from the third decade of the revolution in the requirements of national security, the increasing tendency to monitor, to establish political perimeters of tolerance and expectation, rather than to use power to intervene deeply in shaping the substance of policies, is perhaps the most striking development in congressional behavior.

Between the presidential and congressional perceptions of national security policy lies an ill-defined area. The President strikes a national security theme, but the Congress often does not. Even then, the Congress more often than not asserts its voice on the periphery of fundamentals. These are policies which the Congress views as marginal to national security, as essentially domestic and thus essentially congressional. Or the policies involve cherished powers, such as the power of the purse, for purposes that the Congress is reluctant to accept as continuing necessities of national security. Setting sugar import quotas, tariff issues, restricting immigration, disposing of farm surpluses abroad, internal security prob-

[2] 61 Stat. 496, Section 101 (a).

lems, cultural and informational programs, and, in significant ways, foreign aid are examples of policy areas in which the Congress is more assertive. Needless to add, the Congress gives continuing detailed attention to the administrative organizations through which policies are implemented.

Regardless of the depth of its involvement, whether it chooses to monitor, to attempt to govern, or, more commonly, to blend the two tendencies in varying proportions, the Congress participates significantly in the shaping of national security policies. No major legislature in the world can match the extent of its participation.

THE ENVIRONMENT

Fractions of power

The number and variety of programs needed to support the multiple dimensions of national security involve a large number of the committees and other groupings in the fragmented power structure of the Congress. In justifying continuing foreign-military programs in a typical year of the 1960s, the Secretaries of State and Defense were obliged to maintain close relationships with ten major committees. Important programs or issues also were likely to rest in the jurisdictions of some fifteen other committees.

These standing and joint committees spawned more than seventy subcommittees. A few of the subunits required continuing attention by the Secretaries and their subordinates. Each year, for example, the House Appropriations Subcommittee on Foreign Operations took hundreds of hours of testimony in reviewing foreign aid programs. Thousands of man hours were consumed in preparing for these annual reviews.

In addition to their relationships with many committees and subcommittees, the Secretaries necessarily maintained critical ties with key individuals, with chairmen, with ranking minority committeemen, and with the majority and minority party leaders.

The number and diversity of congressional units invariably acts as a restraint on policy. Fragmentation inspires caution and complicates the search for consensus. So many bases have to be touched and so many points exist where programs and policies can be eroded that an administrator is more likely to choose the conservative approach than one innovating and departing from past patterns. The annual foreign aid programs are reviewed and revised by five units of the Congress and intermittently concern as many as thirty other committees and subcommittees. At least nine fractions of the Congress are interested in the administration of the Department of State. A missile problem can easily spur activity by eight major committees.

Duplication of effort is common. Several committees can intervene, or fail to act, and complicate the conduct of policy. In 1960, for instance,

President Eisenhower sought flexibility in using sugar quotas as leverage in conducting relations with Castro's Cuba and the Dominican Republic, then under Trujillo. The President had the general support of congressional foreign policy leaders. He worked closely with other Latin American states.

The President got discretion with regard to Cuba, but the Congress, approving bills reported by the farm committees, required increased purchases of Dominican sugar. When the Dominican government was condemned by the Organization of American States for acts of aggression against Venezuela, the President requested authority to cut back the Dominican allotment. The farm committees could not agree on a bill. Inaction required the President to allot the substantial sugar bonus to the Dominican Republic.

Innovations in organization

Organizational responses to the new demands of national security have largely been carried out within the traditional committee structure, as modified by the reorganization of 1946. Improved staffing and the proliferation of specialized subcommittees have been the principal organizational changes.

The historic centers of major influence have retained their dominant positions. These include the House and Senate Armed Services Committees (formed in 1947 from the Military and Naval Affairs committees), the Appropriations Committees, and the Senate Committee on Foreign Relations. The Appropriations Committees, and especially subcommittees of the House money group, have gained more influence because of the requirement of substantial funds to support foreign-defense programs. With the new importance of the House, the Committee on Foreign Affairs, with a rich tradition but little business until the 1930s, has gained stature.

Three committees have emerged to cover major new sectors of policy that could not be readily accommodated within the traditional structure. The House Committee on Science and Astronautics and the Senate Committee on Aeronautical and Space Sciences, organized in 1959, are concerned with the largely non-military aspects of outer space, as reflected in the programs of the National Aeronautics and Space Administration. Space issues are not easily compartmentalized into the military and the non-military. It is not surprising that military policy issues pervade the deliberations of the space units as well as the other committees—Armed Services, Appropriations, and Atomic Energy—more directly specializing in such matters.

The third new major unit, the Joint Committee on Atomic Energy, organized in 1946, has developed into perhaps the most powerful and influential standing committee that the Congress has ever created. It is unique. Joint House-Senate committees are rare. They normally have been given only study and reporting functions. The Joint Committee on Atomic Energy, in contrast, reports legislation to either the House or the Senate. Its recommendations are rarely challenged. Its power and influence in the atomic energy sector, which extends significantly into the realms of international diplomacy, are only in a minor way reflected in the business it presents to the House and the Senate. It is of greater importance that the committee has woven itself into the processes of executive deliberation, thus breaking down the normal barriers between the executive and legislative aspects of decision-making.

Modifications of behavior

The Congress processes foreign-military business in much the same way as other public business, but distinctive modes of behavior are displayed in dealing with the basic programs and policies which the Congress embraces as requirements of national security. Recognition of the special roles and burdens of the President, the element of secrecy, the bewildering technology, the hazards in choosing wrongly, the penchant to avoid responsibility, the involvement of foreign nations and cultures, the necessities of multilateral diplomacy, appeals to national unity and interest transcending local and partisan considerations—these and other factors inspire more caution and restraint by the Congress, its parts, and the members than is evident in the handling of other public business.

The restraints are reflected in the behavior of the majority of the members. Senators and representatives enjoy greater freedom from constituent and other pressures in exercising judgment about responses to the foreign environment than they do in such matters as farm and welfare programs and civil rights. The congressman who chooses to exploit his greater freedom in disruptive, irresponsible ways gets extraordinary publicity. The more prevalent pattern of individual behavior, one more important ultimately in the congressional impact upon policy, is disciplined restraint.

Caution and restraint also are evident in the extensive bipartisanship pervading the consideration of foreign-military policy business. While comprehensive bipartisanship, in the sense of close Republican-Democratic collaboration beginning in the early stages of policy initiation, is rare, the less dramatic forms of bipartisanship in a committee, in floor debates, in votes on critical issues, and in the often private contacts with the President and his subordinates have been routine in the processing of national security business.

Other factors in the new dimensions of national security condition the behavior of the Congress and uniquely color its deliberation. Because his powers and, especially, his responsibilities in acting for the nation in the world are directly affected by what the Congress does or fails to do, the President more deeply and frequently involves himself in this aspect of the legislative process than he ordinarily does. Congressional deliberations also are affected by the increasing intervention of foreign nations and their publicity agents in the political processes of the national government, by the revolution in transportation and in communications that permits committees and members to be in Viet-Nam or the Congo during crises or to talk with Soviet leaders within a few hours of flying from Washington, and by the occasional assignment of Senators and representatives to diplomatic roles at international meetings.

These and other features of the congressional environment may best be illuminated by brief studies of the behavior of the Congress and its parts in crisis situations and in such policy areas as East-West relations, defense, and foreign aid.

CRISES

The rhetoric of crisis is invoked in every session of the Congress to spur support for programs. In some circumstances a crisis atmosphere has become almost routine as the leaders work to move bills through a fractured structure that provides so many opportunities to delay, erode, or dilute the recommendations of the executive branch. The Congress generates the crisis atmosphere. On other occasions international events of varying magnitude provoke crises to which the Congress reacts.

The frequency of crises and emergencies since World War II has invariably enhanced presidential power. As the nation has become vulnerable to military attack, the Congress has more willingly conceded extraordinary exercises of executive power. It has no choice. In many situations it now expects to be informed rather than to be consulted. In every emergency, however, lurks the potential of hazardous division and dissension in a political system of separated and diffused power.

Resolutions anticipating crises

On only a few occasions has the President asked the Congress for broad authority in anticipation of a crisis. The risks in asking must be carefully calculated. If the vote is overwhelmingly favorable, potential adversaries are warned that the President has the backing of the nation for whatever he chooses to do. But the debate may be prolonged, division exaggerated, votes close, public confidence shaken, and the backing possibly denied or seriously diluted.

President Eisenhower's request in 1955 for authority to use force, if necessary, to defend Formosa was quickly approved. The resolution was part of a strategy of communicating to Communist China the firm determination of the United States to defend the island stronghold of Nationalist China and vaguely described adjacent areas.

Conveying the unity of the nation and the determination to take risks was evident in resolutions on Berlin and Cuba in 1962. The Berlin resolution expressed the sense of the Congress that the United States was prepared to use any required means to prevent the violation of Allied rights. The Cuba resolution, passed less than a month before the missile crisis of October, 1962, warned the Soviet and Cuban governments that the United States was prepared to use any necessary means, including force, to deal with a Soviet build-up of arms in Cuba and Cuban aggression in the hemisphere. The President did not ask for the Cuban and Berlin resolutions. Once initiated in the Congress, he moved to prevent a narrowing of his discretion and succeeded. The Congress provided constitutional legitimacy for virtually any exercise of executive power. By the Cuba resolution, in particular, the more vigorous congressional proponents, responding to a troubled public, undoubtedly hoped to press the President to take a harder line. When the missile crisis arose, the Congress was not in session, but its resolve to see any crisis through was freshly on record.

The seriousness of the resolutions regarding Formosa and Cuba was underscored in the Senate by joint meetings and reports of the Foreign Relations and Armed Services Committees. The immensely powerful military and foreign policy voices of the Senate were blended. All of the resolutions were approved by huge majorities. They expressed a national consensus.

Congressional resolving in anticipation of crises, whether stimulated by the executive branch or generated within the Congress, entails risks. When President Eisenhower in 1957 asked for approval of his Middle East doctrine, the Congress, under the control of the Democrats, consumed two months to process his proposal. No doubt existed that the Congress would ultimately give him broad authority. The House endorsed the doctrine in only a few hours of debate. Extensive Senate hearings, conducted jointly by Foreign Relations and Armed Services, were followed by twelve days of Senate debate. The President's proposal was thoroughly analyzed and amended. By its debate the Senate performed an intellectual-political function. It explored alternatives and illuminated areas of doubt. Among other things, the Senate voted for a comprehensive review of Middle East policy and, rather than authorizing the President to use force, simply expressed the view of the Congress that the United States was prepared to use armed force if the President decided that it was necessary. The Senate, in a sense, was preventing the President from diluting his military powers and responsibilities. The House quickly accepted the Senate version.

The U-2 incident

Resolutions anticipating crises are rare. More commonly the Congress must react to rapidly moving events. The hazards and strengths of separated and diffused power are quickly exposed.

Acute and sudden crises drastically narrow the range of likely congressional behavior. During the most intense period when the uncertainties are greatest, the Congress provides legitimacy for executive responses and reinforces the unity of the nation. As the emergency unfolds and abates, however, elements in the Congress are tempted to exploit the crisis for partisan advantage. In every crisis the Congress by its behavior affects public confidence in men and institutions. The tests of crises are well illustrated by the U-2 incident and the Bay of Pigs failure.

For the Democrats in control of the Congress, the U-2 crisis offered tempting opportunities for partisan gain. It was a presidential election year. The Democrats recalled the bitterness of the 1952 campaign, when Republicans in and out of the Congress had exploited the Korean War for partisan advantage. The principal Democratic contestants for the nomination were members of the Senate. Vice-President Nixon, who was to become the Republican nominee, presided. And the events were embarrassing—a spy plane shot down in the Soviet Union on the eve of a crucial summit conference in Paris, fake cover stories to mask the purpose of the flight, the Soviet Premier's announcement that the pilot was alive and his general mission revealed, President Eisenhower accepting responsibility for the flight, repercussions in Japan, Turkey, and elsewhere, and the subsequent collapse of the summit meeting. All of these events were telescoped within three weeks.

The Republicans naturally rallied to their President. In retrospect, the reactions of the congressional Democrats were controlled by the behavior of three leaders, Speaker Sam Rayburn, Senate majority leader Lyndon Johnson, and Senator J. William Fulbright, the chairman of the Foreign Relations Committee.

Democratic and Republican leaders were first briefed on the reconnaissance plane's fate on May 9, 1960. From then to the collapse of the Paris meeting and the return of the President to Washington some ten days later, the Democratic leaders called for national unity. When the Soviet Premier suggested in Paris that the conference might be postponed for six to eight months, the three Democrats, joined by the titular head of the party, Adlai Stevenson, cabled President Eisenhower to express to Premier Khrushchev the view of the Democratic party that the conference not be postponed and that "all of the American people earnestly desire peace, an end to the arms race, and ever better relations between our countries." [3] When the Soviet leader's reply assailed the "present Administration," Senator Johnson promptly scorned the attempt to divide the nation.[4] The Democrats, of course, were not solely demonstrating bipartisanship and the essential unity of the nation. They were also avoiding the prospect of being branded as the party the Soviet leader preferred.

Upon the President's return to Washington, the political truce almost collapsed. Democrats in the Congress raised questions about "the blun-

---

[3] *Congressional Record,* 106 (May 18, 1960), 10497.
[4] *Ibid.* (June 2, 1960), 11635-36.

ders" of the preceding weeks. As in all such debates, motives for partisan gain were blended with a desire to learn the facts of a situation that had shaken public confidence.

The Democratic leaders again moved to mute the partisanship of their colleagues by rejecting demands for a full-scale formal investigation in favor of an inquiry by the Senate Committee on Foreign Relations. It was a "self-appraisal," as Senator Fulbright put it, a review and assessment to "learn from the events of the past weeks what we can do to improve our foreign policies and our governmental procedures for their formulation and execution." [5] The inquiry was addressed to the judgments made by the President and his associates and the procedures for making them. Their instrument for the operation, the Central Intelligence Agency, was not investigated. Edited testimony was released daily for public consumption. The Committee's report was sufficiently judicious in drawing conclusions from the facts that four of the six Republican members joined the Democrats to sign it. All of the Republicans expressed mild reservations.

The U-2 affair played only a quite minor part in the presidential election campaign. In retrospect, this largely Senate-managed response to the incident, while illuminating errors of judgment, helped restore public confidence in the competence of government.

The Bay of Pigs

Congressional reaction to the abortive Bay of Pigs paramilitary operation in April, 1961, was, in contrast, extraordinarily passive. Leaders of both political parties firmly backed President Kennedy in his exchanges with the Soviet Premier. The Congress provided legitimacy for the operation and conveyed the unity of the nation largely by silence. In the two weeks before the landing the Congress was silent when newspapers reported the training of anti-Castro units in Florida and elsewhere and their movement to forward bases. The President briefed a small bipartisan group of congressional leaders during the three-day period when the invaders were crushed. The leaders were silent. The House and Senate foreign policy committees conducted short, secret hearings two weeks after the event. They did not report. Only in the aftermath, when more information became available about the nature of the invasion and the deep American involvement, were questions raised in the Congress. Even then the criticism was guarded—part of the general stream of debate on what to do about Cuba. Those who got the publicity suggested that the President had not been sufficiently ruthless.

The exceptional congressional restraint may be explained partly by President Kennedy's swift moves to accept responsibility and to form a

[5] *Events Incident to the Summit Conference,* hearings before the Senate Committee on Foreign Relations, Eighty-sixth Congress, Second Session, 2.

national front. The President, or a prominent associate, met with former Presidents Eisenhower, Truman, and Hoover, former Vice-President Nixon, General MacArthur, Governor Nelson Rockefeller, and Senator Goldwater. "I would say that the last thing you want is to have a full investigation and lay this on the record," said former President Eisenhower.[6] Republican apprehensions about the extent of the Eisenhower Administration's part in planning the affair, fear of war, and, especially, the implication of sensitive agencies, the Joint Chiefs and the Central Intelligence Agency in particular, also contributed to the passivity of the Congress. During the month of April the Congress was also distracted— perhaps with some relief—by a crisis in Laos and the Soviet achievement of whirling a man in space.

Covert operations

The U-2 and Bay of Pigs affairs exposed starkly the unresolved dilemmas of the Congress in performing representative and oversight functions with regard to secret and covert activities. Each affair provoked a dialogue about forming a joint committee on the model of the Joint Committee on Atomic Energy to oversee the Central Intelligence Agency and related intelligence activities of the government. As on past occasions, the proposals met resistance and the debate died.

The Congress has uneasily accommodated itself to the existence of clandestine activities. Most members have no idea where the money for secret and covert intelligence operations lies hidden in the budget or for what purposes the money is spent. Few want to know. Few know much about the Central Intelligence Agency, an agency larger than many government departments over which the Congress seeks to maintain meticulous control.

The Congress had adjusted to mystery by an assumption and by faith in the limited surveillance conducted in secret by a few of its members. The assumption, expressed most clearly in the U-2 hearings, is that the CIA is a servant of the National Security Council, that it does not "make" policy, and that the President and his associates are accountable for the Agency's operations. The surveillance is conducted by subcommittees of the House and Senate Armed Services and Appropriations Committees. Scant evidence exists concerning the extent of their concern and to what degree they monitor the CIA. The chairman of the House money subunit reported that his group had long known about the overflights of Soviet territory. In the Senate U-2 hearings the administration refused to divulge the mission of the particular flight that failed. Senator Fulbright had some advance knowledge about the Bay of Pigs and warned the President against the operation. Most congressmen knew nothing about either vast intelligence operation.

[6] *New York Times*, May 2, 1961.

The Congress, in sum, has not devised satisfactory solutions to the many dilemmas posed by the extensive clandestine activities conducted by the executive branch. Its dilemmas are not simply dilemmas of secrecy. Many Congressmen are privy to secrets, and adequate ways have been devised to safeguard secret materials. The dilemmas posed for the Congress go beyond secrecy to the nature of the activities and the questions they raise for democratic government. The democratic ethic proclaims the self-determination of nations, a public voice through representative institutions in the choice of major means to accomplish national ends, and ways for compelling accountability in the continuing operations of government. The consequences of not employing the black arts on a vast scale in a tumultuous world, on the other hand, are incalculable.

How does the Congress resolve these dilemmas? A few members have spoken out vigorously for broader based continuing surveillance through a watchdog committee. Most members evade the dilemmas and are content to let the President and his associates make the ethical judgments and bear the responsibilities. The troubled for the most part are quiet.

EAST-WEST RELATIONS

The setting

"With the indulgence of the House, Mr. Speaker, may I say at the outset that the decision we make here today is the most crucial to the future of the world." [7] Thus a representative addressed his colleagues who had been convened by the leaders at seven in the morning on the day before Christmas, 1963. At issue was discretion for the President to underwrite credit for Soviet purchases of American wheat. The Democrats provided the votes for the President. All but two Republicans voted "No."

Many Republicans and Democrats were troubled that morning. The issue was politically volatile. All dread the charge of being "soft on Communism." Some had been scarred. Many no doubt recalled, if only fleetingly, episodes of the past—the bitter debates of the early 1950s about who lost China, the searing controversies over the war in Korea, and Senator Joseph McCarthy's dramatic forays. To many the issue appeared to be another indecent assault upon the whole rationale underlying the great programs for conquering space, for spending half of the budget on the military forces, for aiding Viet-Nam and scores of other countries, and for supporting alliances with more than forty nations. Yet many had also felt increasing pressures by farm and business interests to facilitate trade with Communist nations.

This scene reveals in miniature only some of the tensions plaguing the Congress in dealing with the infinitely complex area of East-West rela-

[7] Representative Don H. Clausen, *Congressional Record*, 109 (December 24, 1963, daily ed.), 24330.

tions and especially with the independent tendencies displayed within the Soviet bloc. The dominant instinct of the Congress is to be negative about concessions to Communist states. In this the Congress reflects, and a majority of members share, the prevailing public view instilled over a generation that Communism, wherever expressed or institutionalized, is a monolithic evil.

The search for discretion

In dealing with the legislature on East-West issues the President seeks to conserve as much flexibility as possible. He works to prevent or modify attempts to foreclose the use of important means—trade and aid, for example—to affect the course of change. The Executive wishes to retain the ability to adapt swiftly to circumstances.

The inclination of the Congress is to contract the President's area of maneuver, to set, in an infinite variety of ways, limits of tolerance and expectation. Only rarely have these limits been expressed in hard, inflexible legislative provisions. More commonly the Congress and its parts indicate perimeters of acceptability by debate, by often emotional exchanges and close votes when an amendment to curb the President's discretion is taken up, by investigations, by warning language in committee reports, and by resolutions.

In this intricate interplay of dialogue and action involving the President, his associates, the Congress and its parts, and interested publics, the President has retained some discretion. In making every important move, however, he must anticipate the reactions of the Congress and explain, justify, and report to a degree not required in most areas of public policy. The Congress, more likely than not, will react negatively and vigorously criticize but not check him. It implies grudging consent by inaction. The Congress wants no share of the responsibility for accommodations with Communist states. By its behavior the Congress has made the President the custodian of reality.

Communist China

Only in the case of Communist China has the Congress played a major role over a long period of time to confine narrowly the President's means of maneuver. In the late 1940s and early 1950s the Congress served as the forum for developing and expressing the version of why China went Communist that was to permeate the public most deeply. Communist China's intervention in the war in Korea reinforced hostility to the regime.

Beginning in the early 1950s the Congress went on record each year, often more than once and usually with no dissenting voices, to oppose the seating of Communist China in the United Nations. The resolutions were symbols of the tangled and emotion-laden history of China policy. If they did not always explicitly endorse this resolving, the Presidents expressed no dissent. By these resolutions, by amendments to various laws, and in other ways, the Congress constructed formidable walls for any President, if so inclined, to breach.

Yugoslavia and Poland

Presidential efforts to use the instruments of aid and trade to encourage independent tendencies in the Soviet bloc, and particularly in Yugoslavia and Poland, have especially provoked and perplexed the Congress. By actions and inactions the Congress has expanded and contracted the President's authority. Its behavior, while permitting limited maneuvers, has denied the President and his agents flexibility over time to adapt these instruments quickly to international developments. The situation varies from year to year, depending upon emotion-charged responses to bills and amendments respecting foreign aid, trade, the disposal of farm surpluses, and export controls. At least a dozen major House and Senate committees, in addition to numerous subcommittees, are concerned with these matters. Any member can plunge the House or the Senate into turmoil by proposing further restrictions on Communist states. The negative aspects of congressional behavior are promptly publicized throughout the satellite area.

The explanation for this erratic behavior lies partly in the persistence of the monolithic view about Communism. Then, too, the members are frequently reminded about the captive nations and the suppression of rights by hearings, by reports, by resolutions, by communications from their constituents who fled from Eastern Europe and from their descendants, and by scores of speeches. Both political parties have been wedded to some version of a policy of "liberation."

Thus it was routine in 1959, something akin to hailing National Pretzel Week, for the House and Senate unanimously to call upon the President to proclaim Captive Nations Week and to do so annually "until such time as freedom and independence shall have been achieved for all of the captive nations of the world." [8] President Eisenhower proclaimed the week, urging Americans to "recommit themselves" to support the aspirations of the captive peoples.[9] The resolution and proclamation, hardly noticed in the United States, coincided with a visit by Vice-President Nixon to the Soviet Union and became the subject of heated disputes with Premier Khrushchev.

In conceding discretion for the President to take some advantage of fluctuations in the Soviet bloc, the Congress has required him to justify the exceptions in terms of the "national interests," "national security," and similar criteria. Thus, in the 1962 foreign aid authorization bill, the Congress barred aid for eighteen Communist nations, including Yugoslavia and Poland, but permitted the President to waive the ban if he

[8] 76 Stat. 212.
[9] Proclamation No. 3303 (July 17, 1959), 73 Stat. c 65.

made certain findings, including a determination that the country was not dominated by international Communism and that assistance was "vital to the security of the United States." [10] The fund bill in the same year required the President to report any waivers to four committees and to state the reasons for his actions for publication in the *Federal Register*.

But the discretion the Congress gives may be taken away. In the Trade Expansion Act of 1962, for example, the Congress directed the President to suspend "most-favored-nation" trade treatment for Poland and Yugoslavia "as soon as practicable." [11] He delayed. In the 1963 foreign aid authorization bill, he regained discretion.

Both the President and the Congress prefer a patchwork of laws and provisions regarding trade and aid with Communist states. For the President, the patchwork provides discretion somewhere. For the Congress, the patchwork is politically safer and masks congressional responsibility while permitting the President to cope with reality. Neither wishes to face the perils of gathering the problems and issues into one bill for debate and action.

The Test Ban Treaty

On occasion, the Congress must squarely face an important policy shift bearing on East-West relations and share responsibility with the President. Such was the case in 1963 when the Senate was asked to consent to the ratification of the Test Ban Treaty with the Soviet Union.

In retrospect the consent of the Senate appears almost to have been routine. The principal foreign-military issues in conflict were extensively debated and reconciled within the executive branch before the decision was made to sign the treaty. Within seven weeks of receiving the treaty, the Senate endorsed it by the overwhelming vote of eighty to nineteen. This deceptively easy triumph for the administration was preceded by rich processes of consensus-building in which the Congress, and especially the Senate, played a critical part.

While senators and representatives were usually prepared to comment about disarmament from the late 1940s—questions about fall-out, the United Nations efforts, and so on were likely to be raised in every district —the dominant mood was skepticism even about small steps to mitigate the arms race. Over the years, however, a few members specialized in arms control issues and used committees and subcommittees to educate themselves, interested fellow legislators, and attentive publics that cared to read and listen. The fall-out hearings of a subcommittee of the Joint Committee on Atomic Energy in the late 1950s and the hearings and reports over several years by the Foreign Relations Subcommittee on Disarmament are examples. They built a public record, a reference library of hearings, reports, and speeches for future use.

[10] 76 Stat. 261, Sec. 260 (f).
[11] 76 Stat. 876, Sec. 231.

Discussions about the prospects and difficulties of arms control gradually spread into other crevices of the Congress. The Armed Services Committees and some of their subcommittees dipped into the issues. The annual requests for authority and funds to sustain the Arms Control and Disarmament Agency, established in 1961, stimulated House and Senate debates. In early 1963, when the prospects for a limited ban seemed brighter, the tempo of the dialogue picked up. The House Republican Conference established a Committee on Nuclear Testing. And in May, as the talks with the Soviet Union continued, thirty-two senators joined Senators Dodd and Humphrey to introduce a resolution favoring a limited test ban treaty. The resolution provided an optimistic reading of the political temperature of the Senate when the negotiators moved into the final stages of writing a treaty.

Thus, when the Senate received the treaty, most senators had absorbed some general knowledge about arms control and a few were experts on the technical and foreign-military problems of test ban agreements. The few included influential members of both political parties. In the hearings and debates, the Senate drew upon this reservoir of knowledge and competence to explore the proposal thoroughly and to bring an independent stream of judgment to bear.

Because of the overlapping foreign-military issues and the concern of other committees, the Committee on Foreign Relations invited the Armed Services Committee and the Senate members of the Joint Committee on Atomic Energy to attend its hearings and to question witnesses. Such arrangements are rare in the Senate and impossible in the House. Even with this arrangement, the Preparedness Investigating Subcommittee of the Senate Armed Services Committee, a powerful, virtually independent subunit, conducted its own hearings on the military aspects of the treaty. The subgroup monitored discontent and issued a pessimistic report. Its pessimism, while pressuring the executive branch to explain further and to elaborate understandings, was overcome by the dominant *ad hoc* group assembled by Foreign Relations and by its careful examination and blending of foreign and military policy issues.

The political chemistry of developing Senate consent was subtle and intricate. Only a small part of the story has been sketched. While in retrospect the development of consent was essentially bipartisan, the Republican floor leader maintained a studied detachment as he worked with the administration to build agreement. At his suggestion the President sent a letter to the Republican and Democratic floor leaders giving "unqualified and unequivocal assurances" about aspects of future nuclear weapons policy if the treaty were approved.[12]

No President could have carried the Senate, however, in the absence of the continuing disarmament dialogue over the years in the Congress and

[12] *Congressional Record,* 109 (Sept. 11, 1963, daily ed.), 15915.

with elements of the public. In the hearings and debates on the treaty the Senate served as the final, dramatic place in the political system for constructing the national consensus so essential for supporting an important shift in policy. The Senate promoted public understanding and acceptance of the decision. In the final vote it joined with the President to address the world.

DEFENSE AND FOREIGN AID

Some comparisons

Annually the Congress has four major opportunities to review broad segments of national security policy and to bring its political judgments to bear upon the purposes of the nation and the means it employs to relate to the world. On two of these occasions, when the Congress provides authority and funds for the Defense Department, it can review the state of the common defense. In the other debates, on authority and money to support the foreign economic and military aid programs, the Congress can appraise the effectiveness of major instruments of foreign policy.

Obvious differences between defense and foreign aid programs and the sources of their support largely account for distinctive patterns of congressional behavior. Foreign aid is new, defense old and deeply entrenched in the history and traditions of the Congress and of the nation. More than ten times as much money is spent for defense as for foreign aid. Defense programs are visible; foreign aid programs and their results are not. While in the past the armed forces experienced cycles of feast, famine, and neglect, the extraordinary advantage of offensive over defensive military power and the vulnerability of the nation to military attack have given an urgency and priority to military programs that no foreign aid programs could hope to develop.

In spite of these and other differences, some comparisons are useful. These two broad sectors of public policy compose the main ingredients of national security policy about which the Congress annually legislates. In both, the Congress not only represents the nation but speaks to its allies, Communist nations, and the unaligned. It legitimizes purposes and intentions. Both sectors of policy deeply involve the external responsibilities of the President and the constitutional powers of the Congress. Both fully display the tensions of the political system. Each is exceedingly complex. Regarding both, the Congress rarely innovates. It reacts to programs initiated and coordinated by the Executive. All of the programs must survive annual inspections by the whole House and Senate, and these are preceded and followed year around by scores of hearings, discussions, investigations, inquiries, studies, and reports by numerous committees, sub-committees, and individuals.

Regardless of parallels between the policy sectors and their interweaving in the day-to-day realities of the conduct of international business, the tone and style of the Congress in the defense area contrasts strikingly with its behavior in dealing with foreign aid.

Defense

In the defense area the Congress and its committees admire and encourage long-term planning. The Congress is generous with obligational authority and funds for the services to innovate, to look ahead, and to experiment. Only a fraction of the programs must be authorized each year. Only since 1961, for example, has the Congress required annual authority for the procurement of airplanes, ships, and missiles. While keenly interested in details about real estate transactions, military bases, personnel problems, and other matters relating to the supporting structure of the armed forces, the Congress and its parts probe only cautiously, and then with a special concern for maintaining public confidence, into the strategic elements of military policy relating to the nation's global commitments. Usually only a handful of congressmen vote against major defense bills. Reductions in funds normally are manageable. In final votes in the House and Senate defense bills draw support from all over the nation.

Foreign aid

In the foreign-aid area, the Congress resists long-term financing. When long-term authority has been reluctantly voted, it has been tied to the uncertainties of the annual appropriations cycle. The separate authorization and appropriations processes often appear to produce two different decisions about foreign aid in the same year. In contrast to the caution displayed in military matters, the Congress occasionally attempts to legislate foreign policy positions for the President to assume with regard to particular nations or regions of the world. Fund requests are likely to be cut deeply. Votes, especially in the critical amending stage, are often close. The final votes authorizing the programs and appropriating funds usually attract substantial bipartisan majorities. Since the mid-1950s, however, more than half of the Democrats from the South and, since the late 1940s, some two-thirds of the Republicans from the Middle West have voted "No."

Credibility

These and other differences in the approaches of the Congress to defense and foreign aid have a major impact on the credibility of the policies. By its behavior the Congress strengthens the credibility of the nation's defense posture. At times the Congress has acted, or failed to act, in ways that created serious doubts about the nation's military capabilities. As in all sectors of public policy, a unit of power and even one member, taking advantage of the diffusion of authority and the penchant of mass media for negative and dramatic news, can work to undermine confidence in the armed forces. The dominant moods and actions of the Congress, even in periods of retrenchment, however, have promoted confidence and pride.

In contrast, the credibility of foreign aid programs is shaken by the attitudes of the Congress and by the way in which it employs its processes for review and action. The Congress conveys doubt to the nation and to the world about the worthiness and future of the programs. By its tone and style it tends to undermine confidence in these instruments of foreign policy. The rhetoric of debate is especially extravagant, and the many negative voices of the Congress are widely publicized abroad. The unstable and varying moods of the Congress and its parts compel aid administrators to be exceptionally cautious. Foreign aid appears always to be in crisis.

While politicians in the newer African and Asian nations may have grave doubts, veterans of congressional foreign aid battles and astute observers abroad whose memories go back to the days of the Marshall Plan know that the Congress will approve foreign aid programs each year. Despite the appearance of chaos, strong advocates guide the House and the Senate to agreement.

Foreign aid bills

A brief comparison of the reactions of the Congress to foreign aid and defense bills in the same year will illuminate the contrasting behavior.

When early in 1964 the President signed the bill appropriating foreign aid funds, six months of the fiscal year had already passed. The Congress had provided 66 per cent of the money that had been requested nine months before. Even opponents of all foreign aid were disturbed when the Secretary of Defense in blunt terms described the "absolute chaos" created in military aid programs by the fund reductions voted by the Congress and retroactively applied to the beginning of the fiscal year.[13]

As they waded through the legal thicket built up and repeated through the years in the authorization and fund bills, aid officials examined the many new and modified restrictions. Unless essential to national security, the President was directed to deny Indonesia aid. Aid must be denied to any country which the President determines "is engaging in or preparing for aggressive military efforts" against any other nation receiving aid.[14] As the Senate debates made clear, and as the Cairo newspapers reported in front-page stories, this restriction was aimed at the United Arab Republic. Other restrictions required the President to deny aid to nations expropriating American-owned property and not providing adequate compensation to those countries not accepting the investment guarantee

[13] *Foreign Assistance Act of 1964*, hearings before the House Committee on Foreign Affairs, Eighty-eighth Congress, Second Session, 103.

[14] P.L. 205, Sec. 620 (i), Eighty-eighth Congress, First Session.

program of the United States, and to nations, unless vital to national security, which traded with Cuba. Ceilings were lowered on the amounts of military aid permitted for Latin America and Africa. Language had been inserted to insure that the President would not lend India money for the Bokaro steel mill, a project the President had earlier dropped in the face of congressional pressure.

These represent only a fraction of the curbs. In the politics of compromising House-Senate differences, scores of others had been modified or dropped. These had dealt with such matters as fishing rights, aid and trade concessions for Yugoslavia and Poland, contributions to international organizations with projects in Cuba, and policies to apply when the military seized power from an elected government in a Latin American state. Administrators also had to plow through the warning language of committee reports and the speeches of influential members for further evidence of the limits of congressional tolerance.

Nineteen sixty-three was an especially bad year for foreign aid. By its behavior the Congress seemed to caricature all of the attitudes and weapons it had displayed at one time or another in the past. The dominant mood was rebellion. The bills were passed much later than in previous years. The normal bipartisanship on important matters broke down in the House. The focus of past crises, the subcommittee of the House Appropriations Committee, was almost overshadowed. Many members of the Congress committed to foreign aid worked to modify the programs to accord more closely with congressional opinions which they felt the executive branch had not adequately responded to over the years. The Congress more precisely defined its limits of tolerance and expectation, limits the administration prudently observed in 1964 by submitting a "lean," "tight," "minimal," foreign aid program.

The President got a foreign aid program in 1963 and, despite the turmoil, considerable discretion and generous funds, at least in congressional eyes. Even some obstructions it voted, regarding aid to Indonesia, for example, possibly provided the President useful leverage for the more effective conduct of United States foreign policy. The niceties of diplomacy prevented him from publicly saying so. And these bills provided funds and authority only for the "regular" foreign aid programs. This same year, for example, the farm committees made it possible for the executive branch to utilize more than $1.5 billion in surplus farm products for "foreign assistance."

Defense bills

On the surface, congressional reaction to major defense bills in 1963 seemed to be a formality. A bill authorizing $15 billion for research, development, and procurement of missiles, airplanes, and ships sailed through the House with only thirty-three dissents and was whipped through the Senate by a voice vote. A delay occurred in the Senate. Fo:

the first time in two decades the Senate closed its doors for a secret session to hear a colleague present classified information about missile defenses. He pleaded with the Senate to uphold a committee decision authorizing $196 million for procuring parts for the Nike-Zeus anti-missile missile. President Eisenhower some five years earlier had refused to spend extra money voted for Nike-Zeus. This year the powerful chairman of Armed Services, backing the Secretary of Defense, opposed authorizing extra funds. Shortly, all but sixteen Senators supported him.

On other days, a bill authorizing $1.6 billion for military construction was approved without amendments by voice votes in House and Senate. The bill appropriating $47 billion for the armed forces—less than four per cent below the President's request—drew no dissents in the Senate and only one in the House on roll call votes. In the Senate, a proposal to reduce research, development, and procurement funds by 10 per cent —advocated in terms of reducing spending for "overkill" and providing funds for urgent educational and other national needs—received only two votes out of seventy-four cast.

These were the major activities of the House and the Senate as collective bodies in reviewing the common defense in this particular year. Powerful committees headed by strong chairmen had their way in the formal debates. Most years were not as placid as this one and thus, as in the case of the foreign aid bills, the Congress was drawing a caricature of its basic tendencies.

While the Senate and House were relatively passive, the committees and subcommittees concerned with defense were not. As always, they were engaged in processes of bargaining, persuasion, negotiation, and compromise with their colleagues, the executive branch, and concerned publics. Elements in the Congress lobbied for particular programs and won or lost, depending upon the extent of agreement among the powerful committees. Thus, while the Senate and House Armed Services Committees authorized $363 million for stepped-up development of the RS-70 plane—not requested by the Defense Department, but desired by the Air Force, and a source of past executive-legislative conflict when the unwanted funds were voted—the Appropriations Committees failed to provide the funds.

The Armed Services Committees and Appropriations subcommittees listened to comprehensive briefings on the nation's defense posture. The committees gave their usual detailed attention to military construction and related matters. In other corners of the Congress, the Permanent Investigations Subcommittee of the Senate on Government Operations investigated the manner in which the TFX plane contract (involving several billion dollars and 20,000 or more jobs) was awarded and compelled the Defense Department to make a public explanation. Elsewhere, a subcommittee of the Senate Armed Services Committee was exploring the contract award procedures for a naval airplane. Both subcommittees.

were alert to the possible effects of their inquiries upon future administrative decision-making.

THE FUTURE

These brief studies of reactions to crises, East-West relations, defense, and foreign aid display only samples of congressional activity in the national security policy area. A more comprehensive picture would include the Congress at work on such matters as civil defense, atomic energy, outer space, research and development, administration, cultural exchange, and international organizations. The picture would include neglected facets of behavior—the effects of seniority, the interlacing of members, committees, and subcommittees in intricate patterns of continuing relationships with components of the executive branch, and the many subtle rituals of leadership and partisanship.

The more comprehensive treatment would deal at greater length with the many changes in the Congress since World War II. Congressional participation in shaping policy has gained in quality as a consequence of such developments as the employment of professional committee staffs, the establishment of consultative subcommittees, extensive travel abroad, the involvement of many members in international conferences, improvement in executive-legislative communication, and the dissemination of thoughtful committee- and party-sponsored studies of international problems. A significant development during the Eisenhower Administration was the consolidation of the Republican commitment to the main lines of United States foreign policy as they had been evolving since World War II. The political base supporting the demands of world leadership became more stable.

The more complete picture would impress upon us the seemingly infinite variety and extent of congressional involvement in national security policy. From other perspectives, the picture of the Congress, while no less impressive, diminishes in size.

The concerns of the Congress

Much important activity in the military and foreign policy realms lies beyond any really effective control or influence by the Congress and its parts. The Congress often is relatively passive, moreover, concerning foreign-military developments and situations that it could influence.

Congressional concern, and thus the extent of its activities, is closely related to the extent of public concern. If an issue or situation interests only small publics, only a few members are likely to carry on a dialogue with them. As the attentive publics grow in size and variety, and especially as mass media join to dramatize issues and problems, more members, committees, and subcommittees become active. When concern spreads down from the attentive elements to affect the general public, the temperature of the Congress rises rapidly.

This correlation of congressional and public concern may be illustrated with regard to Viet-Nam. During the 1950s elements in the Congress only intermittently monitored the commitment of the United States. General legislative support was implied by annual approval of the foreign aid programs. In 1954 the negative reaction of Republican and Democratic congressional party leaders was perhaps decisive when they were consulted by the administration concerning proposals to use American planes and warships to help the French on the eve of the Dien Bien Phu defeat. In 1959 a series of newspaper articles charging aid mismanagement spurred House and Senate subcommittee investigations in Washington and in Saigon. A few members of the Congress visited Viet-Nam in the 1950s, but only one, Senator Mike Mansfield, gave continuing attention to the situation. In the eyes of the administration, his voice at times was the voice of the Congress. Only with the extensive commitment of men and resources beginning in 1961 did concern and activity spread from a few to many members of the Congress.

In allotting time, energy, and thought, the great majority of the members of the Congress give higher priority to domestic problems and programs than to the nation's international involvements. Each member is, of course, intensely concerned about the nation's physical security. The big votes for defense appropriations underscore this concern. The members also are quite involved in such domestic national security business as defense contracts. They worry about foreign policy.

Except for the specialists on the committees processing the principal legislative ingredients of national security policy, however, the members focus on the more familiar and politically more important domestic issues. For the member and his constituents, programs to achieve international goals are often unpleasant competitors for resources that might support domestic programs. The human tendency is to give the unpleasant lower priority. The flood of programs demanding the congressman's attention, coupled with the fact that most are mired in a huge volume of constituent business that they choose to perform, virtually guarantees a low priority for international business.

Reform

This scale of priorities is only one of several problems troubling those most sensitive to the world responsibilities of the United States and most concerned about the future of the Congress. While conceding that, in many respects, the Congress has adapted remarkably well and that its adaptability provides a basis for optimism about the future, it can be argued that the Congress displays major deficiencies that weaken the effectiveness of national security policies and programs and impair legislative influence and control in their formulation and execution.

The deficiencies most commonly noted stem from the dispersal of power and the lack of ways for coordinating judgments on interrelated programs and policies. Military, industrial, political, scientific, cultural, diplomatic, economic, psychological, and other factors are now woven together in the formulation and implementation of foreign-military policies. While the Congress has attempted to cope with these realities— the *ad hoc* joint hearings by the Senate's Armed Services and Foreign Relations Committees on the Test Ban Treaty and the Cuba and Formosa resolutions are examples—more commonly it responds or fails to respond to parts of interrelated problems as the diffuse structure and the specialized interests and impulses of committees, subcommittees, and individual members dictate.

Problems that once could be regarded as wholly domestic in their implications but that now bear critically on the nation's international obligations, moreover, are managed by committees which, while increasingly alert to the international aspects of their business, concede excessively to domestic pressures. Use of the executive budget for coordinated discussion and action is, of course, prevented by the congressional practice of splitting the budget into numerous parts for review and action.

The dispersal of related business among a multitude of isolated compartments and inadequate thought to the interdependence of programs and policies not only affect the substance of policies and their implementation; these practices also drain an inordinate amount of the time and energy of public officials.

In looking to the future, it is evident that foreign-military programs and policies will become infinitely more complex and require extraordinary degrees of sophistication and coordination by the executive and legislative branches in their formulation and execution. Scientific and technological considerations—even now often beyond the layman's grasp —will become increasingly dominant. The political system will be confronted by unparalleled tests. If the Congress fails to adapt adequately and imaginatively to this state of affairs, a further decline in its influence is in prospect. Ill-equipped to participate in making critical judgments, it may abdicate fundamental aspects of its representative functions. Its efforts to keep the executive accountable may become a hollow formality. On occasion, it may strike out irrationally to affect programs and policies in ways that might be dangerous for the nation.

These and other diagnoses of the ills of the Congress have provoked a variety of proposals for reform. For some, the extent of the illness requires drastic surgery, nothing less than amendment of the Constitution to provide for a fusion of executive and legislative power as in Great Britain. Disciplined majorities, the direct and continuing confrontation of coordinated executive programs and legislative power, the executive weapon of dissolution—these and other features of the ideal parliamentary system, so it is argued, offer the only adequate cure for the deficiencies of the system of separated, fragmented, checked, and balanced powers in a totally unprecedented era of world affairs.

Less drastic alternatives for the Congress lie in various proposals for a better utilization of the resources of the political parties. The members of the Congress generally resist the prospects of greater party discipline. While the recipes differ, virtually every analysis of the Congress concludes that party reform offers the most promising opportunities for the Congress to arrest its decline, to enhance its voice in public affairs, and to mitigate the hazards of uncoordinated, fragmented, undisciplined, and, at times, irresponsible exercises of power.

Political parties are the only agencies of the Congress that have general, continuing responsibility for everything that the Congress does or fails to do. On many occasions in the past, party leadership has demonstrated the capacity for enhancing the stature of the Congress on the world scene. Yet, the potential of party resources for the development of consensus, for coordinating policies and programs throughout the legislative process, with the executive branch, and between the parties, and generally for promoting greater discipline and responsibility to offset the disintegrated structure of the Congress has only barely and intermittently been exploited.

Proposals for party reform often are linked with others that promise a more unified and constructive role for the Congress. The proposals include expansion of professional staff resources, experiments with a periodic question period in each chamber or before joint meetings of both houses, frequent use of joint committees and joint subcommittees within and between the houses in related policy areas, and formation of a joint committee on national security.

An answer to the question of whether the Congress is adequately staffed depends upon one's conception of its roles and functions. Those opposed to a major staff expansion fear that the search for consensus would be complicated. The Congress could never hope to match executive expertise, but its attempts might result in the development of rival foreign-military policies and dramatically weaken the Executive's tasks in managing relations with the world.

Proponents argue that a failure to expand staff resources will lead to a further decline in the competence and influence of the Congress. As scientific and technological factors increasingly intrude into the shaping and implementation of foreign-defense programs, laymen, whether part of the attentive public, administrators in the executive branch, or congressmen, become increasingly less competent to evaluate them. Unless the Congress is adequately staffed, its options are to take the word of executive expertise—to which the political leaders of the executive branch have perhaps already succumbed in bewilderment—or to stab out haphazardly, irrationally, and in frustration. In either event, the loss is a loss for democratic government.

From this perspective, the Congress should dramatically expand its staff resources. One proposal, for example, urges formation of an institute or academy of experts to advise the Congress and its parts. The academy would draw upon university and other sources of knowledge. The congressional experts would have a vested interest in disagreeing with and testing the recommendations of the executive branch. They could look ahead, plan, and anticipate situations. In the competition and testing, laymen in and out of the Congress would derive a sounder basis for exercising that fundamental, humanizing quality which can be summed up in one word—*wisdom*.

Discussion of reform prospects by members of the Congress has most commonly centered on the proposal for an integrating committee on national security policy. Many variations of the idea have been advanced. Most attention has been given to the formation of a Joint Committee on National Security Policy, composed of members drawn from the House and Senate committees—Armed Services, Appropriations, Foreign Relations, Foreign Affairs, Atomic Energy, Space—with jurisdiction over the principal elements of national security policy. The joint group's domain would parallel that of the National Security Council.

As most commonly advocated, the joint group would not supplant the standing committees. It would study, inquire, review, investigate, and report, giving primary attention to the interrelationships among policies and programs that relate to national security. The group's activities, so the proponents of the reform argue, would fill an information void for the Congress and especially provide coordinated perspectives to guide the members and many standing committees and subcommittees at work on aspects of national security policy. The group could also serve as a high-level vehicle for communication between the executive and legislative branches. Only rarely do the proponents explore whether the joint group might possibly develop into a powerful competitor of the President.

In conclusion

Looking back from the third decade of the revolution in the requirements of national security, it is evident that major changes have occurred in aspects of congressional behavior. The demands of international politics have inevitably enhanced executive power. Drawing upon resources that the Congress could not expect to match, the President initiates and coordinates the major programs and policies that relate to national security. He calculates where the nation's interests lie. The Congress provides legitimacy for these calculations. Regarding fundamental aspects of national security policy, the dominant inclinations of the Congress have become to test, to criticize, to publicize, to compel explanations and justifications, in a word, to monitor. While by no means a certainty in a system of divided and diffused power, the evidence indicates that these trends in congressional behavior will gradually embrace a broader range of policies and programs that bear on the nation's international involvements. Whether in the process the Congress will gain or lose stature, power, and influence will be determined in large measure by the Congress itself.

In reality, national security policy is a blend of all of the nation's policies as they affect the world roles of the United States. It is inseparable from other sectors of public policy. Whether the United States enjoys domestic tranquillity, the blessings of liberty, security, and the other purposes for which the Constitution was ordained depends upon how successfully and imaginatively the political system, including the Congress, responds to the fantastic pace and scope of change in the United States and in the world. Politics and public policy have inextricably become both national and international.

David B. Truman

8

The Prospects for Change

Any deliberate change in a key institution, if it has consequences that are not merely trivial, may be regarded as a reform. But the effects of such changes do not necessarily move in the same direction. That is, they may affect the distribution of power—within the institution or between it and other segments of the government—in differing or contradictory ways. To take an obvious example, if an attempt were made to limit the capacity of the Rules Committee to keep bills from the floor of the House, a time limit could be placed on Rules consideration of bills, like the one in force during the Eighty-first Congress (1949-1951). But if the authority to call up such blockaded bills were given to the chairmen of the standing committees that originally handled them, the effect would be further to enhance the power now dispersed among committee chairmen. The same authority granted to the Speaker, however, would be a step in the direction of centralization, since it would strengthen his hand against the standing committees.

THREE PROBLEMS

Probable effects

An initial problem, then, in examining any proposed change is to estimate the character and direction of its effects. Relatively few proposals, however, are so simple and so uni-dimensional in their consequences that one can predict their effects with a high degree of confidence. Especially if they are part of an omnibus or composite proposal, the problem of estimating *net* consequences seriously complicates the assignment. This may be one reason, as Huitt implies (Chapter Four), why few if any observers predicted that the Lafollette-Monroney bill, which in amended form became the Legislative Reorganization Act of 1946, would result primarily in weakening central leadership in Congress to the advantage of the standing committees and their proliferous subcommittees. The provisions that had this effect were associated with others that conceivably could have operated in the other direction—the legislative budget, party policy committees, and regulation of lobbies— but the latter either failed to work or were dropped from the measure in the process of enactment.

Basic functions

An attempt at anticipating effects is nevertheless essential, even though estimates are difficult and their reliability uncertain. When the attempt achieves some clarity, however, a second and more fundamental set of questions will confront a reflective observer: What are the *needs* of the Congress? What, more fundamentally, are the distinctive functions it is to perform in the governmental scheme? A representative assembly, as Huntington has pointed out (Chapter One), can be a significant component of government without being in a strict sense a legislature, that is, an agency that assumes the chief role in both preparing and enacting statutes. If it is to be more completely a legislature in this sense, the needs of the Congress are not the same in most respects as they are if it is to be primarily a delaying and legitimating body or if it is to act chiefly as critic and modifier of administrative policies.

The problem of basic function is not important for the reason that it is in fact possible to make a formal and official choice among the alternatives. Institutions are rarely created by fiat or by a single conscious choice. It is important rather because incremental choices will lead by steps toward one alternative or another, and both realism and satisfaction are likely to be served if these fundamental questions are kept in view.

Feasibilities

The Congress today is more nearly a legislature in the strict sense than is the national assembly in any other major country of the world. One may, however, question whether it is in any realistic sense possible, under the technical conditions of an industrialized and interdependent society, for the Congress more fully to exercise the legislative function. The point is raised not in order to propose an answer but rather to introduce the third problem to be confronted in assessing proposals for change, the problem of feasibility: Can it be done?

Discussions of reform frequently are carried on with the unstated assumption that anything is possible, that the question of feasibility is essentially irrelevant. Yet proposals for change that would require major alterations in the Constitution almost certainly are beyond the bounds of feasibility. They may have utility as means of agitation and criticism, but they lack more than a toe hold on reality. It is well to remember that in nearly two centuries the nation has not returned to Philadelphia and that the document written there displaced a system that had been in effect less than a decade. Even there the question of feasibility was paramount. It is no disservice to the achievement of that assembly of notables to say that they were not free to adopt any arrangements they chose, that they were obliged to take account of existing distributions of power and to reckon with continuities of practice and of expectation.

The most significant changes, written and unwritten, in the Constitution of the United States came in the wake of desperate crises: the Civil War, the Great Depression, and World War II. Crises of these proportions would almost certainly be a necessary condition for major constitutional changes in the future. But in the contemporary world, crises of these proportions almost certainly would place the whole nation in jeopardy. Reforms contingent upon such upheavals, therefore, cannot be regarded realistically as feasible.

The constraints of feasibility apply equally, however, to less sweeping proposals. For adoption and accomplished effect depend upon the convergence of existing power as the fulcrum of change. The authors of the preceding chapters are not of one mind on the changes that might be made in the Congress, but none would dissent from Ralph Huitt's trenchant observation (Chapter Four) that "a successful reform is a demonstration of effective massing and use of power, not a prelude to it."

CURRENT PROPOSALS AND THE DISPERSION OF POWER

One thread that runs through all of these essays is the dispersion of power, in the past half-century apparently an increasing dispersion, within and between the houses of Congress. Almost regardless of what may be taken, explicitly or implicitly, as the appropriate basic functions of the Congress, restraints upon this dispersion are likely to be at the focus of controversy in the days ahead. If this is the case, the most useful way in which to draw these observations to a close is to review some of the current proposals for change in relation to their probable effects on dispersion.

Neutral effects

Many suggestions for revision, of course, would have no appreciable effect on dispersion, whatever else they might accomplish. In turn, a number of these could be adopted without major difficulty simply because they do not significantly affect the power structure or the political risks of the individual members. In this category would fall most of the suggestions for altering the "workload" of the Congress, such as providing separate days for committee and floor work, delegating to some special tribunal the handling of additional private bills—since 1946 chiefly bills dealing with the immigration and naturalization problems of individuals —and adding to the personal staffs of representatives and senators. They might well lighten the burdens of members, but none of them would touch the power structure at all closely. Some of them would, of course, promote efficiency in the sense that they would save time, but "waste" is after all a relative term, to be measured by what might have been done with what was saved. What appears as a "waste" of time, moreover, may, in a chamber in which power is diffused, be a source of some control by leaders, as the adjournment rush in most legislatures demonstrates.

Also in the neutral category probably should be placed proposals that Congress divest itself of the somewhat anachronistic duty of being the legislature for the District of Columbia. The change would reduce the power and perquisites of two committees; and it would be at least a symbolic loss for those who fear self-government in a city in which white citizens are not a majority, but the effects on Congress would be slight. Equally nominal, for the Congress, would be a requirement of joint hearings by House and Senate committees. If the change could be made, which is doubtful, some time of administration witnesses would be saved, which would be a gain, but the congressional effects would be insubstantial. Unless it were given power over revenue and appropriations, the creation of a joint committee on fiscal policy would likely go the way of the 1946 reorganization's legislative budget or at best become a vehicle for instruction, such as the Joint Economic Committee. (If it were given such power, which is unlikely, it would become a formidable rival to any other points of control in the Congress.)

Finally, it seems likely that proposals in the realm of congressional "ethics"—chiefly conflict-of-interest and "moonlighting" activities—would have a neutral effect as long as they went no farther than disclosure. They might reduce the utility of some Congressmen to outside interests, and they would tend to increase public respect for the Congress—clearly an advantage, especially if they resulted in eliminating the double standard for the legislative and executive branches—but their power implications would otherwise be slight.

Reinforcing dispersion

A considerable number of suggestions, especially some that are urged in the name of "democratizing" the House or Senate, would have the effect of further weakening the power of the central "elective" leadership, the Speaker and the floor leaders. Thus the suggestion, recurrent over the years, that the number of signatures required in the House to make effective a petition discharging a committee from further consideration of a bill be reduced from the present 218 to something like 150 would transfer control from one minority to another (and shifting) one equally inaccessible to control by the elective leaders. Similarly, as noted earlier, under a twenty-one-day rule for calling a bill out of the House Rules Committee in which authority so to act were granted to the standing committees, the effect would be to weaken the Speaker's control of the agenda if he "owned" the Rules Committee. In any case it would in this form enhance the powers of the chairmen of the legislative committees.

In both House and Senate several proposed modifications of the seniority rule, however unlikely of adoption, would tend toward further dispersion. For example, caucus election of committee chairmen by secret ballot or the choice of chairmen by majority vote of the committee members would at best give nothing additional to the central leadership and at worst would strengthen the autonomy of chairmen, especially if an incumbent were regularly re-elected.

Further increasing the professional staffs of the standing committees, whatever its benefits in other respects, would tend to strengthen committee autonomy. Similarly, the elimination of remaining jurisdictional ambiguities among committees would, as did the "reforms" of 1946, reduce further the discretion of the elective leaders in both houses.

Finally, the introduction of electronic voting equipment, frequently recommended by outsiders as a time-saver, especially in the House, would strengthen minority control by facilitating snap votes. Further, it probably would take from the central leadership the time it now has during a long roll call to muster maximum support from the waverers or the negotiators.

Strengthening central leadership from inside

A great many devices can be imagined that would directly increase central control from within the House and Senate or do so indirectly by reducing the opportunities for a minority to block or seriously to delay congressional action. These would in varying degrees assault the collective powers of the present oligarchy, and their prospects are therefore correspondingly limited. In a body where risks are individual and localized, decentralized authority is likely to have a broad base of support, especially among those who have been re-elected at least once. Such decentralization puts within a member's reach the means of helping himself politically—an entirely worthy motive—and it is the more attractive because he cannot clearly see the capacity of any central leadership, in or out of Congress, to do the equivalent for him. A successful assault, therefore, would require a crisis severe enough to isolate the members of the oligarchy and to solidify the rank and file around central leaders willing to spearhead a serious shake-up.

The most promising, though not necessarily feasible, means all would have one feature in common, namely, increased leadership control of the timetable, not only in the chambers, but also in the committees. In the Senate a simpler and more easily invoked rule for limiting debate than the present two-thirds of those present and voting would control the most serious and most notorious threat to the timetable in that chamber, the filibuster. In the House a reinstituted twenty-one-day rule, but one that placed the authority to call up a bill blockaded by the Rules Committee in the hands of the Speaker or the majority leader, would strengthen the position of at least the Democratic leaders in the chamber.

In both houses some alternatives to or modifications in the seniority rule would aid the leaders in relation to the committees and in the chambers generally. A return to the practice under which the Speaker designated committee chairmen in the House and a granting of comparable power to the majority leader in the Senate would of course contribute to centralized control. The circumstances that would have to exist in order to make such a change possible, moreover, would assure use of the power, at least for several years. The less drastic proposal for caucus election of chairman from among the three most senior members of a committee would have the same tendency only if the Speaker and majority leader were able and willing to make their preferences prevail. If they were not, the result would be a reinforcement of dispersion.

Strengthening central leadership from outside

A striking fact about the Congress in this century is that most, if not all, of those developments that have tended toward reducing or restraining the dispersion of power in the separate houses and in the Congress as a whole have come from outside the legislature and chiefly from the White House. In some instances the Congress has been formally a partner in the changes, where legislation has provided the occasion for them, and in some instances not. But in either case the anti-dispersion effects have been secondary, and largely unintended, consequences of lines of action taken by the President primarily to discharge his own responsibilities and to meet the needs of his role.

Thus the Budget and Accounting Act of 1921, which established the executive budget in pursuit of the goal of fiscal efficiency, created for the first time a government-wide fiscal program and gave the President responsibility for its formulation and, equally important, its public presentation. The act did not achieve quite the integration of the appropriating and revenue activities in the Congress that some sponsors hoped for, but it did lead to the setting of rational, if not inflexible, proportions in expenditure. In the course of time, moreover, it created something of a counterbalance to the agency-committee relation that could be useful in as well as outside the Congress. The Employment Act of 1946, though it created no comparable operating functions, placed on the President the responsibility for developing and pronouncing the requirements of the economy as a whole and the government's part in meeting them. Although little more than an agenda-setting device, it is at least that and as such is a check on complete committee freedom in setting the congressional program.

Alongside and reinforcing these formal and legislatively created activities, at least three less conspicuous practices have developed since the 1930s. In the first place, the President's legislative program, as Neustadt has demonstrated (Chapter Five), developed from the needs of a succession of chief executives, but it acquired vigor and, in all probability, permanence because it also met the needs of others—the agencies and, more important, the Congress, including its committees. It has provided the latter with not merely a "laundry-list" but a set of priorities. Its priority-setting qualities, moreover, have been strengthened in consequence of the increased and continuing prominence of foreign policy-national security problems. Presidential priorities are not coincident with congressional ones, but in these areas limits have grown up around committee autonomy and hence around congressional disjunction.

In the second place, as a likely consequence of the President's stake in his program, the growth of a White House staff specialized in legislative liaison has introduced an element of coherence and coordination into congressional deliberations, especially at the committee stage. Again, although it has been little studied, one suspects that its viability depends not merely on presidential desire but also on its utility *in general,* and not necessarily for identical reasons, to committee chairmen, to elective leaders, and even to some agencies. It clearly is not and cannot be a legislative high command, but it seems to have acquired informational and secondary influence capabilities that are centripetal in tendency.

Thirdly, the now well-established practice of regular presidential consultation with his party's principal elective leaders in the Congress works in the same direction. Like the two developments already mentioned, it was initially an outgrowth of presidential needs, but apparently it also has utility for elective leaders, especially if they head a nominal majority in Congress. Particularly if these leaders in name see themselves potentially as leaders in fact—and they need not do so—their relations with the President seem useful. The President's program and priorities are not necessarily theirs, and they do not, if they are prudent, attempt to operate simply as his lieutenants. But they may share with him the handicaps of power dispersion in the Congress, and their collaboration with him may—again if they see themselves as more than the servants of the congressional oligarchy—place limits on its effects, to their joint advantage.

A possible implication of these developments for the further restriction of dispersion is that they may offer something of a pattern for the future. Needs in the Presidency, if they are at least consistent with needs in Congress and among its central leaders, may lead to new practices whose consequence, in all likelihood unintended, could be some further limit on the dispersion of power. One such need, as yet not clearly felt, is suggested by Neustadt (Chapter Five) in his discussion of the common stakes of elective politicians against career officials.

A next step, though it would be a long and difficult one, might be, as Walter Lippmann and Huntington (Chapter One) have suggested, toward a commitment in Congress to bring to a vote, at least by mid-session, any legislation carrying top priority from the administration. The prospect of such a commitment would require more care in the construction of the President's program, since some means would be needed explicitly to distinguish urgent needs from trial balloons, and the invidious judgments that this would require might be too costly politically. It also would require a collegial commitment from the congressional oligarchy that might prove impossible of achievement. But the attempt would at least follow logically from the trends of several decades.

Prospects of strengthening central leadership through jointly acceptable leverage from outside Congress have at least the semblance of feasibility, and not only because of the developments already identified. Evidence suggests that reforms that would rest largely on the initiative of the Congress itself do not command requisite majorities. For example, a random sample of the House in 1963 found a majority supporting only fourteen of thirty-two specific proposals of reform. Of the proposals enjoying such support, only two were ones likely to be of major consequence—reinstatement of the twenty-one-day rule and a four-year term for representatives (which senators certainly would not favor). The remainder, including most of those discussed in these pages, appealed only to a minority.[1]

Whether or not outside leverage leads to a reduction in dispersion, the examples discussed here underscore a central point: The Congress and its power structure cannot profitably be viewed as something separate and isolable from the remainder of the government and the society. They affect and are affected by needs and changes in the society and in the government as a whole. They must, therefore, be looked at within this context.

[1] Michael O'Leary, ed., *Congressional Reorganization: Problems and Prospects* (Hanover, N.H., 1964), pp. 18-21, 58-63.

The American Assembly

The American Assembly holds meetings of national leaders and publishes books to illuminate issues of United States policy. The Assembly is a national, nonpartisan educational institution, incorporated in the State of New York.

The Trustees of the Assembly approve a topic for presentation in a background book, authoritatively designed and written to aid deliberations at national Assembly sessions at Arden House, the Harriman (N. Y.) Campus of Columbia University. These books are also used to support discussion at regional Assembly sessions and to evoke consideration by the general public.

All sessions of the Assembly, whether international, national, or local, issue and publicize independent reports of conclusions and recommendations on the topic at hand. Participants in these sessions constitute a wide range of experience and competence.

American Assembly books are purchased and put to use by thousands of individuals, libraries, businesses, public agencies, nongovernmental organizations, educational institutions, discussion meetings, and service groups. The subjects of Assembly studies to date are:

1951——United States—Western Europe Relationships
1952——Inflation
1953——Economic Security for Americans
1954——The United States' Stake in the United Nations
——The Federal Government Service
1955——United States Agriculture
——The Forty-Eight States
1956——The Representation of the United States Abroad
——The United States and the Far East
1957——International Stability and Progress
——Atoms for Power
1958——The United States and Africa
——United States Monetary Policy
1959——Wages, Prices, Profits, and Productivity
——The United States and Latin America
1960——The Federal Government and Higher Education
——The Secretary of State
——Goals for Americans
1961——Arms Control: Issues for the Public
——Outer Space: Prospects for Man and Society
1962——Automation and Technological Change
——Cultural Affairs and Foreign Relations
1963——The Population Dilemma
——The United States and the Middle East
1964——The United States and Canada
——The Congress and America's Future
1965——The Courts and the Public

The American Assembly Series